NORTH AMERICAN
F-100 SUPER SABRE

Peter E. Davies with David W. Menard

The Crowood Press

Acknowledgements

First published in 2003 by
The Crowood Press Ltd
Ramsbury, Marlborough
Wiltshire SN8 2HR

www.crowood.com

British Library Cataloguing-in-Publication Data
A catalogue record for this book is available from the British Library.

ISBN 1 86126 577 8

This project was given life by the enthusiasm of some of the men who flew or fixed the 'Hun'. Aircrew from many stages of the aircraft's history gave generously of their memories, experiences and records. Similarly, a representative selection of the equally vital maintainers who kept the aircraft operational were keen to pass on their insights and impressions. They are owed a real debt of gratitude for enabling this book to offer an unusually thorough and detailed analysis of the F-100's character and role.

Above all, I am indebted to David W. Menard: 'Mr F-100'. After spending a third of his long USAF career with the Super Sabre he has continued to expand his unique collection of information and photographs concerning the aircraft. I was delighted when he offered to 'ride shotgun' on the project and I have welcomed his guidance and overview throughout. Many of the images reproduced in these pages come from David's collection. Particular thanks are also due to Batur Avgan, Steen Hartov, Clarence Fu and Jean-Jacques Petit for making possible a comprehensive and detailed account of the F-100's 'foreign' service for the first time in a book of this kind.

This book has also benefited from the significant contributions from the following F-100 veteran pilots, maintainers and historians: George Acree, Lance Barber (Wings Over the Rockies Museum), Maj Curtis Burns, Michael Benolkin, CMGT Mike Bilcik, J. E. T. Clausen, John Clarity, Soner Capoglu, Tony Cassanova, Troy Clarke, Larry Engesath, Jack Engler, Robert Fanthorpe, Mehmet Findikli, Jerry Geer, Maj Dick Garrett, Col Bruce Gold, Col Tom Germscheid, Dr John Grigsby, Lee Howard, Lt Col Van Hall, Lt Col Ronald Herrick, Jean-Pierre Hoehn, Chris Hobson, Col Art Johnson, Col Mike Kulczyk, Lt Col Allen Lamb, Col T. G. Lancaster, Thomas E. Lowe, Sgt Bob Macavoy, John J. Maene Jr, Sgt Jay McCarthy, Maj Alex Martin, Col William McDonald, Maj Roy Moore, David Morphew, Maj William 'Moose' Moseley, Gary Nophsker, CMSGT Rich Newell, Al Neubecker, Rod Norman, William Potts, Charles Penley, Larry H. Rectenwald, Maj Donald L. Schmenk, Steve Sopko, Ed Sandelius, Richard Such, Everett Sprous, Peter Schinkelshoek, TSgt Norm Taylor, Col Ronald Thurlow, Tony Thornborough, MSgt Otto Uebel, SSgt Hank Valentine, SSgt Leo van Overschelde, Johan van der Wei, Peter Vanderhoef, Joe Vincent, SSgt Bobby 'Orville' Wright, Vern Wagner, Brig Gen David O. Williams Jr, Wai A. Yip.

Contents

Introduction

In the summer of 2000, an angular, glinting shape blazed through the wide blue skies of Indiana, its bold markings and polished metal surfaces proclaiming that it was no dull, grey twenty-first century warplane. It wore the extravagant red and white décor of the 353rd Fighter-bomber Squadron (FBS), a unit that flew F-100 Super Sabres (although not this one) for thirteen years from 1957. A closer look would have revealed that this F-100F (56-3948) also bore a tiny US civilian registration (N2011V) for its owner, Dean 'Cutter' Cutshall, based at Fort Wayne, Indiana. Its military career had begun in 1957 at the USAF Missile Development Test Center at Holloman AFB and ended with the Turkish Air Force, which it had served since August 1974.

Seeing its proud plumage quickened the pulses of many who recalled the days when USAF fighter units devised such dazzling displays of squadron heraldry and the F-100 was the harbinger of a new era of supersonic flight. A whole generation of fighter pilots had their supersonic initiation in the aircraft and savoured the enormous boost in performance and capability compared with the F-84s and F-86s that many of them had previously flown.

When their supremacy within the US armoury declined, many Super Sabres were passed on and gave the same excitement to the pilots of four other air forces. While most aircrew enthused, there were dissenters who considered the fighter unforgiving and over-demanding. Landing the F-100 was popularly described as a 'controlled crash' and one severely disenchanted pilot wryly suggested that its optimum mission was static display! However, the inevitable attrition while at the base of the supersonic learning curve (and in some of the foreign air forces) was vastly outweighed by the F-100's formidable reputation in the Vietnam conflict. For over six years it was America's 'heavy artillery' in South Vietnam, flying incredible numbers of combat missions with the reliability of a jeep and accuracy that made it first call for forward air controllers (FACs). Many units scored mission totals, flight safety records and availability rates that were the envy of squadrons with newer, more 'fragile' types.

Before that time, the F-100 had pioneered the concept of global deployment of tactical aircraft, using the recently developed asset of inflight-refuelling. Super Sabre units regularly took up short-notice nuclear alert duties at bases around the world, flying thousands of miles to do so.

This book describes how North American Aviation (NAA) designed a day fighter that was the first US service aircraft capable of supersonic speed in level flight. The company also designed into it an ordnance delivery capability that enabled Tactical Air Command (TAC) to use the F-100 as its standard nuclear bomber for several years until later types like the F-105, F-111 and F-4 gradually took over and refined the tactics developed by Super Sabre pilots.

To a public that was generally unaware of these Cold War strategies, the Super Sabre was better known as a spectacular performer in the Thunderbirds aerobatic team. From 1956 until 1963, crowds throughout the world were treated to thunderous displays in which the aircraft's 'cannon shot' hard-light afterburner featured prominently. When the Republic F-105B proved to be an unviable successor, the Thunderbirds stepped into F-100s once again and flew them for another five years.

In Vietnam, in addition to serving as the USAF's main 'ground pounder', the F-100 (or 'Hun' to its pilots) laid the foundations for other essential elements of modern air warfare. The techniques of airborne suppression of enemy air defences (SEAD) were first established by a select group of aircrew flying Wild Weasel F-100Fs against the surface-to-air missile (SAM) threat in North Vietnam. Other F-100F flyers developed the high-speed FAC mission that is also now established as a primary component in the contemporary battlefield scenario.

The F-100 first flew in 1953 – half a century ago – at a time when exciting new aircraft designs were announced every few months. Although it was the first of the Century Series of fighters, it soldiered on far longer than any of its successors in that innovative series of aircraft, apart from a small number of F-104 Starfighters. Within twenty years of the F-100's first flight, supersonic travel at twice the Super Sabre's top speed had become available to commercial airline passengers, and tactical fighters had become multi-mission, all-weather machines. Many of the pilots who had served in the USA's twenty-eight F-100 Wings had graduated to that new, sophisticated generation of fighters but the F-100 still remained a 'first love' and a defining experience for them.

To its groundcrews, the Hun was an aircraft with a few well-defined vices but it was also the last of the 'mechanics' aircraft. Line-replaceable units and complex avionics became the dominant features of the next breed of fighters. After the Century Series and the F-4, designers began to think of fighters that weren't 'hard to fix'.

Conceived in response to the Korean War, the F-100 fought in three other conflicts. Today, the survivors of the breed still resemble the first: menacing, silver fish with gaping mouths, cruising through the empty blue expanses, still hungry for prey.

CHAPTER 1

Fast and Fiery

The USAF's Century Series fighters, beginning with the North American Aviation (NAA) surface-to-air missile F-100, were innovative, extremely expensive and very successful programmes that generated some of the most important aircraft designs of the 1950s. Several, like the Convair F-102 and Lockheed F-104, were truly revolutionary. Others, including the F-100 and Republic's huge F-105 Thunderchief evolved more directly from earlier designs within their respective companies.

From 1948, NAA had equipped the USAF with the F-86 Sabre. A true successor to the company's classic P-51 Mustang, the F-86 appeared just in time to give the USAF a claimed victory-to-loss ratio of 8:1 in the skies over Korea. For many pilots it provided the first experience of swept-wing jet flight and it became the first jet-powered equipment for many of the world's air forces, serving several of them well for over a quarter of a century.

By 1949, the galloping pace of technical innovation in aviation made a supersonic version of the Sabre a vital USAF requirement. On 26 April 1948, NAA test pilot

George S. Welch had taken the prototype XP-86 through the sound barrier in a shallow dive, making it the first Western combat aircraft to beat that mythical limit. In the USA, only the rocket-driven Bell X-1 research plane had already achieved supersonic speed when Chuck Yeager had shown that such a thing was possible on 14 October 1947. (There is a real possibility that Welch actually exceeded the speed of sound early in October 1947, slightly before the 'official' event.) Earlier attempts had claimed the lives of several test pilots including Britain's Geoffrey de Havilland.

A team led by NAA's Vice President (Engineering) Raymond H. Rice had already explored the possibilities of sustained supersonics in level flight. They soon realized that merely improving the F-86 would not be enough. A new design, based on a far more powerful engine than the J47, would be needed. Two innovations were soon specified: an increase in wing and tail sweep to 45 degrees and an afterburning engine for greatly increased thrust. The option of using a secondary rocket motor, as used in the Dassault

A pair of F-100A-5-NAs positioned to show the difference between the original vertical stabilizer (left) and the shortened version on 52-5773.
David Menard Collection

Mirage 1 or Saunders Roe SR-53, was rejected in favour of a large axial (rather than centrifugal) turbine with thrust augmentation greater than the short afterburner used in the F-86D. Early tests with a modified F-86 showed that the '45' wing alone conferred very limited improvements in high-speed flight. Clearly, an entirely new fuselage with much lower drag had to be designed. An axial flow turbine would allow that fuselage to be much slimmer for high-speed flight, whereas a large centrifugal engine such as the proposed Pratt and Whitney (P&W) J48 would have needed a fat, draggy fuselage.

NAA projected an Advanced F-86D in August 1950 as insurance against problems with the Convair F-102 and an Advanced F-86E the following year, both of which were found inadequate by the USAF. In

Power for the Super Sabre

NAA had a variety of potential powerplants for the F-100 from its inception. The earliest proposals were for an up-rated Allison/General Electric (GE) J35 offering 9,000lb (4,000kg) of thrust compared with 5,600lb (2,540kg) or the J35 variant that had powered early Republic F-84 and Northrop F-89 fighters. GE also suggested a developed, afterburning version of their J47 (as used in the F-86 Sabre) yielding 13,000lb (5,900kg) of power. This in turn led to the GE XJ53 that was supposed to blast out a mighty 21,000lb (9,500kg) of military thrust, but never left the drawing board.

At first, the most logical choice seemed to be the 12,000lb (5,500kg) thrust Westinghouse J40, under development for the USN's A3D Skywarrior, F4D Skyray and F3H Demon. The insuperable technical challenges posed by this design led finally to the selection of a new P&W engine, the JT3 that had been under development since 1948 by Andy Willgoos to power the Boeing XB-52 bomber. It first ran in June 1949 and rapidly progressed to thrust figures beyond 10,000lb (4,550kg) – the first turbojet to achieve such a performance. Under the design leadership of Leonard S. Hobbs it became, as the J57, the vital component for many US military jets in the 1950s, powering the B-52, U-2, KC-135, F-101, and F-102 and the Navy's A3D Skywarrior and F4D Skyray. Civilian JT3s powered enormous numbers of Boeing 707s and DC-8s.

P&W's engine, the only government-funded item in the early stages of the F-100 programme, pioneered the use of a 'split' (two-spool) sixteen-stage axial-flow compressor with nine low-pressure and seven high-pressure stages. The two spools were mechanically independent and could rotate at different speeds. This arrangement allowed for higher pressure ratios than previous engines but it also improved specific fuel consumption considerably. P&W chose an arrangement of eight Iconel can-annular burner chambers developed from a system used in the earliest German and British jet engines. Each can held six burners, with cooling air passing along the outside and through a hole in the centre of each can.

In the B-52, extra take-off thrust of around 2,500lb (1,150kg) per engine was generated by the use of water injection for brief periods. A supersonic fighter clearly needed more than this and P&W (with NAA) advocated a long, integrated afterburner section to give a more massive boost. For the F-100, a structure 20ft (6m) long, weighing 5,000lb (2,300kg) was added to the 14ft (4.3m) length of the J57. It added 5,800lb (2,650kg) of kick to the 10,200lb (4,650kg) military thrust of the J57-P-21 used in most Super Sabres. F-100 pilot Charles Weidinger described it as 'the blackest, ugliest afterburner nozzle in aviation history'.

An afterburner was de rigueur for virtually all take-offs to avoid 'excessive ground roll and slow acceleration rates'. It was supposed to ignite within two seconds of selection on the throttle control, and a pilot would have had little doubt of this as he was pressed hard against the back of his seat by a sudden thrust augmentation of over 50 per cent. Unlike the afterburners added to later engines such as the J79, the F-100's afterburner was an 'all or nothing' unmodulated burst of blazing energy. However, it enabled the aircraft to fly a 4g sustained turn until the fuel ran out. Compared with later fighters such as the F-15, that could boast a power-to-weight ratio of 1:1, this was not so impressive, but in the mid-1950s it was quite an achievement for a fighter like the F-100 at 20,000lb (9,000kg) in 'clean' configuration to achieve even half that ratio.

The J57 rapidly became an extremely reliable power source. Any problems in the F-100 installation were usually associated with incorrectly functioning afterburner nozzle 'eyelids', causing surges or compressor stalls.

May 1951, came the much more promising NA-180 'Sabre 45'. Built around the new P&W J57-P-1 delivering 15,000lb (6,800kg) maximum thrust, the design offered Mach 1.3 top speed, a 580nm combat radius at 23,700lb (10,750kg) gross combat weight and four new 20mm guns for the air superiority mission. At first, NA-180 was to have been a radar-equipped interceptor to follow the F-86D, but this role eventually passed to the F-102A. In any case, the NA-180 design team wanted a large air intake in the nose to feed a controlled air mass to the J57 engine, precluding a big radome installation.

The USAF expressed a strong interest but wanted further revisions and a significant number of prototypes (eventually to include two real prototypes and ten 'production test' aircraft) so that development of the potential fighter would be rapid. A large order was in prospect, driven by a new urgency that derived from the burgeoning conflict in Korea. MiG-15 jets had been encountered from November 1950 and the USAF became painfully aware that its best fighter, the F-86, had been virtually equalled by the Soviet Union. By January 1951 NAA had begun design work on the Sabre 45 and November of that year brought a USAF contract for two prototypes and 110 production aircraft. On 7 December 1951, the design was awarded the designation 'F-100'. Although no one could foresee it at the time, this nomenclature, only ten years after Pearl Harbor, fortuitously heralded a whole generation of advanced fighter designs: the Century Series. Sadly, it was also to be NAA's third and final production fighter.

The decision to go ahead represented an act of faith in its assumption that production could begin while the various phases of acceptance testing were still in progress.

The parallel supposition that no major alteration would be needed to the design as a result of the completion of testing was also a calculated risk. For subsequent Century Series programmes, such as Convair's F-102A, this approach became known as the Cook-Craigie plan after the two USAF generals who instigated it. USAF-approved designs could thereby be put straight into production using definitive tooling and jigs rather than relying on the traditional lengthy process of hand-building a series of prototypes that gradually evolved into the production design. The inevitable minor modifications were to be made on the production line without impeding the rapid acceleration of the production line to peak output, using large stocks of components that would have already been stockpiled. It was obviously a high-risk strategy and in the case of the F-102 it meant a major redesign of both delta wing and fuselage after production had begun when tests showed that the aircraft was incapable of supersonic flight in its original form.

Some early changes were made to the Sabre 45 at the initial mock-up stage after a USAF inspection in November 1951. The hydraulic systems were routed separately to reduce battle damage risks and ammunition for each of the four guns was increased from 200 to 275 rounds. A weight saving of 60lb (27kg) came from deleting the tailskid and a further 400lb (180kg) were lost when the USAF dropped the requirement for self-sealing fuel tanks.

NAA had invested in a supersonic wind tunnel in 1949, enabling the company to test aerodynamic models at speeds up to Mach 5.25. This was used throughout 1952 to refine the F-100's configuration. Perhaps the most important change was to the horizontal tail slab, which was moved from an F-86-style position at the base of the fin to a location low on the rear fuselage with consequent improvement in stability and control at high angle of attack. A drag-reducing extension to the fuselage pushed the gaping oval air intake 9in (23cm) further forward and flattened it, while its edges were 'sharpened' to smooth the airflow at the intake lips, thereby increasing maximum speed by 50mph (80km/h). The elongated cockpit canopy was faired into the fuselage behind it, making visibility for the pilot slightly inferior to that in the F-86. However, downward visibility (even in the later two-seat F-

YF-100A 52-5754 at the USAF Academy in April 1963. Stevens via David Menard Collection

The first Super Sabre, photographed on 21 April 1953, a little over a month before its first flight. There are many external differences from the F-100A production configuration, particularly around the rear fuselage and vertical stabilizer contours.
David Menard Collection

Col 'Pete' Everest, who stood to gain a couple of beers from Welch who had bet him that the F-100 would go supersonic on its maiden flight. The prototype leapt ahead of the 'Dog Sabre' until Welch cut his afterburner to allow Everest to catch up. Then at 35,000ft (10,700m) he engaged afterburner once more and within two minutes the F-100 had exceeded Mach 1. Pete Everest got his beers and Welch made a second level-supersonic flight later the same day.

The prototype went on to fly 100 hours in its first six weeks, demonstrating excellent serviceability. Minor rudder flutter was cured by installing hydraulic dampers and the aircraft's rolling and pitching dynamic stability was explored. In other flights, Welch and NAA pilots Joe Lynch and Dan Darnell flew high-speed dives, taking the YF-100A to Mach 1.44 at its fastest. USAF pilots from Wright Air Development Center (WADC) couldn't wait until the forty-three Phase I flights for the manufacturer's test programme were over before getting their hands on the YF-100A. Pete Everest flew it within two weeks of the maiden flight and unofficial Phase II (USAF) testing began soon afterwards. Understandably, there was also a desire on the USAF's behalf for reassurance that there were no defects that were not revealed in Phase I, given that production aircraft were already starting to take shape at NAA's Inglewood plant.

Bucks for Bangs

Although the aircraft employed relatively conventional technology and structure compared with some of the later Century fighters, setting up production for a new supersonic fighter required an enormous investment by NAA. The background for the series was in itself costly, relying on the data generated by the X-1, X-2 and D-558-2 research aircraft that explored the boundaries of supersonic flight. Construction of the F-100 needed massive investment in machinery and forging processes. New lightweight materials, such as titanium, provided increased strength – in 1953–54 NAA used 80 per cent of the sheet titanium produced in the USA. A greater proportion of components were machine-milled for the F-100 than for any previous NAA aircraft. Automatic milling led to simpler structures too: the F-86 wing structural box had 462 components and

100F) was unimpeded by the wing. A pitot tube extended 5ft (1.5m) forward from a position below the intake, providing air pressure data from a point well away from airflow disturbance around the airframe. At the same time, the thickness/chord ratios of the vertical tail and slab tailplane were cut by half to a mere 3.5 per cent.

With the revised mock-up approved on 26 August 1952, the USAF increased its F-100 order to 273 units and construction of the first YF-100A proceeded apace. NAA's design department turned to the

detailed drawings for the production F-100A. YF-100A 52-5754 was completed on 24 April 1953, well ahead of its 26 June deadline and trucked to the AFFTC at Edwards AFB to be instrumented and prepared for its test programme.

Early on 25 May, '754 was towed out to Rogers Dry Lake and test pilot George 'Wheaties' Welch (who had shot down four Japanese aircraft during the December 1941 attack on Pearl Harbor and another fourteen and a half later in WWII) lit up the J57. Flying 'chase' in an F-86D was Lt

Another view of the unmarked YF-100A-1-NA on 21 April 1953. Three days later the aircraft was complete, including a long instrumentation boom on the upper intake lip. David Menard Collection

YF-100A-1-NA 52-5754 is prepared for another test flight as George 'Wheaties' Welch (on the crew ladder) discusses a cockpit item with Lt Col 'Pete' Everest. David Menard Collection

Test pilot George Welch with the first Super Sabre. He took '754 for its first flight on 25 May 1953. David Menard Collection

over 16,000 fasteners whereas the integrally stiffened F-100A wingbox used only 36 parts and 264 fasteners. The wing used skins made from metal sheets that were tapered from root to tip (like the F-86's) but also machined into integrally stiffened upper and lower skins for the first time on any fighter. The fuselage sides were each made from a single alloy sheet, formed in a massive stretch press and assembled together like a giant model kit. At the front of this structure was the sinister, hungry-looking air intake.

However, the F-100's chosen mission made it a less expensive project than most of the later Century Series types. The decision to make it a day fighter meant that no search radar was fitted (apart from the small gun-laying set squeezed into the upper surface of the intake) so the Super Sabre became the last US fighter to date with an intake in the extreme nose. The overall simplicity of the aircraft's avionics and armament represented a cost saving compared with the complex systems required, for example, for the all-weather F-101B, F-102 and F-106. However, the F-100 shared with those fighters the enormous R&D bill for advancing the US aircraft industry to the point where it could produce a range of groundbreaking designs like the Century Series jets.

Wings and Wires

Most of the innovative structure in the F-100 was designed to address the problems of making the aircraft supersonic, stable in both low and high-speed flight, capable of a safe landing speed and relatively manoeuvrable. Experience dictated the use of inboard ailerons to avoid the 'control reversal' effect that could occur when the aerodynamic loads imposed by outboard ailerons made thin, high-speed wings twist. Later designs tended to use spoilers instead. The ailerons were powered and very sensitive to pilot-induced control movements. The use of a simple, two-skin wing structure initially precluded the fitting of trailing-edge flaps, though these were to appear on the revised wing of

YF-100A '754 on take-off for another engineering test flight with a single instrumentation boom. The bulge at the rear of the fin tip is a fuel vent. David Menard Collection

Hun's Teeth: The M-39 Gun

The Super Sabre's main armament was the M-39 gun, tested in F-86F Sabres in Korea as the T-160 and put into production at GE's Pontiac Division in 1953. It fired about 1,500 electrically detonated 20mm rounds per minute, with 200 rounds per gun, allowing around eight seconds of firing. The M-39 was one of the F-100's most effective innovations and it also equipped the F-101A Voodoo, later F-86H Sabres and (as the M-39A3), the Northrop F-5. Probably it would have found other uses but the M61 Vulcan 'Gatling' gun entered service while advanced variants of the Pontiac gun were under development and became the standard gun for many of the next generation of US combat aircraft. On several occasions consideration was given to installing the M61 in later-model F-100s, but its four M-39s were invariably thought adequate for the ground-attack role that became the Super Sabre's main task.

The weapon was based on the German WWII Mauser MG-213C, a totally new design using a revolver-type cylinder to fire its shells, giving a considerably increased rate of fire. Post-war, other manufacturers adapted the design. In the UK, the Royal Small Arms Factory produced the Aden Mk.4 and the French made the DEFA 552 cannon, both weapons using 30mm ammunition and firing at about 1,200 rounds per minute.

The designers of the M-39, working to contracts at the Illinois Institute of Technology, opted for a smaller 20mm calibre to give a higher rate of fire. M50-series ammunition was fed from a belt (from the left or right side) into a five-chamber, gas-operated revolving cylinder and from there to the barrel (with right-hand twist rifling) situated at the six-o'clock position relative to the cylinder. Each 3.56oz (101g) projectile departed from the gun at around 2,850ft (870m) per second muzzle velocity. The weapon was 6ft (1.8m) in length and weighed around 178lb (80kg).

A later version, the Ford Aerospace Tigerclaws, improved the basic system – increasing the rate of fire to 2,300 rounds per minute, reducing the weight by 20 per cent and doubling 'endurance life' to 10,000 rounds.

In the F-100, ammunition was supplied from four magazines, situated two each side of the cockpit in close proximity to the pilot. Although the usual limit was 200 rounds per box to prevent cooking-off of rounds, some Super Sabres (F-100D-1 to D-15, D-35, D-40) could carry 257 per magazine. The F-100F's two M-39 or M-39A1 guns were limited to 175 rounds each and many aircraft would have carried fewer rounds for training sorties. In the F-100F, the gun barrels tended to vibrate in their blast tubes, causing mild buffeting. The weapons were manually charged before the aircraft rolled out for take-off; automatic charging from the cockpit was not allowed for. Loading the ammo was an all-manual task.

Armourer Richard G. Such, with the 431st Munitions Maintenance Squadron (MMS) based at Tuy Hoa in the Vietnam War, recalled:

It took me seven seconds to load 200 rounds in a magazine. Most of the other guys on my crew could load them just as fast. We loaded HEI [high explosive incendiary] 20mm shells only – we never loaded tracer for our F-100s. Our squadron had the best firing rate in South East Asia and we received a commendation for this. We only had a 5 per cent dud rate over the millions of rounds we loaded.

Expended ammo links were retained in compartments adjacent to the guns but the cases were ejected through tubes flush with the lower fuselage with enough force to prevent damage to the underside of the aircraft. The four guns were mounted virtually upside-down in compartments vented by slots in the fuselage. Their barrels were housed within the blast tubes and in single-seat F-100s they could be fired as an upper or lower pair or all together.

A gun compartment purging system drew air from the main air intake duct through automatic doors to clear explosive gases from the compartment during firing. The doors opened when the pilot squeezed his trigger to the first detent position (which also initiated the gun camera) and continued to admit air for five seconds after firing ceased. If the purge doors failed to open automatically, a micro-switch prevented current flowing to the gun-firing circuits. Another micro-switch neutralized the gun circuits once it sensed the aircraft's weight on the nose landing gear and a separate ground fire switch, protected by a safety-pin, had to be operated before the guns could be fired. In flight, the lower speed limit for gun firing was 250kt to prevent a build-up of gases in the gun-bays.

When static gun testing was required, all hatches for the guns and ammo bays had to be removed to allow adequate ventilation. Venting of the gun-bay in flight was vital as a build-up of gun gases during long bursts of firing could cause an explosion in the bay. Gun seal problems did occur and these affected F-100Ds of the 481st Tactical Fighter Squadron (TFS) during their 1965 deployment to Vietnam. During a mission to relieve troops in contact, Capt Joe Reynes, having made long strafing attacks on enemy troops, heard a loud explosion from his aircraft during the final pass. Looking out at the wings he saw that both gun-bay doors had blown off from the fuselage and impaled themselves on the inboard stores pylons each side. Although one door had jammed the left leading edge slat and fuel was leaking from the wing, he managed to make a safe return to Tan Son Nhut AB.

aerodynamic loads on the wing. Each leading edge had five slat sections: two outboard and three inboard, sliding up and down their guide rails independently. When the outboard sections were closed the inboard sections stayed open 2 degrees, providing an aerodynamic slot to enhance stability. In normal flight the slats would be up (or closed) except on the rare occasions that F-100s operated at very high altitudes where aerodynamic loads were reduced. At lower speeds, depending on the angle of attack, the slats would drop partially or fully open to reduce the stalling speed, enable better turning manoeuvrability or increase lift for take-off. A similar system was used on later-model F-86s and the A-4 Skyhawk. The slats were simple and reliable. Minor problems could be rectified by cleaning the guide rails with a rag but occasionally the roller bearings needed changing. At worst, the guide rails or slats might need re-aligning to stop them from jamming, 'a real Pandora's box' according to maintainer John Clarity.

A one-piece, powered and geared horizontal stabilizer was located at the base of the rear fuselage and like the ailerons it was activated by two independent, irreversible hydraulic systems. Aerodynamic loads could not be transmitted back to the pilot via the control stick so an artificial 'feel' system was incorporated in each control system, using string-loaded bungees. It provided awareness of the loads that were being placed on the airframe via the flying controls and prevented the pilot from accidentally overloading it.

The same system was also used to trim the aircraft in place of traditional trim tabs. Trim was effected just by altering the neutral position of the pilot's control column via trim switches on top of the column to give optimum stick and pedal forces. A separate take-off trim button on the pilot's left panel repositioned the artificial feel system to the take-off position. To provide the correct take-off trim position for the horizontal stabilizer, a white triangle symbol appeared on the rear fuselage and groundcrew had to check that the stabilizer was aligned with it. F-100s generally had to be hand-flown all the time: trimming for hands-off flight was barely possible.

Production F-100s had a stabilizer with a mere 3.5 per cent thickness/chord ratio although the first production F-100A was tested with a 7 per cent unit in case the stabilizer fluttered during tests on 8 December

the F-100D/F as hydraulically operated surfaces that could be lowered to a 45-degree full-down position in about ten seconds using a flap handle near the throttle control. Some aircraft had an intermediate 20-degree position for use at take-off or for inflight-refuelling, though this position could be set on any flap-equipped F-100 by using the flap-position circuit breaker.

F-100A/C models had only the Kruger leading edge wing slats for use in low-speed flight and manoeuvring. This system required no hydraulic or electrical power; the slats were operated simply by

A short-tail F-100A-5-NA receives attention during AFFTC's accelerated Phase VI flight test programme. USAF pilots and maintainers participated in this 552-hour series of service tests. David Menard Collection

1953 when the aircraft was required to reach Mach 1.45 at 35,000ft (10,700m). As the system matured with the experience of test flying, it incorporated pitch damping to neutralize pitch oscillations independently from inputs from the pilot's 'stick'. This system cut out when underwing loads other than 275 or 335gal drop tanks were carried. Both damping systems were activated by buttons on the pilot's left horizontal panel and neither system could be engaged during take-off or landing, which prevented the systems inadvertently signalling excessive flying control inputs in the case of a system failure.

The powered rudder, like each of the ailerons, was built in two sections that combined together in operation. In the case of the rudder, the division was chordwise with a hinged joint. Production aircraft had flutter dampers fitted to the rudder and hydraulic, electrically controlled yaw dampers acting upon the rudder control valve in aircraft that were not equipped with an autopilot. The F-100's rudder was such a powerful control surface that it enabled the aircraft to perform a complete 360-degree roll without the use of ailerons.

All the main flying controls were operated by a pair of independent, simultaneously operating 3,000psi hydraulic systems, each with its own engine-operated pump and each supplying half the power requirements of the flying control actuator units. The rudder drew power from the Number 2 hydraulic system, though it was later coupled to the utility system. Power on the Number 2 system could be maintained by a ram-air turbine (RAT) if the engine failed. The RAT's intake door, inside the main engine intake duct, then opened to feed air to the small turbine unit. Another door, situated on the fuselage spine behind the cockpit, also opened to exhaust this airflow. The RAT could be energized by external airflow at speeds down to 150kt, providing sufficient pressure in the control systems to maintain very basic operation. In less favourable situations where any sort of manoeuvrability was necessary, ejection was usually a safer option for the pilot, bearing in mind that an F-100 with a 'frozen' engine and landing gear extended could glide for only about 25 miles (40km) from a starting altitude of 30,000ft (9,000m).

A large 'barn door' speed brake extended from the flat, central lower fuselage. Hydraulically operated by two actuators, this surface could open and close within a couple of seconds. It could be extended at any speed, although a relief valve prevented it from opening at very high speeds (above 500kt) to prevent damage. The brake was available to slow the aircraft in all flight regimes or on approach, albeit with an increase in buffeting.

Hydraulics powered the landing gear too, extending or retracting the three units in about seven seconds. During testing, that cycling time could be reduced to less than four seconds by increasing the pressure in the system to 5,000psi. Each main wheel had hydraulic, multi-disc brakes with an anti-skid system. The dual-wheel nose-gear had a steering unit, which acted as a shimmy damper when steering was not engaged. An electrically actuated tail-skid extended and retracted simultaneously with the landing gear. Operation of the undercarriage was via a handle with an unmistakeable 'landing wheel'-shaped tip, on the left auxiliary panel in the cockpit. Landing gear positions were shown by indicators in early aircraft and later by the conventional three green lights. A black and yellow emergency handle would lower the gear if the normal system malfunctioned, with an emergency accumulator supplying hydraulic pressure to lower the nose-gear. If this accumulator had been used, a red metal rod protruded from the fuselage at the left of the nose-wheel well. Pushing the rod back in re-set the nose-gear hydraulic selector valve. An 'emergency up' button allowed the undercarriage to retract, bypassing the 'weight on wheels' switches and enabling the gear to retract while the aircraft was on the ground. In practice, only the nose-gear would actually fold up in that (hopefully unlikely) situation. Pilots had various audio warnings if the landing gear was not extended with the aircraft below 10,000ft (3,000m) and 205kt. On take-off, this system would not cut in while the engine was in afterburner.

Super Speed

The first production F-100A (52-5756) with NAA senior engineering test pilot George Welch at the controls, made its public debut on 29 October 1953 having left the production line on 25 September. Welch drove the aircraft through the sound barrier for the Press, breaking some windows and leaving more than one reporter rather breathless. Clearly the new fighter was ready to give its manufacturers a shot at the ultimate publicity tool of the

er. Less than a year later, Peter Twiss pushed the speed margins up spectacularly by hitting 1,131.76mph in the Fairey Delta 2 research aircraft off the coast of the UK.

Phase II

The forty-three flights in the manufacturer's Phase I tests were made by George Welch and two other NAA pilots. Maj Gen Albert Boyd flew the first official USAF F-100 sortie on 11 August 1953 and the seven-stage, USAF Phase II trials ran from 3–17 September.

In all, thirty-nine flights were made by project pilot Pete Everest and six other USAF pilots including Chuck Yeager. While the team praised the Super Sabre's overall performance in their twenty hours of demanding testing, there were a few reservations. Visibility over the nose was thought to be poor at high angles of attack, low speed handling was criticized and some pilots were unhappy about the fighter's longitudinal stability at high speeds. Yeager went as far as to say, 'That airplane just isn't stable. You can't fly formation with this thing'. Everest identified the problem as an over-sensitive control system with roll and yaw coupling and a tendency for the left wing to drop suddenly when near stalling speed. Directional stability appeared to deteriorate most when the aircraft was test-flown with underwing fuel tanks. The problems only became apparent when the USAF pilots wrung the jets out harder than they would be used in normal service life, but they were difficulties nevertheless for a potential combat aircraft. Everest was also unhappy about the combination of high landing speeds and slow control responses at lower speeds: no problem for an 'old head' like him, but a potential disaster for the inexperienced. He wanted the release of the aircraft to USAF squadrons to be delayed until remedial action could be taken.

Naturally, NAA defended their new product strenuously, as did many of the USAF service pilots. Bob Kemp, the chief project engineer, was receptive to many of the pilots' reservations about the new aircraft. At Welch's suggestion (according to Chuck Yeager) a number of other USAF fighter jocks were invited in to check out the F-100. Predictably, their response to the supersonic, afterburning beast was enthusiastic. Dutch Kindelberger visited

'754 received a good polish for its world speed record flight on 29 October 1953. Record-breaker Lt Col 'Pete' Everest, then Chief of the Flight Test Operations Laboratory at Edwards AFB, poses with the aircraft. An alternative instrumentation boom arrangement is evident here. USAF via David Menard Collection

time – success in an international speed record attempt.

LCDR James Verdin, project pilot on the USN's Douglas F4D-1 Skyray, had surprised the F-100 team by taking his delta jet to 752.9mph over a 1.86 mile (3km) course, beating recently set records by Britain's Neville Duke and Mike Lithgow. With the USAF's honour on the line, Pete Everest flew F-100A '754 at 75ft (23m) altitude over the Salton Sea, reaching 755mph (1,247km/h) over a 9.3 mile (15km) course on 29 October. It was enough to secure a new record for the F-100 and on one run Everest exceeded 767mph

(1,234km/h), Mach 0.97, faster than the F4D-1's best. However, it was the last record to be flown at such risky altitudes, although in August 1961 a USN crew flew a record-breaking F4H-1 Phantom flight at 902.769mph, never exceeding 125ft (38m) above ground level. By that time, F-100 pilots were practising nuclear strike flights across Europe at altitudes of 50ft (15m) or lower, but the next F-100 record flight was conducted at 35,000ft (10,700m) where Col H. A. Hanes reached 822mph (1,322km/h) in an F-100C on 20 August 1955. It was the world's first supersonic speed record, flown by an operational fight-

Making its first take-off from Los Angeles international airport en route to Edwards AFB, the second F-100A-1-NA 'roasts the runway'. USAF via David Menard Collection

but it was to cause major problems in that it unexpectedly reduced the fighter's 'weathercock' stability factor.

The 479th made the most of their new steed's performance in training. At this time, the USAF's day fighter capability was still dominated by sixteen F-86 Wings and a dozen with Republic F-84Fs. George's three supersonic hot-rod units were the place to be. However, their Commander strongly emphasized safety and sought to build a sound technical support base for the new jet. After the Korean War many enlisted mechanics returned to better-paid civilian jobs, leaving the still-expanding USAF short of personnel. Operation *Toolbox* was launched to provide skilled maintainers for aircraft like the F-100.

Sadly, the Super Sabre's service initiation took place against a background of accidents as the test programme continued. With tragic irony, the worst of these took the life of George Welch. He was scheduled, on 12 October 1954, to perform the final test in a series that would take the fighter close to the limits of its structural endurance in a manoeuvre that combined maximum g and maximum Mach number. Flying the ninth production F-100A (52-5764) Welch attempted to take the airframe to its load limits of 7.3g by pulling out of a steep supersonic dive at 23,500ft (7,200m). Having failed to reach the exact parameters on his first flight, he repeated the test later that morning. He radiochecked with NAA's Palmdale Flight Test

the Pentagon to play down what he took to be minor criticisms of the aircraft by some of the Phase II testers. His view won the day with USAF commanders, who were in any case eager to see the prestigious F-100As perched on their flightlines. The cycle of production and delivery went ahead while five phases of the acceptance tests were still to be completed. The initial batch of 110 F-100As was to be followed by two further orders bringing the total to 203.

The urgent need to deliver F-100s and introduce a whole new generation of pilots to modern fighter combat tactics caused NAA to seek a second production source for the F-100C and subsequent F-100D. On 11 October 1954, it was announced that the former Curtis-Wright plant at Columbus, Ohio had been chosen and Super Sabres followed FJ Furies off the line at this, NAA's Columbus Division. One batch of twenty-five F-100C-10-NH aircraft emerged before F-100D production began there, with Block numbers also using an '-NH' manufacturer's code suffix rather than the '-NA' of Inglewood aircraft. In fact, when F-100 production ended at the 2,294th machine, the total came to only 25 per cent of the number of F-86 and FJ fighters delivered – NAA had hoped for a much bigger run.

On 29 September 1954, the 479th Fighter (Day) Wing (FDW) was activated at George AFB using sixty of the F-100As that had already left NAA's Inglewood

plant. The Wing had operated F-86F Sabres and its 436th Fighter (Day) Squadron (FDS) received its first new aircraft when its Commander, Lt Col M. G. Long, landed Tactical Air Command's (TAC's) first F-100A (53-1541) at George. In natural metal finish with USAF insignia on the nose, FW-541 had the abbreviated vertical stabilizer of early F-100As. Reduced in height, aspect ratio and rudder span compared to the YF-100A's, the revised fin saved a little weight

'FW' buzz numbers first appeared on the F-100A's nose, then on the rear fuselage but heat from the afterburner quickly obliterated them. Finally, they were painted on the centre fuselage where they stayed until 1965. F-100A-10-NA 53-1538 was used by the USAF's ARDC. David Menard Collection

F-100A-5-NA 52-5775 with Nellis AFB's CTAF emblem on its tail. This aircraft was also used by the WADC at Wright Field as an EF-100A in 1954. At that time it had the short vertical stabilizer. Norm Taylor Collection

The 140th F-100A nearing completion on the Los Angeles production line.
David Anderton Collection via David Menard

Centre that he was about to commence the dive over the Rosamond Dry Lake, Mojave – and then no more was heard from him. The aircraft was seen to explode at 20,000ft (6,000m) and two parachutes were sighted, one of them the braking chute with part of the rear fuselage still attached to it. On the other parachute was the fatally injured Welch, his body lacerated by debris from the disintegrating F-100.

The accident investigators began an exhaustive analysis of the myriad tiny pieces of wreckage and interviewed 170 witnesses. The crew of a B-47 Stratojet, returning from the practice range at Salton Sea, had observed the fatal dive as the F-100 arced over from 45,000ft (13,700m) and then came apart at less than 20,000ft (6,000m).

Among the fragments was a small cine camera, part of the test instrumentation. It had been focused on the aircraft's left horizontal stabilizer and its last few frames of film showed the shadow of the F-100's vertical fin pass very rapidly over the tailplane. Combined with some salvaged film from an oscillograph in the cockpit recording control forces and positions at the time of the disaster, this evidence showed that the aircraft had entered a supersonic side-slip that massively overstressed the airframe and tore it apart. The F-100A had comparatively short flying surfaces and a long, heavy fuselage, with its principal axis of manoeuvre running from nose to tail. It had entered a supersonic pullout and the aerodynamic loads then moved to other axes, causing the aircraft to roll and exacerbating the yaw that had already been present throughout the dive. It is also possible that the structure of the two-section ailerons, whose upward-moving panels moved further than the downward-moving sections, caused uneven drag across the wings and added to the yaw. As the yaw worsened with an increasing angle of attack during the pullout the vertical stabilizer was unable to provide adequate directional stability and the aircraft could no longer be controlled.

Although Welch's F-100A had been pushed beyond the parameters of normal service flying, the accident triggered severe problems for the programme. With over seventy aircraft in service and mass production under way, a rapid solution was urgently needed. Although the USAF had officially accepted the fighter, NAA would have to bear part of the burden of any modifications that might be deemed necessary after an

Slick Chicks

The RF-100A 'Slick Chick'. This aircraft was lost in a crash near Bitburg on October 1956. via Larry Engesath

Although the 36th FDW initiated the F-100 air superiority/attack variants into United States Air Forces in Europe (USAFE) service, the first Super Sabres in USAFE were in fact a trio of highly secret spy planes; the RF-100A reconnaissance Huns. In the early 1950s, the USA needed aircraft that could make deep, high-speed penetration flights over Soviet territory to investigate its burgeoning defence build-up, particularly its intercontinental ballistic missiles (ICBMs).

While Clarence 'Kelly' Johnson at Lockheed went to work on his U-2 design to meet the need in the long term, NAA responded to a USAF request to equip six F-100As with five Chicago Aerial Survey cameras each – two split-vertical 36in (91cm) K-38s, a pair of tri-camera K-17s and a prime-vertical, tri-camera K-17C. While not as advanced as the Hycon 'B' cameras under development for the U-2, these instruments could resolve images of golf balls on a grass course from 53,000ft (16,200m) altitude. The aircraft needed an optical viewfinder (above the instrument panel in place of the A-4 gun sight) to sight its cameras, a speed of 530mph (853km/h) at 53,000ft to evade the defences and an endurance of 5½ hours.

The F-100A had only just entered production at the time, but the USAF's late-1953 request was urgent and a seven-man NAA team directed by Don Rader was given a mere three weeks to modify the new fighter as a camera-ship. The M-39E guns were removed to provide the obvious locations for two cameras, with two more in the ammunition bays and one in the right-hand expended ammunition compartment. Their associated electrical heating and control equipment went in the left-hand expended ammunition bay. The aft electronics bay (behind the ammunition boxes) was used for an extra 830gal fuel tank. To provide further range, inboard pylons (similar to those on the F-100C but with extra sway-braces attaching them to the fuselage) were fitted and plumbed for 200gal fuel tanks to complement

This view emphasizes the twin bulges for the camera installations and the sway-braces connecting the inboard pylons to the fuselage. via Larry Engesath

the standard 275gal 'supersonic' tanks. In order to squeeze the last few miles, an extra 30gal of fuel were pumped into the fuel venting system through a new filler cap on the upper dorsal fairing, providing just enough JP-4 to start the engine and taxi to take-off without cutting into the main fuel supply. F-100As could not be refuelled in flight and in any case tankers could not have accompanied them on their dangerous overflights.

The gun sight radar was removed and the AN/ARN-6 radio compass, fuel control amplifier, main power inverter and battery equipment displaced from the elec-

tronics bay were installed there instead. The voltage regulator and some other electrical control panels moved to the left-hand ammunition bay. In the cockpit there were changes to the side consoles to remove the armament control panel and add controls for an airborne navigation system that continuously computed the aircraft's position using data from the F-100's own sensors. An MM-2 attitude gyro replaced the equivalent Type J-8 model and a pedestal mount, installed on the cockpit floor between the pilot's legs, held the camera controls and an emergency drop-tank release lever. Another handle on the right-hand forward cockpit rail operated an emergency system to open the external doors on the camera bays.

Although two of the cameras were mounted horizontally, using angled mirrors to acquire their imagery, the forward fuselage would not accommodate the five cameras without modification. It was therefore deepened (primarily between Stations 80 and 267) with a pair of boxy 'jowl' fairings incorporating motor-driven, protective doors for the optics. There were new doors, and panels extending the ammunition and electrical bays outboard of the original fuselage mould line by about 5in (13cm) each side. (For their earlier RF-86F recce variant

NAA used similar but smaller bulges in the side-panels of the F-86F to squeeze in a very cramped camera array.) The RF-100A's camera viewfinder used a metal tube projecting through the engine air inlet to a small window beneath the nose. Flying at such an altitude required the pilot to wear a pressure suit as a back-up to the cockpit pressurization, with consequent cockpit modifications and the 5½ hour endurance parameter meant a big increase in the gaseous oxygen supply.

A final structural modification was a pair of bolt-on 12in (30.5cm) wing-tip extensions (taking the span up to 38.8ft/11.8m) to help with the altitude requirement, an

Slick Chicks (*Continued*)

1 RADIO EQUIPMENT
  TRUE AIRSPEED COMPUTER
  A2 AMPLIFIER
  BATTERY AND SUMP JAR
  POWER INVERTER
  SPEED CONTROL UNIT
  YAW DAMPER AMPLIFIER
  YAW DAMPER POWER SUPPLY
  I.M.C. POWER SUPPLY*
  ASN-6 COMPUTER
  ASN-6 AMPLIFIER

2 REMOVE FAIRING FOR ACCESS TO SURFACE CONTROLS

3 TRI OBLIQUE CAMERA

4 GENERATOR VOLTAGE REGULATOR
  POWER CONTROL PANEL
  GENERATOR FIELD CONTROL RELAY
  ELECTRICAL CONTROL PANEL

5 IMAGE COMPENSATION MOTOR

6 EMERGENCY BRAKE ACCUMULATOR AIR FILLER VALVE, AIR GAGE AND DUMP VALVE

7 OXYGEN FILLER

8 SPLIT VERTICAL AND AIR CONDITIONING EQUIPMENT

9 CAMERA REFRIGERATION EQUIPMENT

1 LATERAL ACCELEROMETER
2 RT-263/ARC-34 RECEIVER-TRANSMITTER
3 F-137 INVERTER
4 R-101/ARN-6 RECEIVER
5 RT-82/APX-6 RECEIVER-TRANSMITTER
6 ACCELEROMETER AMPLIFIER
7 YAW DAMPER POWER SUPPLY
8 CP-188 ASN-6 COMPUTER
9 PILOT'S INSTRUMENT PANEL
10 TRI OBLIQUE CAMERAS
11 FUEL GAGE AMPLIFIER
12 ELECTRIC BAY FUEL CELL
13 YAW DAMPER AMPLIFIER

14 A-2 AMPLIFIER
15 MA-1 TRUE AIRSPEED COMPUTER XMTR
16 BATTERY
17 AM-916 ASN-6 ELECTRONIC CONTROL AMPLIFIER
18 RADIO FUSE BOX ASSEMBLY
19 OPTICAL VIEW FINDER
20 CAMERA CONTROL PEDESTAL
21 IMC MOTOR*
22 SPLIT VERTICAL CAMERAS
23 TRI VERTICAL CAMERA
24 CAMERA AIR CONDITIONING EQUIPMENT COMPARTMENT
* IMAGE MOTION COMPENSATION

P-100A-1050-00-1

10 FUEL VENT FILLER
11 FUEL FILLER
12 HYDRAULIC SYSTEM
   EMERGENCY DOOR ACCUMULATOR
   AIR GAGE, TRI OBLIQUE CAMERA, AND FUEL GAGE AMPLIFIER

13 TRI VERTICAL CAMERA
14 SPLIT VERTICAL CAMERA
15 TEMPERATURE SENSING BULB
* IMAGE MOTION COMPENSATION

P-100A-1050-00-2A

These NAA drawings give an idea of the camera and equipment layout in the RF-100A.

RF-100A 53-1551 cleaning up after take-off before delivery to the 7407th SS in West Germany. via Larry Engesath

addition that would appear on production F-100As together with the extended vertical stabilizer also used on the RF-100A. The wing was also strengthened internally to take a pair of drop tanks on the inboard pylons. All RF-100As had the J57-P-39 engine.

The half-dozen selected F-100A-10-NAs were rebuilt with a great deal of skill and improvisation. The project, code-named *Slick Chick* on 7 December 1954 and conducted with great secrecy, involved aircraft 53-1545/48, -1551 and -1554. The serials are important since the aircraft frequently bore false serials (such as 53-2600) during service to confuse the opposition. Known unofficially as RF-100As, they were always simply F-100As on USAF records to thicken the security blanket.

With flight testing completed by mid-1954, pilot training was initiated and the 'Slick Chicks' were handed over to the USAF in spring, 1955. Three were destined for use in the Pacific area with the 6021st Recce Squadron at Yokota where they arrived on 2 June 1955. The others were shipped to the UK aboard USS *Tripoli* and then flown from Burtonwood to Bitburg, West Germany on 16 May 1955. Their parent unit was the 7407th Support Squadron (SS), already flying RB-57A spyplanes out of Rhein Main AB.

Detachment 1 of the 7407th SS, commanded by Maj Bert E. Dowdy, began test flights with its 'Chicks', partly to ascertain that the use of continuous afterburner for more than the recommended fifteen minutes was possible. The J57-P39 engines were also 'tweaked' to give 16,000lb (7,250kg) thrust. Later, they were replaced with the up-rated J57-P21 engines of production F-100Ds, but the Detachment reverted to the 'Dash 39' model (since it gave better performance above 40,000ft/12,000m) until the 'Dash 21A' was refitted once again in 1957. Detachments were made to Furstenfeldbruck, Rhein Main and Hahn in West Germany, and (allegedly) Incirlik in Turkey.

In all, Detachment 1 flew over 800 missions, many of them high-speed dashes over the border to photograph Soviet missile installations. Speed was the 'Slick Chicks' only defence and pilots frequently encountered anti-aircraft fire and attempted interceptions by Soviet fighters. Like their SR-71A successors they were there and gone before the defences could respond effectively. There were no losses over hostile territory but 53-1551 crashed 15 miles (24km) north of Bitburg in October 1956, probably due to a mechanical fault, with only 213 flight hours on its record. The pilot ejected successfully. It was replaced by an F-100C (55-2711) for training purposes. During one mission the pilot remained in afterburner for almost thirty minutes to avoid Soviet interceptors, causing such severe heat damage to the aft section of his aircraft that a new rear fuselage section had to be bolted on.

When Detachment 1 was shut down at Bitburg on 1 July 1958, the RF-100A had already been superseded by the higher-flying Martin RB-57F and Lockheed U-2A/C. Improvements in Soviet air defences made the relatively heavy, unmanoeuvrable RF-100A too vulnerable. However, the loss of Gary Powers' U-2 in May 1960 showed that even the stratospheric Lockheed design was not immune to a new generation of Soviet surface-to-air missiles (SAMs) and better fighter tactics. The two surviving RF-100As plus the two remaining from those based at Yokota (53-1548 was lost on 23 June 1955) were returned to NAA's Inglewood plant in June 1958 and all four were transferred under MAP to the Republic of China Air Force's (RoCAF's) 4th Reconnaissance Squadron where they remained until late 1960. All were subsequently scrapped.

urgent examination of the F-100's stability problems. Project pilot Jack Simpson was one of several USAF pilots who had already expressed grave reservations about the short tail. On a November 1954 gun sight test, Simpson's F-100A entered a nose-right yaw during a split-S manoeuvre and ended up going almost sideways at transonic speed. Metal from the right side of the vertical stabilizer was torn away.

The basic 'fix' agreed upon was simple: a 26in (66cm) increase in wingspan and a taller vertical stabilizer with 27 per cent greater area. In effect, this meant a return to the taller, higher aspect ratio fin used on

Three of the new breed of 'Mach Busters' step to their jets at George AFB. On the left is Col Foster L. Smith who later became a USAF Maj General. The line-up of 436th FBS F-100As has the squadron's 'Mach Busters' tail insignia. Scalloped intake designs in squadron colours and 'speed lines' behind the squadron emblem were added later. David Menard Collection

A whole generation of fighter pilots experienced the new world of supersonic flight as they progressed from their T-33A trainers to the new F-100A. USAF

the YF-100A. It had been abbreviated on early production aircraft to save weight and drag. This in turn meant reduced rudder area since the fuel vent above the rudder had been moved lower on the fins of early F-100As. All seventy squadron F-100As had to be modified, plus 108 at various stages of production. George's F-100As were grounded from 11 November 1954 until early February 1955 and the modification programme continued into May of that year. The first modified aircraft was the thirty-fourth off the line, an F-100A-10-NA, but aircraft in the latter part of production Block 20 were the first to have the changes incorporated during production. Other improvements included at this stage were a retractable tail-skid (from F-100A 52-5766 onwards), a yaw damping system (from late Block 15 F-100As) and pitch damping (Block 20). From the 167th aircraft onwards the J57-P-7 was replaced by the -39 variant, though there was no thrust increase.

Despite all this, Dutch Kindelberger joined Douglas Aircraft's designer Ed Heinemann at the White House in December 1954 to receive the highly prized Collier Trophy. NAA's share of the award recognized the F-100 as representing 'the greatest

achievement in aviation in America'. The modifications had in any case greatly improved the F-100's handling characteristics and would eventually almost remove the risk of pilot-induced oscillations.

Unfortunately, the difficulties persisted. A strike at NAA's Los Angeles factory seriously disrupted production from October to December 1953, and there were further accidents. On 8 November, shortly after Welch's crash, Air Cdr G. D. Stephenson, Commander of the RAF's Central Fighter Establishment, was killed when the

F-100A (53-1534) he was evaluating at Eglin AFB sustained loss of control through pilot-induced oscillations and disintegrated. The next day, Maj Frank N. Emory ejected from F-100A 52-5771 after loss of control during a Phase IV gunnery test. In all, six losses and two fatalities preceded the USAF's decision to ground the fleet while the structural modifications were carried out.

In February 1955, NAA test pilot George F. Smith became the first man to survive a supersonic bale-out: all the more remarkable since he was dressed in Levis and a sports shirt. He had agreed to give production aircraft F-100A 53-1659 its initial flight during a chance visit to the factory on his day off. At 35,000ft (10,700m) a minor hydraulic fault locked the control column as the aircraft entered an uncommanded dive. Smith apparently ejected at 780mph (1,255km/h) – just five seconds before the Super Sabre smashed into the sea, landing near a Sea Scout vessel. He had a catalogue of internal injuries and lost nearly 28lb (13kg) in weight as a result of the colossal air pressure on ejection but, he lived to fly again.

By the end of 1955 all the production F-100As had been delivered, and in September the 479th FDW finally reached initial operational capability (IOC) at George AFB. Other F-100As had arrived at Nellis AFB (52-5761 was the first visitor in August 1954) for the use of the 3595th Combat Crew Training Wing (CCTW) and for R&D work within that unit. F-100As served with Air Material Command and other test units, but the most extensive use of the surviving USAF examples was to be in the three Air National Guard units: the 152nd Fighter

A very rare shot of an F-100A-20-NA used by the 323rd FBW for transition to the F-100D at Bunker Hill AFB in 1956. The markings (a squadron colour band in red, blue or yellow with black check borders) were designed by Maj Bill Dillard, the original leader of the 48th FBW Skyblazers team in their F-84G/F-86F years. David Menard Collection

A neat quartet of F-100A-10 and -15-NAs on the prowl. The lead aircraft (53-1589) later flew with the Republic of China AF after service with the Arizona ANG's 152nd TFTS and it was preserved as '0218' at Taiwan's National University. John Maene Collection

Interception Squadron (FIS), Arizona ANG (May 1958 – until 1969), the 118th FBS Connecticut ANG (mid-1960–January 1966), and the 188th Fighter-bomber Squadron (FBS) New Mexico ANG (April 1958–early 1964). Of the 203 F-100As accepted by the USAF only those at George AFB served with a front-line Wing. Fifty were lost in accidents and over half the total production run (122 F-100As and four RF-100A reconnaissance variants) was eventually transferred to the RoCAF. By the end of 1955, the USAF had already decided that the F-100 was better suited to the fighter-bomber role. Project *Hot Rod*, flown at Eglin AFB by Air Proving Ground Command pilots, found shortcomings in the F-100A's operational capability that made it less than ideal for the air superiority role. Four years later, a similar decision was made concerning the Lockheed F-104A interceptor after only a year's service with Air Defense Command (ADC). It had another short USAF career as the F-104C fighter-bomber, also with the 479th TFW after it ceased F-100 operations and was then shifted to the export market. However, in USAF service the F-100 was to prove one of the most enduring and effective attack aircraft it had ever possessed.

450th FDG F-100C-5-NAs on the ramp at Foster AFB. FW-775 is the Wing Commander's aircraft with fuselage bands complementing the red, white and blue tail colours. David Menard Collection

CHAPTER 2

Swords Unsheathed

F-100C-1-NA 53-1777 was TAC's first F-100C, delivered on 14 July 1955. It took part in the 4 September 1955 Bendix Race from George AFB to Philadelphia, averaging 610mph (980km/h) on the 2,325 mile (3,740km) journey with Col Carlos Talbott as pilot. The aircraft was later lost in a crash at Foster AFB. John Maene Collection

F-100C

More than a few disenchanted fighter pilots have observed that because the heavy hand of Strategic Air Command (SAC) ruled the USAF in the 1950s and early 1960s, fighter aircraft were all too quickly turned into bombers. They also point to the escort fighters (like the F-101 Voodoo) that were originally intended to protect SAC's fleet in flight and the interceptors whose main task seemed to be to protect SAC bomber and missile installations. There were certainly insufficient 'pure' air superiority fighters between the F-86 Sabre of the early 1950s and the mid-1970s F-15 Eagle to satisfy fighter pilots from the dogfighting tradition, and the F-100 was no exception after it was re-roled from a defensive to an offensive mission.

Following a comparatively short run of F-100A air superiority fighters, the USAF wanted a new version, the F-100C, with a substantial attack capability to replace its nuclear-capable but under-powered Republic F-84Fs. Beneath the evolving 'big stick' of the nuclear triad of intercontinental ballistic missiles (ICBMs), bombers and submarine-based missiles, strategic planners required a tactical layer of response that was based closer to the action than SAC's airbases. This would enable smaller nuclear and conventional weapons to be directed very rapidly at, for example, a Soviet armoured advance into Western Germany. Fighter-bomber aircraft for this role required high speed at low altitude to avoid counter-air defences,

An early F-100C-1-NA pre-delivery. The 'US Air Force' stencil remained on the tail-fin of most F-100As, F-100Cs and some early F-100Ds. *John Maene Collection*

Factory-fresh F-100C-10-NH 55-2724, one of the twenty-five F-100Cs built at NAA's Columbus, Ohio facility as preparation for its use as a second source for F-100Ds. Braking parachute doors beneath the rear fuselage are open. This aircraft was later used by the Thunderbirds team. *John Maene Collection*

and adequate range to give their pilots a chance of something better than a one-way mission. At first this mission fell to F-84 and some F-86 units.

The F-100A's range was insufficient for the task and the only place for more fuel was in the wing, a 'dry' structure in the original F-100 design. North American Aviation (NAA) had already conducted feasibility studies for a 'wet' wing (giving the equivalent range extension of two 275gal tanks) during the F-100A design phase. In July 1953, the company was asked for further wing redesign to include strengthening for extra stores pylons, bringing the total to three each side. The inboard pylons could only accept stores short enough to allow the undercarriage to retract behind them. These pylons were bolt-on installations, lacking the explosive jettisonable facility of the F-100D pylons. The redesigned wing had leak-proofing sealant injected into all spars and boltholes in the fuel-retaining areas of the structure. These tanks added 422gal, which made a total of 1,189gal of internal fuel including the forward, intermediate and aft fuselage tank sections. All were refuelled via a new single-point receptacle low on the left fuselage behind the wing-root and fed to the engine through a small (1.6gal) inverted

The F-100C concept gave the Hun a primary fighter-bomber capability and the third aircraft, 53-1711 was used to test its maximum ordnance-carrying muscle. Triangular sway-braces are fitted to the inner sides of all pylons, the largest attaching the long inboard pylons to the fuselage. David Menard Collection

The F-100's original standard drop tank was the NAA Type III 275gal 'banana' tank with integral pylon. 53-1710 was the second F-100C-1-NA used for Phase II tests at AFFTC, Edwards AFB and it won the Mackay Trophy with a record speed of 822mph (1,322km/h) on 20 August 1955. John Maene Collection

flight tank (allowing short periods of negative g flight) within the centre fuel tank. A detachable inflight-refuelling probe was added inboard beneath the right wing as another range extender. At first this was a short, straight, tubular installation that provided pilots with some real problems in operational use when they tried to insert it into the trailing fuel-line 'basket' behind a tanker aircraft. Col Tom Germscheid flew F-100Ds with this short probe at Cannon AFB in 1957:

It was virtually impossible to see the end of the probe from your normal cockpit position. You could get a glimpse of it if you squinched your head forward against the upper right side of the canopy but it was almost impossible to fly the tight formation required for refuelling from this position. The result was that you had to guess and estimate where the probe was. You would fly up to the drogue and stabilize about 10ft back from the basket, then make vertical and lateral adjustments in your position, stabilize again and then advance the throttle to give you a pretty good overtake on the basket. You had to hit it with pretty good acceleration to engage the basket latch. Often, turbulence around the airframe would cause the basket to move. You would look for the fuel hose to 'snake', when you hit the basket. If you didn't see it snake as you advanced the last ten or so feet you had probably missed the drogue and the basket was probably beating up your wing-slats or the fuselage sides. If you just hit the lip of the basket it would do a loop and hit the canopy or the top of the fuselage. We had a number of shattered canopies during refuelling. On a practice refuelling near Cannon AFB a refuelling drogue became entangled in an F-100's horizontal stabilizer. The drogue hose broke and an inertial reel zapped it back into the tanker's refuelling pod, igniting a fire on the tanker whose nine crew members successfully bailed out. The F-100 jock painted a KB-50 silhouette on the side of his bird.

If you hit the basket with too much acceleration you would overshoot and bend the probe or even tear it off the F-100. Around 1958 NAA came out with a modification to extend the probe about 4ft, moving the contact point with the drogue forward and into less severe turbulence. It was somewhat easier to see the lengthened probe from the cockpit. Later, they put a bend in the probe, raising the tip up about 3ft. You could then see it from the cockpit out of your peripheral vision and this made refuelling a piece of cake.

One theory has it that an accidentally bent probe gave pilots the idea that it

Wheelus-based F-100Cs of the 7272nd FTW initially wore dramatic red and yellow markings, replaced by the more formal dark blue bands (as seen here) and then by a simple Wing patch. Author's Collection

Inflight-refuelling was the key to the F-100's success as a 'global warrior'. F-100C 54-1830, flown by a 322nd FDG pilot, has made a successful connection using the original, short refuelling probe. USAF via David Menard

would be easier to see a deliberately 'kinked' version.

Our KB-50D tankers' top speed was around 250kt, not far from our stalling speed when loaded up. The KB-50D had three drogues – two on the wings and one tail pod: that was definitely the easiest position to refuel from. Wing turbulence from the tanker caused the wing-mounted drogues to become pretty evasive. While at Cannon I participated in a test for refuelling F-100s off a KC-97, SAC's primary refueller at the time. A drogue on a short hose was attached to the end of the KC-97's 'flying boom', and we merely had to fly into position and the boomer would 'fly' the drogue on to our probe. Piece of cake!? Almost – the problem was lack of tanker airspeed. They had a hard time reaching 200kt. We had to descend to around 10,000ft to refuel. When we got loaded up with fuel our angle of attack would increase and we ran out of power to hang on the boom. We would call, 'Toboggan' and the tanker started to descend, thus reducing our angle of attack. Then we would stay on this descent course until we got our full load of gas. This was the precursor to later refuelling from the KC-135 Stratotanker, which was a piece of cake.

An additional range booster was the 'buddy' refuelling system, developed by NAA in roughly the same timeframe as Ed Heinemann's similar system for his A-4 Skyhawk. This system, the first for a supersonic fighter, was cleared for the F-100D but not used operationally.

Other innovations for the F-100C included improved yaw and pitch damping systems resulting from F-100A experience. These gyro-based stabilizers could be activated from the cockpit. A hydraulic actuator and bungee 'feel' device were installed at the base of the vertical stabilizer. Early F-100Cs were still limited in rate of roll to 200 degrees to avoid 'barrelling'.

The original J57-P-7 engine was replaced by the J57-P-21 from the 101st production aircraft following the first test flight of this powerplant in an F-100C in September 1955. An interim J57-P-39 variant was used in some of the earlier F-100Cs. The 'Dash 21' and the later J57-P-21A (used in the F-100D) supplied 10,200lb (4,650kg) of sea-level static thrust at military thrust and about 16,000lb (7,250kg) with afterburner, improving the F-100C's high-altitude speed by 35kt and knocking 10 per cent off its time to climb to 35,000ft (10,700m). At that altitude it was the fastest Super Sabre, clocking 795kt in an air superiority configuration and beating the heavier F-100D/F by 20kt.

Avionics comprised AN/ARN-21 tactical air navigation (TACAN), AN/ARN-6 radio compass, AN/ARN-31 ILS, AN/APX-6A (later AN/APX-25) identification, friend or foe (IFF) set and AN-APG-30A radar ranging for the A-4 gunsight. The M-1 bombing system (later supplemented by an MA-2 low altitude bombing system (LABS), invented by Maj John A. Ryan) controlled delivery of the F-100C's maximum bomb load of 5,500lb (2,500kg) and this could include nuclear weapons. Progressive update programmes equipped some F-100Cs with a Minneapolis-Honeywell MB-3 autopilot and, ten years after the variant entered service, cluster bomb unit (CBU) and air intercept missile (AIM)-9 Sidewinder capability for the surviving examples in Air National Guard (ANG) units. Tactical Air Command (TAC) squadron F-100Cs never received the TO 1F-00C-563 update to enable them to fire the AIM-9. However, F-100Cs were cleared for MK series bombs up to 2,000lb (900kg), high velocity aircraft (rocket) (HVA(R)) projectiles and chemical tanks,

Checking the straight refuelling probe on a 322nd FDG F-100C, crewed by S/Sgt Fields. The pylon (to the left) is for a bulky 450gal tank. David Menard Collection

though the most usual under-wing load was actually a pair of 275gal fuel tanks.

Although the new inboard stores pylons (Wing Station 55) were meant to carry range-stretching 200gal type IV fuel tanks, these had an adverse effect on longitudinal stability. Instead, a pair of bulky 450gal type II or 335gal type III tanks could be used in place of the standard 275gal NAA type III 'supersonic' tanks on the intermediate wing pylons (Wing Station 106). The type III 335gal variants were simply 275gal tanks with a 28in (71cm) plug in their forward sections for the extra fuel.

If the big 450gal 'bags' (mainly used on F-100Ds) without internal baffles were hung on the intermediate pylons, they had to be fully fuelled or totally empty. Otherwise, fuel sloshing to and fro could unbalance the aircraft beyond its cg limits during take-off. Pilots were in any case instructed to use internal fuel for take-off, switching

to drop tanks after climb-out to altitude. A further limitation was that guns could not be fired with empty fuel tanks on the inboard pylons.

F-100C, D and F models had a further set of pylons on the outboard wing stations (STA 155) for ordnance up to 750lb bombs or 200gal tanks, though the latter were seldom carried. External ordnance and tanks apart from the 275gal pattern had some inevitable negative effects on the F-100's stability. In pilot Alex Martin's opinion, 'The 275gal tanks were so common you barely noticed them after a while but the 450gal ferry tanks, rocket launchers etc. were worse. But if you needed to, one punch on the jettison button and you were clean'.

Don Schmenk, who flew the F-100 extensively in Europe and Vietnam, noted that, 'Inboard stores made the airplane "squirrelly". It wasn't too bad with

F-100C-20-NA 54-1921 of the 7272nd FTW at Wheelus AB was one of the
high-speed target tug aircraft provided for gunnery training of USAFE squadrons.
Author's Collection

inboard, intermediate and outboard stores
but it was bad with inboard stores only,
which was an unusual load'.

F-100D

Further development of the design in
response to TAC requests in May 1954
brought about the F-100D variant, in
which the 'D' could have stood for 'definitive' since it was the final and principal
single-seat production version. A total of

1,274 were manufactured after the run of
476 F-100Cs and 203 F-100As. The first
production F-100C flew on 17 January
1954 with Al White in the cockpit following the first flight on 1 March 1954 of
a 'dry wing' prototype (F-100A 52-5759)
that tested the other F-100C systems. The
first flight of 53-1709, the initial F-100C,
could have happened earlier as it was ready
in mid-October of the previous year.
Delays resulted from the series of F-100A
accidents. Production of the C model was
completed in July 1956 and by that time

the prototype F-100D had flown (24 January 1956, piloted by Dan Darnell) and D-
model Super Sabres began to appear on
the flight lines of the 405th Fighter-
bomber Wing (FBW) at Langley AFB,
replacing Republic F-84Fs.

Externally, the F-100D had the same
fuselage length as the F-100C, but
increased fin height added 4in (10cm) to
the overall length measurement. There
was extra vertical tail area, taking the
overall height from 15.3ft (4.7m) to 16.2ft
(4.9m) and a larger fairing was added
above the rudder to house an AN/APS-54
tail warning antenna. The increased
height gave slightly more area to the rudder, which retained the external-ribbed
structure of most F-100A/C rudders. More
obvious when seen in plan form was the
change in the wing's rear outline to incor-
porate inboard, trailing-edge flaps. An
increase in overall combat weight to
30,000lb (13,600kg), about 1,200lb
(550kg) more than the F-100C, meant
that the previously flap-less wing would
not have allowed a safe landing speed. In
an aircraft whose landing characteristics
had already been described by some as a
'controlled crash', it was vital to prevent
an increase in touch-down speed

Getting Down

Converting to the F-100D in 1957, Tom
Germscheid found that the new jet was:

… definitely a challenge to land. Approach and
landing speeds were higher than previously
experienced in F-84s and F-86s. Approach in
the F-100 was generally around 175kt indicated. The flaps definitely made the F-100D easier
to land than the F-100A and C models. Almost
everybody tended to add a few knots for the wife
and kids. Landing visibility was not very good
once you started the flare and got the nose up.
The tendency was to flare too high, especially at
night and reach stall speed while still 50ft in the
air. This resulted in a *very firm* touch-down,
often leading to a 'porpoise' (or 'J. C.') and aircraft damage. I recall a Wing Commander at

Pumping LOX into a 506th TFW F-100D. The yellow
paint on the intake of this 458th FBS aircraft is
peeling away, revealing the red of a previous owner,
probably the 457th FBS. Col M. Kulczyk

Early 21st FDS markings are painted on Maj Pete Fernandez' F-100C 54-2096. They included blue and white bands and the squadron insignia. David Menard Collection

A sparkling bare-metal F-100C-1-NA (53-1739) of the 334th FDS, 4th FDW at Seymour-Johnson AFB in 1958. Squadron markings are blue. Author's Collection

Cannon AFB rounding out high on a night landing, getting into a 'porpoise' and shearing off the nose-gear. He slid the length of the runway on his nose and stopped with the barrier cable against the canopy, which he had raised during the slide. The word quickly spread that the 'Old Man' took the barrier with his teeth! As a result of this venture, the Wing was restricted from landing at night. We got our 'night-time' by taking off at about 0300–0400 hrs and landing as it was getting light. This lasted until we got a new commander!

The F-100's fairly heavy windshield framing was an inevitable consequence of the construction methods available at the time, and although it provided strength for emergencies like that it did tend to add to the landing problems by restricting forward visibility on approach. The basic toughness of the F-100 airframe was shown on another occasion when a 20th Tactical Fighter Wing (TFW) F-100D landed at Wethersfield with its nose-gear locked in the 'up' position. According to Tom Germscheid:

The touch-down area of the runway was foamed but unfortunately the aircraft floated over the foamed area and landed beyond. The pilot did a good job of lowering the nose to the runway where it slid on the pitot boom for several thousand feet before coming to a stop on the centreline. Damage to this bird was limited to a replacement pitot boom.

Even with all three landing gear members in place, an MA-1 emergency barrier arrestment could be injurious. If the

The F-100D introduced a revised wing to include trailing-edge flaps. Ailerons were moved further outboard as a result.
Wing fences were absent from early F-100Ds such as this one. The 'USAF' lettering was in Insignia Blue (FS15044).
At the base of the tail-fin is a small opening for the drag chute cable connection. David Menard Collection

F-100D-70-NA 56-3057 leads a line-up of 388th TFS, 312th TFW aircraft from Cannon AFB en route to the Far East on 30 August 1958. The squadron, led by Col Arlie Blood, used yellow markings on noses and tails. MA-2 APU vehicles are connected ready for engine start time. USAF via David Menard

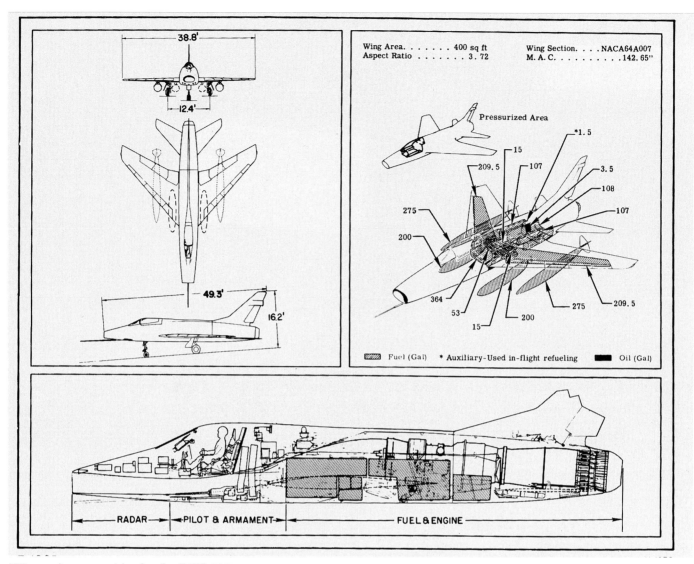

1957 general arrangement drawing of an F-100D. USAF via John Maene

canopy was lost or open, the upper strap of the barrier could slide over the nose and into the cockpit. Pilots were advised to lean forward into the windshield to prevent the strap from throttling them. It was also standard practice to blow off all external fuel tanks before taking the barrier.

Col Art Johnson commanded the 309th Fighter-bomber Squadron (FBS) as it converted from the F-84F Thunderstreak, 'an easy aircraft to fly. With the wide gear legs it was a piece of cake to land'. Checking out in the F-100A and F-100C at George AFB in 1957, he found little difference between these two variants and the F-100D in clean configuration:

There probably wasn't a noticeable difference in stalling speed between them with the flaps up on the D but there was a significant difference

with the flaps down for landing – sort of like night and day. We didn't use flaps for take-off so any difference there would be due to the extra weight of the F-100D.

The extra wing-root chord of the F-100D because of its flaps changed the span-wise airflow over the wing and required single wing fences to be fitted above the wings near the outer end of each aileron. These were factory-fitted to F-100Ds and F-100Fs, though some early 8th TFW aircraft were not at first equipped with the fences.

The F-100C pilot's manual specified 180kt for final approach and touch-down at 150kt with 22,500lb (10,200kg) gross weight. F-100D touch-down figures were a little lower: 190kt was a more typical approach speed. However, as Maj Curtis

Burns observed, 'These figures were all test pilot stuff anyway. For fighter pilots flying the airplane speed is life'. According to Lt Col Ron Herrick, 'one killer was the flight control system on the flare to landing with the engine at idle. If you made a violent pitch correction on or before the touch-down it could result in a violent ending'.

After runway contact was successfully established, the braking parachute was needed to kill the knots. It provided very rapid deceleration, causing the pilot to 'hang in his straps'. In the F-100C, a landing run without the chute took all of 5,500ft (1,700m) using moderate (70 per cent) brake pressure, no wind and a dry runway. Use of the chute reduced this to 4,300ft (1,300m) although, as Curtis Burns found, 'The F-100Cs we flew had a relatively unreliable drag chute. My

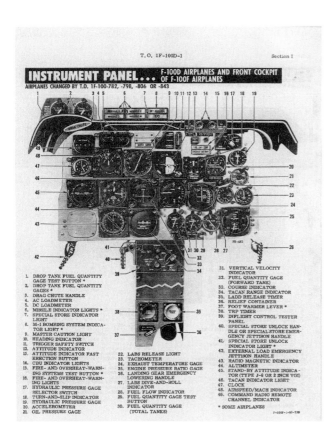

F-100D front cockpit panel and key. USAF

F-100F rear cockpit panel and key. USAF

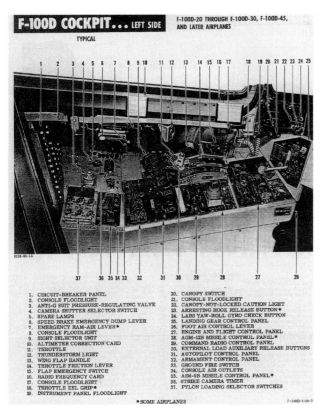

F-100D left side cockpit panel and key. USAF

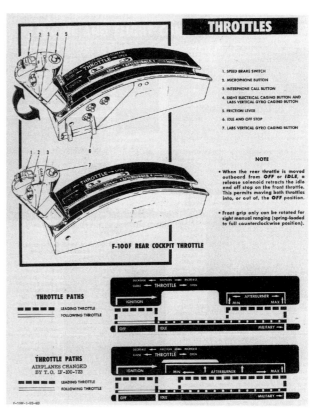

F-100D throttles and key. USAF

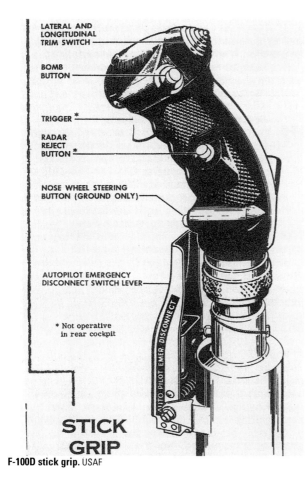

F-100D stick grip. USAF

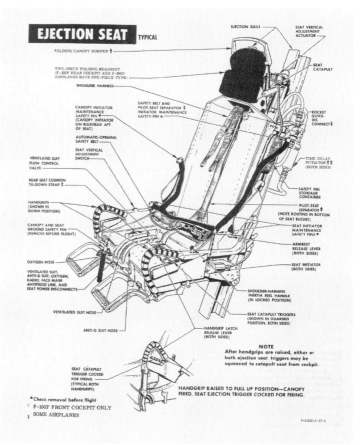

F-100D/F ejection seat. USAF

F-100D-20-NAs 55-3503 and -3507 (later used by the Thunderbirds) refuelling from an AFFTC KB-50D tanker in fair weather conditions. In less favourable weather this could be a far more demanding task. David Menard Collection

Many F-100Ds were 'cocooned' in protective coating for the sea journey to PACAF units and this had to be removed by Japanese civilian employees using high-pressure water lances. Here, 55-3563, its panel joint-lines sealed with tape, gets the treatment at **Kizaruzu AB.** David Menard Collection

impression is that it failed in about one in a dozen landings'. Occasionally, the difficulties arose from the sleight-of-hand needed to deploy the chute. Bobby Wright crewed F-100Cs for the 136th Tactical Fighter Squadron (TFS): 'The chute handle was designed so that the pilot had to invert his hand to deploy the chute and then reverse his hand to twist the handle and release the chute from the aircraft. It was quite possible to screw up and eject the chute too early'. Ron Herrick recalled the F-100 as, 'quite sporty on landing, with the not-too-trusty anti-skid and a drag chute that had about twenty mods to its operating sequence so that you could never assume that it would work'.

Sometimes it was preferable to avoid using the brake chute, as Alex Martin explained: 'When on cross-country missions and a quick turn-around was needed we

Burns, the first generation anti-skid braking system was:

> … not as reliable as we would have liked … I had an anti-skid fail on me once, blew a tyre and swerved off the runway at Landstuhl. I was lucky, as the landing gear didn't fail. At least one squadron mate had an anti-skid failure, blew a tyre, departed the runway and wiped the landing gear off.

Alex Martin pointed out that 'most experienced pilots didn't turn on the anti-skid; they could do better manually. However, it did help the young or 'clanky' to avoid locking the brakes and blowing a tyre'. The Hytrol anti-skid system used a three-legged 'spider' device attached to the wheel hub and transmitting wheel-speed data from the wheel rim to a sensor in the axle. This enabled the system to even up the braking pressure on both wheels and prevent excessive braking. Lee Howard, later an F-100D pilot in Vietnam, found that it was 'never an accepted standard to exceed the recommended landing speeds. The old bitch was too hard to stop with the correct numbers, but just don't get slow!'

No fighter can be free of problems and vicissitudes, and in many respects the F-100 was already a safer and more dependable steed than many of its contemporaries. Lacking the persistent unreliability of the early radar-equipped jets and the poor manoeuvrability of other Century Series fighter-bombers, it was soon forged into TAC's principal strike fighter. Its early pilots quickly learned to manage the aircraft's habits and generally avoided the areas where it could 'bite' them, though this sometimes had to be done the hard way. Since the F-100 era there has been time to focus on reliability, safety and ease of operation in designing fighters. In the 1950s the emphasis was on speed, innovation and keeping well ahead of the opposition.

In terms of equipment, the F-100D initially carried the same radio, radio compass and IFF equipment as the F-100C and a slightly updated TACAN. Additional items to enhance its fighter-bomber role included a new centreline hardpoint (from the 184th aircraft) that could take a Mk 28 Special Store (nuclear), an MN-1 practice munitions dispenser or a camera pod.

The ejection seat was improved to give zero-altitude, minimum airspeed ejection with a ballistic rocket catapult providing 7,500lb (3,400kg) of thrust. It included automatic pilot-seat separation and an

F-100D-20-NA 55-3545 emerges from 'de-cocooning' before delivery to the 8th FBW at Itazuke AB. David Menard Collection

shaved the touch-down speed (normally 148–150kt in an F-100D), held the nose-gear up and didn't deploy the drag chute'. The parachute was stored in a compartment in the lower rear fuselage. Crew chief Rich Newell recalled that it was 'always fun lying on your back in the snow or rain putting the chute into the plane'. When the packed chute popped out through its spring-loaded retaining doors, a cable, attached to it and to a hook in another compartment at the base of the fin's rear edge, was yanked out of a recessed channel through a row of small, spring-loaded, stainless steel doors placed vertically on the rear left fuselage, just ahead of the exhaust nozzle. Crew chief Jack Engler recalled the system as 'a real pain to rig, with over 40ft of heavy steel cable, bell cranks and turnbuckles for tensioning'. Packing the chute into its compartment meant facing 'all the soot, oil and corrosion that was present under the engine'. Dave Menard explained the technique thus: 'Installing a drag chute meant lying on your back and shoulders, using your feet to hold the chute in position while the pins were installed and then closing the doors with your shoes while everything in your trouser pockets dropped out!' However, in Vietnam combat Jack Engler found the system 'gave us little trouble. I don't ever remember one failing to deploy, though 11,000ft runways gave the drivers some peace of mind too'. An electrically improved drag chute control system was tested for the F-100 but not adopted.

F-100Cs had to be flown all the way down, with a slight flare over the runway threshold as power was cut to idle. The lack of any significant aerodynamic braking put a load on the multi-pad disc brakes, which many pilots considered to be barely adequate for the F-100 generally. Braking had to be kept as light as possible to prevent overheating of brakes and tyres, leading to possible tyre explosion. For the F-100D/F the flaps had to be raised immediately after touch-down to increase the load on the landing gear and improve brake efficiency. According to Curtis

The first two-seat Hun, 54-1966, converted from an F-100C-20-NA and designated TF-100C. An F-100D vertical stabilizer was one of the modifications. John Maene Collection

MA-6 automatic-opening safety belt in place of earlier manual models. However, ejection at altitudes below 2,000ft (610m) was still discouraged and 10,500ft (3,200m) remained the recommended safe minimum to allow for any equipment malfunction. In the F-100D, ejection was initiated by squeezing one or both of the independent triggers located beneath the 'tiger striped' handles on the sides of the seat, after first holding the canopy switch at 'open' until the canopy broke away. If the transparency stayed put the drill was to press the head against the headrest, tuck in the chin and eject through the canopy. Normally, the pilot had to release his hand-grips immediately after ejection as the seat-belt release was supposed to trigger one second after the seat blasted out. Manual release was provided as a back-up.

The seat was sometimes needed very suddenly. Ron Herrick had to eject from an F-100D when his stabilizer suddenly went fully 'nose down' at 10,000ft (3,000m). He managed to acquire limited control, using only throttle and roll control. The accident is thought to have been caused by a bolt that retained the stabilizer control valve working loose after its fibre lock nut had been replaced with a castellated type shortly before the flight. Another pilot, Mike Ryan, had a similar experience at Foster AFB when his stabilizer suddenly forced his aircraft into a negative 'g' dive. Both pilots ejected safely, Mike on to terra firma and Ron Herrick into 12-foot seas from which a fishing boat plucked him in the nick of time. The F-100D's seat was electrically adjustable, unlike those in the F-100A and C which, according to Ron, 'Were manual and would occasionally 'bottom out' violently at a critical time'. However, unlike some pilots, he found the seat quite comfortable and the cockpit 'tremendous for its day, but the longer one sat in it the tighter the squeeze. The seat cushion and survival kit were well designed and a quantum improvement over the F-86 where you sat on the emergency oxygen bottle and liferaft with no cushion!'

Hun for Two

The final production F-100s became some of the most useful and versatile Super Sabres. The F-100F emerged, perhaps belatedly, in response to the high accident rate incurred during the early years of training. In the first 100,000 flight hours, the F-100 had ninety-five major accidents, the worst record for a principal US supersonic type. However, only six involved fatalities compared with eighteen for the Lockheed F-104. Like the other Century Series two-seaters (apart from the TF-102) the F-100F required a tandem second cockpit but little other major structural change. Overall length increased by 3ft (1m) and fuel capacity was not reduced. Maximum take-off weight increased about 1,000lb (450kg) to 39,120lb (17,750kg). The deletion of the upper pair of guns helped to restore the cg since single-seaters usually flew with either full ammunition or equivalent ballast for this purpose. Ordnance was limited to around 5,000lb (2,300kg), 2,000lb (900kg) less than the F-100D. A minor difference was that the F-100F's pilot tube was electrically heated to prevent icing whereas the equivalent part in the F-100C/D was heated by bleed air piped in 'microbore' tubing from the engine.

Design studies for the F-100F began in May 1954 and NAA volunteered to convert an F-100C (54-1966) at the company's expense to the dual-cockpit configuration. The USAF responded with an order for 259 'TF-100Cs'. The modified aircraft was first flown on 3 August 1956 with Al White in its front seat, which in service aircraft was intended for the student pilot. It achieved supersonic speed in level flight. This prototype had the F-100D-style tail-fin but retained the 'flapless' wing. Seven months later, the first production F-100F took to the air, flown by NAA test pilot Gage Mace on 7 March 1957. The sole 'TF-100C' crashed a month later during a spin test but NAA pilot Bob Baker punched out uninjured.

The USAF wanted its two-seat Huns to retain their combat capability, albeit in reduced quantity. The ordnance load still included provision on the centreline pylon for a nuclear bomb and the wing stations were unchanged, though the two remaining guns each had twenty-five rounds less than those in the F-100D. Operational training units at Nellis AFB began to receive F-100Fs at the end of May 1957, and 339 examples were delivered before production ended in 1960, forty-five of them for export. There was a corresponding reduction in F-100D production to allow for the USAF two-seaters. A belated attempt to re-instate production was projected in 1964 with NAA's unsuccessful plan to allow the building of a further 200 two-seat F-100s (with Rolls-Royce engines) under licence in France.

By 1958, most operational squadrons had a couple of F-100Fs for continuation training, familiarization flights and all the other support jobs. Don Schmenk instructed in both the T-33 and F-100F, finding the latter 'a little more challenging to land from the rear seat since forward visibility was a little more restricted, though I don't recall having any problems'. Despite the belated introduction of the two-seater, the accident rate in F-100 training remained high and more than 25 per cent of F-100Fs were eventually lost.

Mods and Rockets

The USAF's urgent need for F-100s worldwide meant that batches of aircraft were accepted for service while further detail development continued rapidly, and equipment updates were therefore made ad hoc on the production line.

By 1962, the standard of equipment for successive batches was so various that a fleet-wide programme called Project *High Wire* was instituted to induce some standardization (many early F-100Ds, for example, came off the line without

Sidewinder capability). Officially it comprised two simultaneous operations, first to rewire the aircraft to a common standard, second to provide heavy maintenance and inspect and repair as necessary (IRAN) so that relevant updates could be incorporated. The F-100 was the first USAF aircraft to be maintained by the IRAN method, which became standard practice for later types like the F-4 Phantom II. It reduced overhaul times and costs, keeping more aircraft ready on the ramp.

The rewiring operation was extensive and included stripping and replacing all wiring in the cockpit to a common scheme. Costing over US$150m, *High Wire* ran from April 1962 until June 1965, taking each F-100 out of service for around two months. Inevitably, the situation was not simple and not all F-100C/D/F airframes went through the process though around 700 were originally slated for rework. Those that did had their production Block numbers 'wound on' by one digit – for example, F-100F-1-NA became F-100F-2-NA. In some cases, special modifications still applied only to limited numbers of

F-100D and F-100F jets on the NAA production line. David Menard Collection

The definitive F-100F first flew on 7 March 1957 and 339 were produced. Perhaps the most versatile Hun variant, it was used as a conversion trainer, SEAD aircraft, FAC platform and regular strike aircraft with VIP transport as a supporting role. John Maene Collection

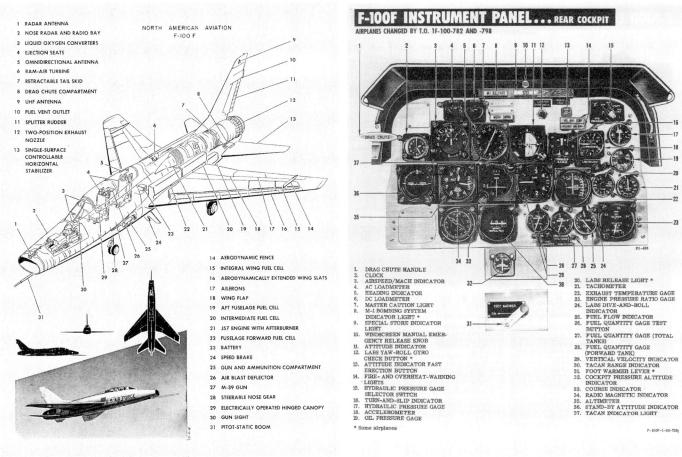

NORTH AMERICAN AVIATION
F-100 F

1 RADAR ANTENNA
2 NOSE RADAR AND RADIO BAY
3 LIQUID OXYGEN CONVERTERS
4 EJECTION SEATS
5 OMNIDIRECTIONAL ANTENNA
6 RAM-AIR TURBINE
7 RETRACTABLE TAIL SKID
8 DRAG CHUTE COMPARTMENT
9 UHF ANTENNA
10 FUEL VENT OUTLET
11 SPLITTER RUDDER
12 TWO-POSITION EXHAUST NOZZLE
13 SINGLE-SURFACE CONTROLLABLE HORIZONTAL STABILIZER

14 AERODYNAMIC FENCE
15 INTEGRAL WING FUEL CELL
16 AERODYNAMICALLY EXTENDED WING SLATS
17 AILERONS
18 WING FLAP
19 AFT FUSELAGE FUEL CELL
20 INTERMEDIATE FUEL CELL
21 J57 ENGINE WITH AFTERBURNER
22 FUSELAGE FORWARD FUEL CELL
23 BATTERY
24 SPEED BRAKE
25 GUN AND AMMUNITION COMPARTMENT
26 AIR BLAST DEFLECTOR
27 M-39 GUN
28 STEERABLE NOSE GEAR
29 ELECTRICALLY OPERATED HINGED CANOPY
30 GUN SIGHT
31 PITOT-STATIC BOOM

F-100F INSTRUMENT PANEL... REAR COCKPIT
AIRPLANES CHANGED BY T.O. 1F-100-782 AND -798

1. DRAG CHUTE HANDLE
2. CLOCK
3. AIRSPEED/MACH INDICATOR
4. AC LOADMETER
5. HEADING INDICATOR
6. DC LOADMETER
7. MASTER CAUTION LIGHT
8. M-1 BOMBING SYSTEM INDICATOR LIGHT *
9. SPECIAL STORE INDICATOR
10. WINDSCREEN MANUAL EMERGENCY RELEASE KNOB
11. ATTITUDE INDICATOR
12. LABS YAW-ROLL GYRO CHECK BUTTON *
13. ATTITUDE INDICATOR FAST ERECTION BUTTON
14. FIRE- AND OVERHEAT-WARNING LIGHTS
15. HYDRAULIC PRESSURE GAGE SELECTOR SWITCH
16. TURN-AND-SLIP INDICATOR
17. HYDRAULIC PRESSURE GAGE
18. ACCELEROMETER
19. OIL PRESSURE GAGE

20. LABS RELEASE LIGHT *
21. TACHOMETER
22. EXHAUST TEMPERATURE GAGE
23. ENGINE PRESSURE RATIO GAGE
24. LABS DIVE-AND-ROLL INDICATOR
25. FUEL FLOW INDICATOR
26. FUEL QUANTITY GAGE TEST BUTTON
27. FUEL QUANTITY GAGE (TOTAL TANKS)
28. FUEL QUANTITY GAGE (FORWARD TANK)
29. VERTICAL VELOCITY INDICATOR
30. TACAN RANGE INDICATOR
31. FOOT WARMER LEVER *
32. COCKPIT PRESSURE ALTITUDE INDICATOR
33. COURSE INDICATOR
34. RADIO MAGNETIC INDICATOR
35. ALTIMETER
36. STAND-BY ATTITUDE INDICATOR
37. TACAN INDICATOR LIGHT

* Some airplanes

FOOT WARMER ON

F-100F-1-00-72R

General arrangement drawing of F-100F. USAF via John Maene

F-100F rear cockpit panel and key. USAF via John Maene

**F-100F-16-NA 56-3930 in the standard TAC acrylic silver finish that was applied from January 1960 onwards. Small flashes
of unit identity persisted, such as the patch of colour on the tail of this aircraft in 1966.** Peter M. Bowers via John Maene

Early 308th FBS markings on F-100D 56-3361 consisted of yellow flashes on the nose and a yellow panel with a two-digit identifier, SAC-style on the tail. Joe Vincent Collection

Seen here in its later service with the 524th TFS, 27th TFW, F-100F-21-NA 58-1227 was flown by General Blair as *Excalibur* 4, the first single-engined jet to cross the North Pole during Project *Julius Caesar* in August 1959. Later, it became one of the first four F-100F Wild Weasel SEAD aircraft. David Menard Collection

aircraft. One of these was the zero-length launch (ZEL) capability adaptation that applied only to the last 148 F-100Ds off the production line.

In the mid-1950s, strategic planners became increasingly aware of the vulnerability of their airfields in Western Europe, many of which were located quite close to the Soviet Bloc's borders. Their runways would have been first-choice targets for the increasingly powerful weapons systems (including tactical nuclear devices) being developed in the Soviet Union. NATO jets required up to 10,000ft (3,000m) of clean, FOD-free runway to take off with their own retaliatory nuclear weapons, and even a chance hit on the 2 to 3 per cent of an airbase's area that comprised active runway could delay a strike mission beyond the point where it would serve any purpose. While some designers turned their attention to advancing the vertical take-off and landing (VTOL) technology that led to the BAe Harrier and eventually to the Lockheed Martin F-35, others sought quicker solutions. Essentially, the idea was to disperse the USAF's nuclear-capable F-100D force so that aircraft could be launched (literally) without runways. When the F-100 was first conceived, nuclear delivery was the prerogative of heavy SAC bombers. However, rapid advances in reducing the size of nuclear bombs while simultaneously increasing their power by up to a hundredfold meant that fighter-portable weapons were available by 1957. A year later, TAC revealed that it had tested the NAA zero-length system and intended to equip all F-100 Wings with ZEL-capable aircraft and launchers.

With a single Mk 7 'nuke' on its left intermediate pylon and a 275gal tank on the opposite side, a ZEL F-100D had a massive Rocketdyne M-34 solid rocket booster attached to hardpoints beneath its rear fuselage. It was then mounted on an angled ramp and its pilot climbed up a hazardously tall ladder to his cockpit. With the landing gear extended and engine in afterburner the rocket was fired, adding an extra 130,000lb (59,000kg) of thrust, over eight times the fighter's normal power. The F-100 leapt into the air in a 4g climb. Four seconds later, with the fighter at 275kt, the giant firecracker burned out and was jettisoned. On return from his mission, assuming it had been a two-way trip, an operational pilot would have had to locate a suitable runway or eject.

Two F-100Ds (56-2904 and 56-2947) were suitably modified for testing at AFFTC. NAA's Al Blackburn bravely conducted the initial blast-off in '2904 on 26 March 1958 and went on to complete sixteen flights. Another four were made by Capt Robert F. Titus (later a Vietnam MiG killer). On one of Blackburn's launches the big M-34 hung grimly on to the aircraft's tail, making a normal landing

56th TFS groundcrew at Myrtle Beach AFB remove the crew boarding ladder from F-100F-16-NA 56-3952, with a centreline pylon attached. This aircraft was later operated by the Turkish AF. Norm Taylor Collection

One for the modellers: the variety of metal tones is evident on this 'plain Jane' F-100D-65-NA. In later service it acquired camouflage and the 'HS' codes of the 612th TFS, 37th TFW. It crashed into the sea after a CAS mission near Da Nang AB on 21 October 1967, killing its pilot Capt Joseph Hemmel. David Menard Collection.

impossible as it dangled several feet below the F-100's tail section. Blackburn had to take to his parachute while '2904 pancaked on to the desert. The other ZEL F-100D, '2947, passed into TAC service, flying in Vietnam with the 615th TFS as *Linda Bird*. Joe Vincent, who recalled flying other ZEL-capable F-100Ds in Vietnam, noted that they still had a folding, spring-loaded throttle extension handle, painted black and yellow, that prevented a pilot from accidentally pulling back on the throttle. Don Schmenk enlarged on this:

> The handles were held at the full throttle position like the Navy uses for catapult launches to prevent the transverse g from the launch causing a loss of power when you needed it most. When you advanced the throttle to full power you could wrap your fingers around the handle with your thumb behind the throttle.

ZEL tests continued until late August 1959, including a launch from a specially hardened shelter at Holloman AFB. A Luftwaffe F-104G was also ZEL-tested at Edwards AFB after West Germany showed an interest in the project.

Various stores configurations were tested on the F-100D including 200gal tanks on the inner pylons. It was found that a ZEL Hun could be attached to its ramp and prepared for a mission inside 2 1/2 hours and that launchers could be made sufficiently mobile to be moved by road. Even so, logistical problems and overall cost brought this innovative and spectacular experiment to

ZEL F-100D-60-NA 56-2947 blasts off from a shelter designed to resist an atomic attack at Holloman AFB on 26 August 1959. A *Blue Boy* Mk7 shape appears beneath the left wing. NAA test pilot Al Blackburn made the flight. USAF via Ron Thurlow

56-2947 poised on its launch vehicle, shows the attachment of the Rocketdyne booster unit and the elevating cradles to support the main undercarriage. The problems of entering the aircraft's cockpit in this position are all too evident. Col D. Elmer

an end and the USAF eventually turned its attention to variable geometry aircraft with short-field performance and 'rough terrain' undercarriages. Out of this line of thought came the GD F-111.

One small but important modification retrofitted to F-100s under *High Wire* was a simple, spring steel arresting hook under the rear fuselage. This hook was retained in the 'up' position by an electrical solenoid, and once released it could not be raised again in the air. However, solenoid failure on the ground was not unknown and for groundcrew the hook could become, 'potential energy just waiting to fall on some careless soul', according to crew chief John Clarity. The aircraft's brake parachute could be unreliable, and damage to chute-less F-100s that ran out of runway had been considerable. Pilots were supposed to deploy the chute at speeds below 150kt (5kt below the normal landing speed), avoiding over-robust use of the chute handle to avoid accidental jettisoning of the parachute. With the tailhook, an emergency landing could be made with a BAK-6 or BAK-9 cable arresting system engaging the hook at landing speeds up to 170kt and near-maximum landing weight. In practice, it was preferable to jettison external fuel tanks to reduce that weight.

Ongoing updates to the F-100 continued throughout its career, including the installation of Minneapolis Honeywell MB-3 autopilots in the cockpits of 658 F-100C/D aircraft by mid-1958. This system incorporated links to the pitch and yaw damping (stability augmentation) systems and added HOLD options for altitude, heading and attitude to be maintained automatically using a 'chicken-head' switch on the left horizontal panel. An emergency disengage switch was located on the main control column. The autopilot could not be used in training at altitudes below 200ft (60m) in case of a 'hard over' failure, as there would be insufficient altitude to effect a manual recovery. One of the autopilot's main functions was to operate in the LABS weapon delivery mode so that an 'auto LABS' pull-up, bomb delivery and rollout to recovery altitude could be selected.

Other updates included improved brakes with automatic anti-skid and a better oil distribution system. The original Sundstrand constant speed drive (CSD) used the same oil supply as the engine. If the unit failed and dumped oil this meant that the main oil supply to the engine would be drained too. Meanwhile, Pratt

---

Bullpup

Other modifications to the aircraft gave sixty-five F-100Ds the ability to fire the Martin (Marietta) AGM-12B (GAM-83A) Bullpup command-guided, air-to-ground missile. Conceived during the Korean War as a means of attacking inaccessible targets in mountainous terrain, this 570lb (260kg) rocket-propelled weapon could deliver a 250lb (115kg) warhead at a 12,000yd (11,000m) range at speeds up to Mach 1.75. Suitably modified F-100Ds could carry two missiles on their inboard pylons. Guidance was visual; the pilot could see two small flares attached to the missile's tail fins that increased in brilliance as range from the aircraft lengthened. Course-correcting signals were transmitted to the Bullpup's canard stabilizing fins from a pulse control system and antenna in the F-100D after the missile's booster rocket had accelerated it to its 'flight' speed in a three-second burn.

Bullpup-capable aircraft had a small missile control panel on the left cockpit side-panel including a miniature, cube-shaped 'joystick' which gave simple 'up, down, left, right' signals. Once the missile had gone ballistic, the commands would most often be 'up' signals to keep it in flight. Launch was initiated by switching the missile control switch to READY and selecting one of the two missiles. The missile launch was then set to GUIDE and the missile was fired (from altitudes up to 25,000ft/7,625m) using the normal gun trigger. Once the missile's motor had burned out, the F-100 pilot used the flares on its tail to guide the rapidly rolling Bullpup to its target. Some pilots found that the brightness of the flares tended to obscure their vision of the target, making attacks on small targets such as vehicles more difficult. Good visibility was required for a successful attack, which made the missile a fair-weather weapon. Also, its fairly small warhead meant there was little point in firing it against reinforced targets. To guide the missile, a pilot had to hold his main control column with his right hand and manipulate the missile joystick with the other, leaving him no hands to manage that other crucial device, the throttle handle. The other disadvantage was that the F-100 had to fly straight and follow the Bullpup's course, thereby exposing itself to ground defences. As Joe Vincent remarked, 'That was not a very wise thing to do for adding Oak Leaf Clusters to your Longevity Ribbon'.

Although training on the Bullpup was conducted enthusiastically at Luke AFB from 1960 to 1966 (using a Martin simulator to reduce the cost of live firings) it had been dropped by 1969 apart from brief coverage in the conventional weapons syllabus. Better weapons were on the way, but this early experience with the Bullpup enabled the development of a later generation of stand-off missiles such as GBU-15 and AGM-130. For the F-100, Project *High Wire* increased its range of cleared ordnance to include, for example, later models of AIM-9 Sidewinder (AIM-9E/J) and around twenty types of CBU dispensers, increasing the F-100D's range of weapons to around seventy-five types. SUU-7/As were the initial CBU dispensers to be cleared for the aircraft, referred to as CBU-1/A or CBU-2A/A, depending on their contents. For ferry flights with empty canisters a nose-cone could be fitted to reduce drag.

In Vietnam, the AGM-12B was used on occasion in the early stages of the war. Pilots of the 481st TFS on a 1965 temporary duty (TDY) to Tan Son Nhut AB fired several to maintain their qualification with the system but they found the weapon unreliable. In most firings it went ballistic and missed the target. 1st Lt Peter Vanderhoef was one of the pilots:

I remember we all got to fire a Bullpup one time down in the Delta, south of Saigon. None of us were scheduled to hit a tight target and it was probably fortunate because mine went ballistic as did most of the others, which gave us a slick 500lb bomb that cost the price of a Cadillac – around US$5,000. The only thing we were able to hit with it was the ground.

Other units had better luck with the missile, but it had virtually disappeared from F-100 bases by 1967 though a total of 1,944 of the missiles were fired during the war by an assortment of aircraft.

---

and Whitney (P&W) continued to improve the reliability of their J57 engine with changes to the fuel pump and valves to reduce the cases of flameout and afterburner lighting difficulties. There had been cases of F-100C engine explosions on take-off as the fuel/air flow passed through a 'null' point at about 200kt causing a build-up of vapour in the rear fuselage. This was solved by the simple expedient of drilling seven small holes in a line across the underside of the fuselage.

The final USAF batch of twenty-nine F-100Fs (58-1205 to 58-1233) had an improved AN/ASN-7 navigation computer, PC-212 Doppler radar navigation system (RADAN) and modified flaps to give 40 degrees deflection rather than the usual

45 degrees. Although the gyro stabilization in the Doppler system was thought by some to be hard to keep in working order the aircraft were useful. According to Alex Martin:

When we had to deploy as a unit the Commander would get one of the F-100Fs with the Squadron Navigation Officer aboard and lead the gaggle. When we received a couple at Kadena I remember a lot of running them around the Far East including Australia, flying dignitaries around and doing some free advertising for North American Aviation!

A number of F-100Ds had a similar navigation system installed in an aft electronics compartment in the lower rear fuselage,

Yellow markings adorn F-100C-1-NA 53-1762 of the 336th FDS *Rocketeers,* **4th FDW in this squadron line-up.** Col D. Elmer via David Menard

parallel with the leading edge of the tailplane. This area was cooled by a small bleed-air operated turbine or by ram-air through an intake in the lower leading edge of the vertical stabilizer. These F-100Ds, known as NAVS (Doppler navigation system) aircraft, had an AN/APQ-102 Doppler radar subsystem to provide continuous ground-speed measurement and drift information, and an AN/ASN-25 dead-reckoning computer. The latter calculated dead-reckoning problems using data from the Doppler radar and the standard J-4 compass, controlled from the right horizontal panel. The system gave the pilot a form of 'great circle' navigation, supervised via two panels on his right horizontal console and four instruments on the main front panel.

Sabre-Toothed Tigers

While NAA honed their 'Super Sword', the USAF continued to train and deploy new F-100 Wings. F-100A and C models provided pilots at Luke AFB with supersonic experience, while Korean War MiG-killer Bruce Hinton led five squadrons and a Fighter Weapons School at Nellis AFB under the auspices of the 3595th Combat Crew Training Group (CCTG) until June 1958. Nellis had received its first F-100 (52-5761) on 21 August 1954. Many pilots came from F-84 and F-86 units, including Tom Germscheid, who recalled:

I graduated from single-engine jet pilot training and got my 'wings' in December 1956. Follow-on assignments were granted according to class standings. The F-100s were just coming into the inventory at that time and all of the top-standing graduates were hoping for an F-100 slot. Unfortunately there were none for our class, just several for the F-84F and F-86D. I grabbed one of the F-84F slots since it looked more like a fighter than anything else that was offered. I went to Luke AFB for a three-month checkout and initial combat crew training. I enjoyed the course very much and got my 'Mach busters' pin

after pointing the 'hog' straight down with full power from about 40,000ft. The instruments fluctuated a bit as the airspeed hit about Mach 0.98. I guess I passed the Mach but I didn't stay around long enough to check!

Follow-on assignments were again given according to class standings. This time there were a bunch of F-100 slots and I quickly jumped on one of them and went to Nellis in April 1957 to check out in the F-100A. This was a fabulous time. The F-100F had not yet entered the inventory so everything was single-seat. This time we could bust the Mach straight and level, or maybe in a slight dive, in a clean bird. Most of our flights were in clean configuration [no stores carried].

Coming to the F-100A after flying the F-84F was like strapping a 15,000lb rocket on your 150lb ass and blasting off. Everyone was impressed with the afterburner take-offs. The burner was lit after starting the take-off roll as the brakes would not hold the bird in afterburner – maybe a sign of poor brakes. It was always a real kick in the butt when the 'a.b.' lit. The start of formation take-offs was always

The vital MA-2 mobile air starter unit was the preferred method of starting up an F-100. The alternative cartridge start (available in most F-100Ds) produced toxic fumes that required the pilot to wear his oxygen mask. Col Art Johnson

that if you were near, but not necessarily in the contrail level, going into afterburner would lay a couple of hundred feet of white condensation that was very visible to a potential target. ... The acceleration was significant [50 per cent] but the effect on aircraft attitude was easily handled. Our training allowed us to anticipate and react to it in the same way we did to opening the speed brakes, dropping the gear or lowering flaps. We even had occasions where we would go into afterburner while in close formation.

When a pair of F-100s took off, a pilot would be very aware of the penetrating roar of his wingman's afterburner, though cutting in his own a.b. made little difference to his cockpit noise level. (A bigger long-term noise problem came from the MA-2 starting unit which, in Ron Herrick's opinion, 'ruined many people's ears before they realized it'.)

The F-100's speed and acceleration under 8 tons of thrust were a revelation to many pilots coming from F-84F Thunderstreaks. Art Johnson:

> The F-84F was not exactly a great air-to-air interceptor. I remember one mission where we were on alert to intercept a flight of SAC B-47 Stratojets as they passed near. It took so long to get to their altitude that we never did get within firing range. The intercept was a total bust.
>
> The afterburner made all the difference in the world between the F-84F and the F-100. We were suddenly in fighter pilot heaven with no worries about take-off roll distances.

Pilots soon learned to tame the F-100's less attractive habits too. In a hard turn, particularly to the left, engine torque could exacerbate inertial coupling and cause the aircraft to enter a roll into the opposite direction. Combined with the aircraft's natural adverse yaw condition this could make an F-100A in a high-g turn suddenly tumble out of control. The standard recovery technique was to release the stick pressure and let the aircraft fly out of the situation. Snap rolls, abrupt manoeuvres and extreme yaw angles were off limits for all F-100 models. According to Art Johnson, 'Spins were prohibited and we were told that no one had ever recovered from a spin in the F-100F'. Alex Martin, at Nellis in 1956–57 recalled that in general:

> The F-100's flying characteristics were good. Remember, most pilots transitioned from the F-84, F-86 or T-33 so the ones from the F-84

interesting as it was difficult to get the afterburners on all birds in the formation to light at the same time. Formation Lead would give the predatory hand signal for afterburner and then nod his head forward. At night he would call the signal over the radio. As a wingman I quickly learned to hesitate a microsecond or so before stroking my burner on take-off as it was very awkward if your burner lit before the formation leader's and you found yourself out in front. A good Lead always retarded his engine a couple of per cent from full rpm and that way you wouldn't fall behind if your bird was not as fast.

When afterburner was engaged by moving the throttle outboard, fuel pressure caused the engine exhaust nozzle 'eyelids' to open. On the J57 they were either open or closed; there was no intermediate position. Occasionally they failed to open or close properly and if they failed to open when afterburner was selected you got a violent compressor stall. If they failed to close when afterburner was de-selected you had a big loss of thrust, which happened more often than failing to open in the first place. I lost a Flight Leader (Warren Emerson) and his back-seater in an F-100F at Cannon AFB when they lost afterburner at lift-off and the eyelids stayed open. The procedure for lost afterburner was to bring the throttle inboard immediately to close the eyelids when you recognized that the a.b. had gone out. That F-100F crew either didn't identify the problem soon enough, or the eyelids failed to close for some other reason. In any

case they couldn't get enough altitude to clear a boxcar grain bin off the end of the runway. They might also have saved themselves if they had jettisoned fuel tanks sooner.

Normally, afterburner was disengaged after we got the bird cleaned up and reached climb speed. Using afterburner really guzzled up the fuel, though I recall one flight in a clean F-100A at Nellis where we did a max performance take-off and climb to 40,000ft in afterburner all the way. I was impressed. In-flight operation of the afterburner was always exciting in both F-100A and D. If your angle of attack was too high you often got a good compressor stall. There was a loud bang and your feet were often knocked off the rudder pedals. A large fireball would be seen out of the tail of your bird. It was especially spectacular at night. I always gritted my teeth a little when selecting afterburner in manoeuvring flight. If it failed to light you left a fuel vapour trail behind your aircraft. This would quickly give away your position during ACM [air combat manoeuvring] if you were not otherwise in sight of your adversary. We sometimes used this tactic to help get the flight joined back up when we lost sight of each other. Sometimes we would ask the gunnery target-dart towing F-100 to mark his position in this way if we couldn't spot him.

Curtis Burns added:

One irritation in afterburner use at altitude is

Four 20mm guns were the F-100's main armament in air-to-air combat and they were important weapons for later air-to-ground missions, including flak suppression. Here, an F-100C has its guns boresighted on a target screen at Nellis AFB in June 1957. Peter M. Bowers via David Menard

thought, 'Wow!' The F-86 pilots were more impressed with the kick in the rear you got from hitting the afterburner. You could fly the F-86 or T-33 with your feet on the floor. Not so with the Hun, especially at slow speeds. It was honest, let you know when stalls were imminent and like the F-86 it would fly itself out of a spin if you let it go. At slow speeds in ACM the bird turned best with the rudder pedals, keeping the stick centred so you didn't get drag from the wrong aileron.

Managing a high-performance fighter like the F-100 without the sophisticated fly-by-wire control systems of contemporary jets required the seat-of-the-pants techniques and instincts of an earlier generation of fighter pilots plus the reactions needed to cope with a very complex cockpit and events happening at supersonic speeds.

Gunfighters

In the days before air-to-air missile technology took over the air combat arena, prowess in air-to-air gunnery and ACM remained the principal index of success in the fighter pilots' world. The F-100's M-39 guns were later supplemented by the guided air rocket GAR-8 (AIM-9B) Sidewinder missile but traditional air-to-air and air-to-ground gunnery occupied much of the combat training time. Despite its occasionally uncertain directional stability in manoeuvring flight, the F-100 was a very strong contender in this area and its guns were to be a powerful air-to-ground weapon during its extensive combat career in South East Asia. Tom Germscheid:

The F-100 was a good and fun gunnery platform. Along with the pitch and yaw dampers the taller

vertical stabilizer on the F-100D made it a more stable machine. The dampers, when working properly, were a big help. Gunnery scores were a function of two things: the skill of the aircrew and the boresight and harmonization of the 20mm guns. Stable air conditions also helped. Everyone fought to be on the 0600 air-to-ground mission! That's when the record scores were racked up. Turbulence around clouds or even in clear air was definitely a factoring air-to-air success. Success on the 'rag' or 'dart' target was often like WWI or WWII. If you could press in close enough without getting a foul or eating a piece of the dart you got good scores.

A 'rag' was a 30×6ft (9×1.8m) nylon mesh banner with a bull's-eye marking, towed behind a T-33 or F-100 on the end of a 1,200ft (365m) cable. The A/A37U-5 (or U-15) tow-target 'dart' consisted of a launcher attached to the F-100's left

F-100D-65-NA 56-3002 *Bad News*, fitted with AIM-9 rails and a pair of HVAR rockets on each one. The 'saddleback' fairing is removed and perched on the aircraft's spine, the usual pre-flight location. David Menard Collection

outboard pylon (Wing Station 155) and a steel/nylon cable reel on the right outboard pylon. In the cockpit the switchology for CBU ordnance and the standard 'bomb button' controlled the system and jettisoned it if necessary. The lightweight, dart-shaped target and its towline could be lowered to the ground after use on a 14ft (4.3m) diameter parachute for recovery and re-use so that the F-100 could land without it. The target could be launched from the aircraft at about 200kt and released to the ground at 175kt in straight and level flight. Once the target was deployed, the tow F-100 could fly at speeds up to 475kt. If the target failed to separate from the F-100 at the end of a gunnery session, a landing with the dart in tow was possible, although the dart would shatter on contact with terra firma.

At Nellis AFB, an Instructor Pilot (IP) usually took three students for air-to-air gunnery training. Each would arc towards the 'rag' target from a distance of about 3,000ft (900m), opening fire at 800–1,000ft (245–300m) range from a 30-degree closing angle and then pulling up and away to allow the next pilot his shot. In time-honoured manner, each pilot's shells would leave a distinctively coloured paint-trace on the target and hits were counted later.

Firing the guns with radar ranging for the A-4 sight involved a series of setting-up processes, not least of which was allowing a warm-up time of up to fifteen minutes for the radar and gun sight. The gun camera and gun sight filament were switched on and the rheostat adjusted to the correct level of brilliance. A sight function selector control was then set at GUN and the target speed switch was adjusted to allow for the relative speeds of the target and the attacking F-100. The sight was then uncaged, the camera switch set to 'bright', 'hazy' or 'dull' and the trigger switch to GUNS/CAMERA. The next

job was to set the WINGSPAN lever to correspond to the size of the target so that manual ranging could be used if the radar went down. Once the target was in clear sight, the electrical 'caging' button was pressed to stabilize the sight reticle and target tracking could then begin. The idea was to hold down the caging button and continue tracking a point some distance ahead of the target at a distance that approximated to the 'lead' that the gun sight would allow for in aiming the guns at the moving target. An indicator light came on at the lower left of the A-4 sight mounting to show that the radar had locked on to the target. The caging button was then released, and assuming that the target could be tracked smoothly, the pilot could open up with his primary armament. It was important to remember that firing the guns at supersonic speeds could cause the F-100 to shoot itself down. If a manoeuvre in combat required the pilot to push his aircraft's nose down slightly after

Sidewinder

When F-100s carried air-to-air missiles they were usually AIM-9B Sidewinders or slightly later variants. From 1957 the USAF acquired the USN's SW-1A (AAM-N-7A) as the GAR-8 (guided air rocket), re-named AIM-9B in June 1963 under the standardized designation system. It continued in service until 1968 when it was replaced by the slightly modified AIM-9E and then the AIM-9J in 1972.

The General Electric (GE)/Ford AIM-9B was a passive, infra-red homing missile, 9ft (2.7m) long and 5in (13cm) in diameter. Its range was limited to 2 miles (3.2km), though later models were effective at up to 11 miles (17.7km). The 10lb fragmentation warhead was borne on its brief, 20-second flight to the target by an Aerojet rocket motor and detonated by either contact or proximity fuses. The 155lb missile was mounted on the inboard pylons of the F-100, either singly or in parallel pairs hung from a Y-shaped double launcher. The same launcher could take an AIM-9 on one 'arm' and on the other a TDU-11/B 5in HVA rocket that could be fired from a single tube seconds before the AIM-9 to act as an infra-red target for the missile. Each TDU-11/B had four tracking flares on its aft section to provide a heat-source target for the Sidewinder's uncooled PbS infra-red seeker.

'Moose' Moseley, an IP at George AFB, 1959–61, made one of his squadron's earliest Sidewinder firings:

Sidewinders were new and had seen little use. We had some 'cold carry' missions to listen to its [infra-red] IR-activated tone and I had one live firing to qualify. I tossed a 5in HVA(R) with tail flares out yonder at 30 degrees nose-up and fired a 'snake' [AIM-9] as the target neared the horizon. A kill. But nobody wanted to go fight someone with them.

F-100C 54-1794, fitted with the taller F-100D-style tail fin was one of six F-100Cs used to test the Sidewinder installation. F-100Ds 54-2138, -2144 and -2145 were the first to be modified for Sidewinders, which were introduced on the Inglewood line at aircraft number 184 (55-3502).

Sidewinders were aimed using the A-4 sight with a fixed reticle (caged) and the missile's familiar 'rattle' tone let the pilot know, via his communications amplifier, that its seeker head had picked up a target. A cockpit panel with four lights showed which missile was selected, or unfired, and a missile master switch that was previously set to STANDBY to supply electrical power to the missile, was switched to READY when the target was in range. The AIM-9 was fired with a press of the usual trigger on the pilot's control column and this also cut in the gun camera. A 'station by-pass' control selected the next available missile or by-passed a dud, and a 'safe launch' button could salvo all missiles, unarmed and unguided, in an emergency.

In training, live Sidewinder shots were comparatively rare but practice 'lock-ons' could be made with the radar sight and missile seeker head. On one tragic occasion this caused the loss of a SAC B-52 bomber; ironically the F-100's only confirmed air-to-air shoot down in USAF service. The 188th TFS, New Mexico Air National Guard was the first ANG unit to receive Super Sabres when it transitioned to F-100As in 1958. Ist Lt James W. van Scyoc was flying F-100A 53-1662 on 7 April 1961, running practice intercepts from Kirtland AFB on a 95th BW B-52B. On his sixth simulated Sidewinder launch, van Scyoc's fighter suddenly launched its No.2 AIM-9B and it impacted on the left inboard engine of the mighty bomber. Aboard the B-52B (53-0380 *Ciudad Juarez*) the pilot, Capt Don Blodgett, felt his aircraft lurch to the left as his cockpit caught fire and the left wing separated. Fragments from the Sidewinder killed the two navigators and a student electronic war officer (EWO). The rest of the crew managed to escape though most were injured. A Board of Investigation inquiry concluded that a cracked plug in the F-100A's missile firing circuit had allowed moisture to enter, bypassing the 'safe' No.1 missile and somehow triggering the second one.

Although the AIM-9 was the F-100's principal missile, the Hughes AIM-4B (GAR-2) infra-red missile, used by the F-101 Voodoo and F-102 Delta Dagger, was evaluated on an F-100.

used to haul out bat manure while he was flying down in the Grand Canyon. Another F-100 collided with a commercial airliner at 30,000ft over Las Vegas.

Art Johnson noted that his squadron, the 309th FBS at George AFB, only loaded 100 rounds in each gun (usually in just two guns) for this kind of training and for Weapons Meets, 'mostly to keep from burning out the gun barrels prematurely'. Ground targets on the range for gun passes were the standard 20×20ft (6×6m) canvas spreads with a bull's-eye marking. Attacks were usually low-angle strafe profiles in a 10degree dive.

In 1958, Tom Germscheid graduated from Nellis AFB to the 429th TFS, 474th TFW at Cannon AFB (then known as Clovis AFB) where he spent the next four years. The Wing was still transitioning to F-100Ds with the squadron's yellow and black décor on their tails.

We went to the NAA factory at Palmdale, California and picked up our new F-100Ds. The 27th TFW (formerly 312th TFW) was also stationed at Cannon/Clovis from 18 February 1959. After the 474th got their F-100s the 27th transitioned too. We had about 200 Huns on the Cannon ramp by 1958. A bunch of us new 2nd Lieutenants who had been through the F-100A course at Nellis had more time in the F-100 than most of the old heads who were transitioning from the F-86H. We thought we were big stuff, although in reality we were an accident waiting to happen. We lost a lot of birds in the first couple of years, mostly to pilot error: a lot of dumb things.

Other F-100 class graduates went to the 479th Wing (the world's first supersonic fighter Wing) at George AFB, the 4th TFW at Seymour-Johnson AFB, and the 450th FDW at Foster AFB to fly the F-100C; or to F-100D squadrons at Myrtle Beach (354th TFW, commanded by WWII and Korean War ace Francis S. Gabreski), England AFB, Louisiana (366th TFW and 401st TFW), Langley AFB's 405th FBW, the 31st FBW at Turner AFB, Georgia (later at George AFB as a re-numbering of the 413th FBW), or the 506th FBW at Tinker AFB, Oklahoma commanded by Col Joseph L. Laughlin, which briefly owned F-100Ds from September 1957 to December 1958.

At Cannon AFB aircrew used the Melrose range for 'air-to-mud' training. As Tom Germscheid explained:

firing, he also had to remember to turn slightly to one side in order to avoid intercepting his own shells as they slowed down in flight and began to head for the ground on the same trajectory as the fighter.

When the F-100 did enter combat several years later, its air-to-air firepower was hardly ever needed but the guns were to be a major asset in countless attacks on ground targets. As USAF fighter squadrons progressively converted to the F-100, air-to-ground skills were also trained extensively as part of a full syllabus of combat skills. Tom Germscheid:

About once a year each squadron would deploy to Nellis AFB for air-to-air training. The month-long deployment was always a great time

and something we looked forward to – great flying and Las Vegas had a lot to offer to the boys from the high plains of New Mexico. Since there were more pilots than airplanes in a squadron some would drive their cars there, or get some of the groundcrew to drive our cars to Las Vegas so we would have wheels while we were there. On the Nellis ranges we could qualify in all the air-to-air events: 20mm on the 'rag', 20mm on the manoeuvring dart and GAR-8 Sidewinder missile. We also did a lot of ACM as well as some air-to-ground. We thought we had the world by the tail.

There were some incidents too:

One of the students clipped about 3ft off the vertical stabilizer of his F-100 when he hit a cable

The 31st FW Weapons Team at Nellis AFB in 1958. Left to right: Lt Bud Holman, Maj Chuck Horton, Col Gordie Grahm (team leader), Maj Art Johnson and Capt Walt Bruce. Squadron colours appear on the speed brake of 56-3196 as well as on its nose and wing tank. Five of the Wing's aircraft were painted in this scheme for several weeks.
Col Art Johnson

Showtime

In the late 1950s, with F-100 units adopting ever more eye-catching paint schemes, the real showplace for a squadron's talents was a Fighter Weapons Meet. Art Johnson organized and participated in his unit's Fighter Weapons Team at the 1958 competition. They won the world's first all-supersonic fighter Tactical Fighter Weapons Meet at George AFB and then went on as TAC's representatives in the World Class Fighter Weapons Meet at Nellis AFB in October.

We were still a nuclear bomb Wing and had squadrons on constant alert at airfields in Germany, armed with Mk 7 nuclear weapons through to the end of 1958. However, we also trained for the air-to-air mission and both skip and dive conventional bombing. The 1958 Meet included simulated nuclear and conventional missions, with LABS and M-1 toss bombing attacks. Air-to-air included supersonic firing against dart targets towed by other F-100s and subsonic against 'rag' targets. All the F-100D models were equipped with LABS delivery gyros and the automatic LABS feature using the autopilot (which was not too reliable when I flew the birds). I did better in the Weapons Meet using manual LABS. None of our F-100Ds had Sidewinder capability in 1958. The F-100D Wings, such as Gabby Gabreski's wing at Myrtle Beach had not been equipped with LABS or nuclear delivery hardpoints. They had a strictly conventional mission, although they were later given the nuclear mission as Gabby and all his pilots came down to Turner AFB to go through the Special Weapons delivery course I taught for the Wing. [Gabreski's Wing converted to the F-100D in 1957. His personal aircraft was F-100F 56-3869.]

On bombing and gunnery missions we would strafe and skip-bomb at 500kt at low level, which at elevations like Las Vegas gave us a pretty fast ground speed. The standard entry for a LABS nuclear attack was 500kt in afterburner, on the deck below 500ft. You needed the afterburner to make an Immelmann from the deck with that 3,000lb 'Blue Boy' dummy version on the Mk 7 nuclear weapon plus an external tank on the other wing. We also needed the afterburner to go above Mach 1 in air-to-air gunnery. Mach 1.2 was about it for the F-100 in level flight.

In the 1958 Weapons Meet at George I ended up in a tie for first place with my team-mate, Walt Bruce. They decided to have a fly-off against dart targets to settle it the next morning. I flew the mission in an F-100F with General Weyland in the back seat. I don't recall whether

Conventional weapons events included low-angle strafing, dive bombing with a 45-degree dive angle, skip bombing, 2.75in FFAR [folding fin aircraft rockets] (30-degree dive) and 5in HVA rockets. Nuclear events included 'over the shoulder' [nuclear delivery] (OTS) which was our primary delivery method. We called these 'idiot loops' and we did millions of them. A good yaw damper was a great asset in 'over-the-shoulder' delivery. There was also high-angle dive delivery (60–90 degrees from about 25,000ft) and level retarded nuclear delivery from about 2,000ft.

One of the training devices carried by the F-100 was the MA-3 triple-mounted rocket launcher. Carried on the outboard pylons, these could each take three HVA single rounds or three pods of Mk-4 2.75in FFARs (totalling forty-two missiles).

We generally fired one rocket at a time from the triple tube, simulating the firing of fifty 2.75in rockets. The accuracy of a single rocket was very questionable. Sometimes one of the three folding fins would not deploy and the rocket would go wild. I guess they figured that if you dumped fifty of them in one shot you were bound to hit something. They were designed for armoured

vehicles, radar and communications, vans, etc. The triple rocket launchers were somewhat high-drag, especially when empty and they limited the F-100 to Mach 0.8 below 20,000ft.

An alternative rocket launcher was the nineteen-shot LAU-3/A and one could be hung on each outboard pylon. Aiming of all rockets was done with the A-4 sight and an intervalometer fired one rocket each time the bomb button was pressed, or salvoed rockets from pods. For bombing practice, a dispenser was used that could also launch FFARs.

The SUU-20/A dispenser, which carried four 2.75s and six 25lb practice bombs or simulated retarded bombs ('beer cans') or any combination of the two types of bombs, greatly reduced the drag and permitted high-speed manoeuvring such as ACM after a bombing mission. The bottom of this dispenser had doors that opened and closed to simulate arming a nuclear store. The doors often malfunctioned, sticking in either the closed position (which meant an aborted mission) or open, which restricted where you could fly with a hung bomb. They later came out with a low-drag dispenser [MN-1 or MN-1A] without the rocket tubes and doors.

Brand new F-100D-85-NHs await collection from NAA's Columbus, Ohio factory. This was the last block of F-100s produced there. Allen T. Lamb

Walt flew his regular F-100D. I had shot gunnery in the F-100F before but this was not my regular bird for the Meet. I managed to embarrass myself by missing the target, with the Commander of Tactical Air Command in my back seat! Maybe the guns were not harmonized right or maybe I just screwed up. I didn't blame it on the F-100F as I never noticed much difference in the way they flew compared with the single-seater.

The dart target mission [at the Weapons Meet] was a one-to one affair. It was not possible to attack a dart with the tow-plane in straight flight without endangering the tow-plane. Each attacking fighter had a chase plane from Nellis who told the tow plane when to initiate evasive manoeuvres. The chase pilot was also a judge who decided if the airspeed of the attacking F-100 was supersonic or within the prescribed area. A foul in any respect garnered a zero for the mission. The tow plane first went into a supersonic diving turn while the attacker fired at the dart, then into a climbing turn while the attacker manoeuvred for a second pass at a lower speed, but not less than Mach 0.9. A hit on either of the passes was a win for the mission – not as easy as it sounds. The dart was not a big radar target for the A-4 ranging gun sight and not a large area to hit. However, after a bit of experience you never missed one.

The wisdom of honing these skills was emphasized a few years later when F-100 pilots were poised to attack real targets in Cuba during the Missile Crisis of October 1962. Among them was Lt Col David O. Williams (later a Brigadier General), who led the 524th TFS, 27th TFW from Cannon AFB to McDill AFB, Florida where the whole Wing sat cockpit alert during November of that year:

Each flight of four F-100s was assigned a Soviet missile site for its target, or a Soviet air defence installation. Each aircraft carried two napalm canisters on the inboard stations and two LAU-3 rocket pods on the outboard stations with nineteen 2.75in FFARs in each pod. Fortunately, diplomacy succeeded or there would have been a real blood bath and God knows where it would have led.

Worldwide Warrior

KB-50J tanker pilot piles on the knots to stay with a trio of 354th TFW F-100Ds feeding from its three hoses, September 1958. David Menard Collection

Pacific Alert

The F-100's tactical nuclear role and its inflight-refuelling kit, allowing up to three refuellings per mission, made it the first fighter to be capable of deploying the nuclear deterrent virtually anywhere in the world at 12-hours notice. The world situation in the 1950s and early 1960s provided plenty of occasions on which that show of ultimate strength was required. For F-100C/D pilots that meant a lot of time away from home base.

Flying from Clovis AFB from 1961 to 1964, Alex Martin reckoned to be on temporary duty (TDY) for 270 days a year. Before that, he spent four years at Kadena AB, Okinawa with the 18th Tactical

Fighter Wing (TFW), beginning in 1957 just after it had converted from F-86F Sabres. The Wing had stood alert during the Formosa Crisis in February 1955 and as the tension continued it re-established itself on Super Sabres. In 1958, as Communist Chinese pressure continued, other F-100 units moved to Taiwan including the 511th Fighter-bomber Squadron (FBS) from Langley AFB that did a TDY at Ching Chuan AB. Two squadrons of the 354th TFW at Myrtle Beach spent three months at Kadena supported by F-101C Voodoos. For the 18th TFW the plan was to start a:

... quick strike' alert area at Kadena where strike-ready pilots and nuclear-armed aircraft would be able to launch against studied, pre-planned targets within fifteen minutes. This fledgling operation was honed over the years, but at first it involved a taxi-around on a practice scramble every day with a 'nuke' on board. That got changed. I remember some of the nuclear weapons started to drip high explosive as we sat on hot concrete in mid-summer. They fixed this by putting an umbrella over the weapons to keep them shaded. Twelve aircraft were on the alert pad during the normal DEF-CON [defense condition]. All mainland targets were memorized (with alternate targets) and this was tested regularly, as well as the authenticating procedures. During ORIs [Operational Readiness Inspections] we would launch with the Blue Boy shapes and the rest of the fleet would load up and fly to 'go/no-go' points and authenticate. There were set maximum times for everything. It would drive the opposition nuts when their secret agents reported our launches and saw us all fanning out towards the coast carrying 'nukes' (simulated of course).

8th TFW F-100D-20-NAs at Itazuke AB where the Wing converted to Super Sabres at the end of 1956. David Menard Collection

Alex Martin (left) and Roy Moore. Alex Martin

We'd orbit, get aborted and sail home. Alert pilots would come on duty, pre-flight their F-100Ds, set all the switches to 'go', have the power units hooked up [to start the engines] and their personal gear in the cockpit. Then they'd go to the alert shack that had beds and a kitchen. They could get off the turf in fifteen minutes easily; closer to ten was normal.

Yokota in Japan also hosted F-100 deployments including Operation *Mobile Zebra* in November 1957, when sixteen F-100Cs and the same number of F-100Ds made the sixteen-hour flight from George AFB. While the nuclear weapons themselves were shaded by umbrellas, a device of only marginally greater practicality would have protected the pilots on nuclear missions. Instead, a white flash shield, pulled forward over the interior of the cockpit canopy, was the only available protection. Maintainer John Clarity viewed this contraption ironically as:

... a real pacifier to the pilots on a mission without likelihood of return. This piece of junk would supposedly preserve them from the ther-

mal and light forces which would have overtaken them as a result of a bombing technique that left them too close to the 'ground zero' they had just created. The system was so shoddy it had no place in a machine preparing to destroy a large part of the planet.

The hood was installed solely for thermal protection, as explosive force was not thought to be a problem that would affect pilots. The maximum yield for F-100 delivery was set at one megaton.

For Roy Moore, flying F-100Ds with the 80th Tactical Fighter Squadron (TFS), 8th TFW Headhunters from Itazuke AB, nuclear alert was also a requirement for his Wing's area of responsibility in South East Asia and it carried its attendant hazards.

In the early days of carrying nuclear weapons on fighter aircraft there were no controls, i.e. the pilot, if he got airborne with a 'nuke', could drop it and detonate it. The powers that be were concerned that one man could have total control of so much destructive power so they started thrashing around, looking for some way to control the pilot even after he was airborne with the

The 18th TFW's attractive arrowhead insignia used red, white and blue segments (top to bottom). Individual squadron colours were painted on the nose – in this case yellow and black for a 12th TFS F-100F-20-NA with 200gal tanks inboard. David Menard Collection

weapon. In 1958 a lock handle was installed in the cockpit that had to be pulled before the weapon could leave the airplane. (There must have been a nuclear 'training shape' [Blue Boy] inadvertently dropped somewhere?)

When locked, the handle did prevent anything from being jettisoned or released from the centreline and left intermediate (Type 8) pylon.

The first attempt to control the pilot in flight was to put a combination lock on that 'special store' handle that had to be unlocked and removed before the handle could be pulled. That all sounds like a great idea: the pilot could get airborne with the nuclear weapon but actual control of the weapon could remain in the hands of cooler-headed folk on the ground. They could radio him the combination to the lock if they decided that the right thing was for him to deliver the bomb on target.

The problem was that the special weapons handle in the F-100 was just about level with the top of your boots. To see the numbers on the

combination lock it was necessary to bend over, well below the level where you could see the instrument panel. To try and fly the plane with your head below your knees is to know instant vertigo. It was almost, but not quite impossible to work the combination lock and maintain control of the airplane. I was never able to do it in less than fifteen minutes and that was with a great deal of risk to myself and the airplane. The system didn't stay in force for long. PAL (permissive action link) enabling was perfected somewhere around 1959 and with that system they would radio you with a four or five-digit code to enter into the PAL keyboard.

The F-100 was by no means alone among 1950s fighters in having a cockpit that was less than user-friendly. However, training and experience were great compensators, as Maj Curtis Burns explained:

We used to do everything by touch, because when you are flying tight wing position it's not too wise to look down into the cockpit. To change the UHF radio channel, for example,

you merely had to take your hand off the throttle and move it about 1in to the right on the left-hand console to turn the channel switch, counting the channel numbers up or down from the one you were on to the channel you were changing to.

The *Headhunters* initially flew Block 15 F-100D with MA-2A low-altitude bombing system (LABS), a yaw/pitch damper and no centreline pylon. Lt Col Ronald Herrick referred to them as:

... half-assed Ds because they had some F-100C systems. This caused a problem in PACAF [Pacific Air Force] when the Mk 28 nuclear store was introduced and the Block 15 aircraft were sent all over PACAF and eventually replaced. The Thunderbirds team used some of them (after repainting in team colours) on a Far East tour, while theirs were in IRAN [inspect and repair as necessary], but didn't take them back to the States. NATO countries also got early D models. The rest of the 8th Wing (35th and 36th TFS) had Block 20 aircraft.

In September 1963, a group of 523rd TFS pilots led by Lt Col David O. Williams collected a batch of 8th TFW F-100Ds from Itazuke and ferried them back to McClellan AFB for *High Wire* updates.

The nuclear priority dominated F-100 training in the Pacific area and reduced the time available for traditional tactics. Alex Martin:

In keeping with the nuclear mission we did little ACM [air combat manoeuvring], few conventional deliveries and mostly we were into OTS ['over the shoulder' nuclear delivery].

Air combat training was also reduced because:

Budgets were being cut and we didn't want to lose aircraft or pilots doing crazy stuff like ACM. Of course, we did our own! The upper levels of USAF command were rarely fighter jocks, mostly ex-SAC [Strategic Air Command] and they forgot what a fighter pilot needs to stay sharp, even if there is an occasional loss.

Ten years later, this was a philosophy that was to cost the USAF dearly in the Vietnam conflict.

At Kadena most F-100 pilots got in 20–25 flying hours per month, flying sorties of 1³/4 hours on average. There would be an hour's briefing before a mission and at least thirty minutes afterwards. 'We used

a bombing range on Taiwan and one near Clark AB. There were just enough sorties to keep us combat-ready in conventional ordnance delivery including 2.75in rocket firing, dive and skip bombing and gunnery.'

Conversion to the first batch of F-100s in PACAF was a fairly arbitrary process in some cases. Ron Herrick recalled his first F-100D flight in the days before F-100Fs were available:

At that time I was three years out of pilot training and I had been a T-33 instructor. When I got to Itazuke they were in the process of converting to the F-100D from the F-86F. I was the only one who had gone through Nellis to check out and I became a guinea pig. The F-86 was still there and they gave me unrestricted access to go chase myself around the sky. After about thirty hours on the F-86 I went through ground school on the Hun and was then briefed for hours. They finally said I was briefed enough and off I went. The afterburner was a real kick with a clean bird. The only real surprise was turning from the base leg to finals for landing as no one had remembered to tell me about the 1g buffet so I got a ribbing about my large landing patterns.

Life in a Pacific F-100 squadron had its moments of light relief from the grim business of nuclear alert.

At Clark AB in 1959 there was an on-going competition with the 509th FIS. We buried a

bomb in the front yard at their Ops building with a sign to let them know where the bomb had come from. They glued a large beer-advertising sticker on the drop tank of one of our planes. One of our pilots, Wayne Abbott had a bad landing and got out OK but his F-100D was a total loss from fire and the remains were moved to the salvage yard. They took the burned-out F-100 remains and spread them across the big parade field in front of Thirteenth Air Force Headquarters. They did a very convincing job so that people on the way to work the next morning were convinced that an F-100 had made an emergency landing on the parade field during the night. Since some very heavy equipment was necessary to handle the F-100 carcass it was clear that more than a few men were involved in perpetrating this joke.

A large number of man-hours were wasted on some of these practical jokes and the Wing Cdr finally put an end to them after the 509th broke into our Ops building one night and moved everything other than the classified safe on to the roof of the building. Each item was placed directly above its proper location in the building below.

In 1957, Roy Moore became one of the first 80th FBS pilots to transition to the F-100D, a process that the entire 8th TFW accomplished without losing a single aircraft or pilot.

I had three flights in the single-seat F-100D and became an Instructor Pilot after my third flight. I suppose we didn't have much choice since there were no pilots in the squadron with F-100 time. We transitioned the whole squadron [from the Republic F-84G] without losing a plane or pilot though. I think we did lose one nose-gear strut when a pilot made a hard landing and tried to force the plane back on to the runway.

While at Clark AB, Roy took a flight of four F-100Fs to Bangkok:

... to give VIP rides to members of the Thai Government and military, including the top general in the army and even the King's concubine – the first female pilot in Thailand. They rescinded all flying restrictions while we were there and in fact encouraged us to 'boom' the airfield at very low altitude, although the F-100 was difficult to keep at supersonic speed at sea level. I don't know why we didn't break a lot of glass, but I never heard any complaints.

On one flight I was told to fly non-stop from Clark AFB to Bangkok without inflight-refuelling. We had to file a flight-plan to go around

Roy Moore (left) after giving a check-ride to the senior officer of the Royal Thai AF in F-100F 56-3813, still in 72nd TFS décor with a red tail flash. The unit became the 510th TFS in spring 1959 with purple markings. Roy Moore

Special Stores and LABS

The F-100's principal nuclear weapon was the 1,600lb Mk 7 store, though in 1956–57 some bases still had 1,100lb Mk12s left over from their F-86F/H days. The weapon was 15½ft (4.7m) long with a 30½in (77.5cm) diameter and a variable 'yield' of 2–60KT. For comparison, the Mk1 *Little Boy* used at Hiroshima yielded 13KT (the equivalent of 13,000 tons of TNT). Mk 7s could be carried beneath the F-100C/D/F or F-101A/C Voodoo, or smaller aircraft like the F-84F/G and AD5-N. Detonation could be set for 'airburst' (timer or radar) or 'contact' (with the ground). The bomb casing had three stabilizing fins, the lower one being retractable to enable the weapon to be carried under a fighter.

Summary of F-100 Atomic Weapons Armament Differences

Model	LABS Type	Nuclear Weapon	Carriage Station/Pylon
F-100C (early)	MA-1	Mk 7	Left intermediate
F-100C (late)	MA-2	Mk 7	Left intermediate
F-100D (early)	MA-2	Mk 7	Left intermediate
F-100D (late)	AN/AJB-1B	Mk 7, 28, 43, 61	Left intermediate/centreline
F-100F	AN/AJB-5A	Mk 7, 28, 43, 61	Left intermediate/centreline

Early F-100Cs: F-100C-1-NA, -5NA.
Early F-100Ds: F-100D-1-NA– -15NA, -35NH, -40NH.
Late F-100Ds included: F-100D-20-NA – -30-NA, -45NH – -55NH, -65NA – -75NA, -80NH, -85NH, -90NH.

Mk 7 airburst could be set via an internal timer that began to run when the bomb was released. Radar fusing used one of two settings, selectable from the cockpit, with the bomb's internal radar reading the required altitudes for detonation. The Mk 28 and Mk 43 could be set for airburst using a radar altimeter fuse only for ground contact detonation. The Mk 43 also had an internal timer for 'laydown' mode, a delayed detonation on the ground. The Mk 61 used airburst (radar controlled), ground contact or laydown detonation.

MA-1 LABS had only the vertical gyros and the switches for LABS operation were on top of the instrument panel. It had no low-altitude drogue delivery (LADD) capability and was very difficult to use for OTS delivery. MA-2 LABS added yaw/roll gyros.

Late F-100Ds and F-100Fs could also carry the Mk28 (B-28) weighing 1,980lb (900kg) with variable yield of 1MT and the possibility of free-fall or parachute-retarded delivery (contact or airburst). This was replaced by the Mk 43 (B-43) weighing 2,100lb (950kg) and containing a 1MT warhead. Its 12½ft (3.8m) shell of 18in (45cm) diameter had a steel nose-spike inside a nose casing to secure the bomb in position for a 'ground-burst laydown' detonation. For the laydown option, the nose-cone separated immediately after release due to the parachute deployment slowing the weapon.

All these devices were later supplanted by the tactical B-61 'Silver Bullet' (1966), but by then the F-100's Tactical Air Command (TAC) nuclear role had passed mainly to later types such as the F-4 Phantom, F-105 Thunderchief and F-111 Aardvark.

F-100Cs and early F-100Ds carried the Mk 7 only on their left intermediate pylon, which had the requisite release and control wiring. A counter-balancing 275gal tank appeared on the opposite intermediate station, often with a 200gal tank on each of the outboard and inboard pylons too. This was known as the nuclear '1-E' configuration and it tended to cause asymmetry problems in flight that Curtis Burns equated to 'borderline instability'. Landing with all the external tanks still in place produced some interesting trim problems because of the asymmetric drag. On later F-100Ds and the F-100F, the fuselage centreline hardpoint could also be used for a 'special store' (nuclear weapon) or a practice bomb dispenser.

Early F-100Ds were identified by the main landing gear doors hanging vertically when open. The later, centreline pylon aircraft had doors that did not open so far and hung at an angle. Production aircraft with the centreline pylon had a provision to inhibit speed brake operation when a store was loaded on the pylon. The speed brake was later modified with a larger cutout to allow speed brake operation with a store in place.

The Mk 7 weapon had its own T-270 control panel in the cockpit and the later weapons used the T-249 and variations. The usual bomb button on top of the control stick, with proper armament switch selection, released the 'nuke'. To jettison, the JETTISON button was used to release all stores and then all pylons in sequence. Three AUX JETT buttons could jettison stores without jettisoning their pylons. Pylon jettison was only possible on the F-100D/F; those on the F-100C were bolted in place.

A T-63 *Blue Boy* (so-called because of its colour) training shape duplicated the aerodynamic characteristics of a Mk 7 but comprised a 600lb (270kg) concrete core inside the bomb casing. More often, standard 25lb BDU-33 practice bombs would be used for training. These were carried in a dispenser or individually on a B37K-1 rack that could take four bombs. Similar training shapes were available in limited quantities for the later weapons.

Two main methods of nuclear delivery were available. LADD used parachute-retarded, delayed action bombs (such as the Mk 28 RE) in a 200ft (60m) above ground level (AGL) approach with a pull-up to 45 degrees to release the weapon so that it ended up over the target. The escape was made by rolling inverted and manoeuvring to a 45-degree dive to the deck. This delivery required an identification point (IP) short of the target. The distance was then used to convert to two time parameters in seconds. The first time (PULLUP TIME) was the time at 500kt, indicated (KIAS), from the IP to the initiation of a pull-up to a 45-degree climb. The second time (RELEASE TIME) was the time from the start of pull-up to weapon release. The pull-up signal was via the A-4 sight and the green weapon release light extinguishing. Weapon release was indicated by the green RELEASE light and the A-4 sight illuminating.

A LABS delivery allowed the F-100 pilot to toss his nuclear weapon at a target up to 10 miles (16km) ahead of him, or the OTS delivery. He then made a half-loop at 4g and accelerated away from the bomb's trajectory at maximum speed, putting as many miles as possible between his aircraft and the impact point. Afterburner would be needed for this though it was rarely used at low altitude at other times because of its enormous appetite for fuel at low level. The long-range requirement for most of these missions would not have allowed the pilot enough fuel to return to base. Instead, he was provided with map references for a safe area where he could bale out and be recovered.

The most common variation on the LABS delivery was the more usually-employed OTS release where the pilot overflew the target at about 5,000ft (1,500m), ascertaining that it was the correct one and then pulling up into a 4g Immelmann. The bomb was released as the F-100 passed the correct degree setting (pre-set on the vertical gyro). Two release angles could be set. The armament control panel with the AJB-1/5 LABS equipment on the left console had a MODE SEL switch, which determined the release function. The LABS equipment was controlled by the MODE SEL switch, offering LABS, LABS ALT or LADD settings. The LABS option could be set for any angle of release, whereas the LABS ALT could only be used for OTS. In practical use, the LABS setting was to offer an alternative release setting for a different aircraft weight at the release point. LABS/LABS ALT release was controlled by the vertical gyros as long as the pilot kept the bomb button pressed down. As the bomb ascended in a long arc to 15,000–20,000ft (4,600–6,000m) before falling on its target, the Super Sabre pilot had a chance to dive for the deck and run from the detonation. The autopilot, installed mainly to enable F-100s to fly long transits to deployments, could be coupled to the MA-2 or AJB-1 systems to give an Auto-LABS delivery. Project *Green Door* in May 1957 introduced field modifications to improve the Auto-LABS system and the autopilot.

Ron Herrick set up and taught at the PACAF Nuclear School at Itazuke AB, Japan for three years. After that he was Officer in Charge (OIC) of the Nuclear Weapon Training at Luke AFB. He received his training at Sandia Laboratories as a Nuclear Delivery Instructor. He also flew 1,200 hours in the F-100, followed by 200 combat missions in F-4D Phantoms. He explained in more detail what was involved in an F-100 OTS LABS mission:

LABS was activated by the MODE SEL switch on the pilot's left console. This in turn activated the vertical gyro (which had the appropriate release angles on it) and also displayed (after uncaging) roll and pitch information from the LABS vertical gyro on the LABS indicator. If the gyro had not erected properly [in 13 seconds] the 'cage' button on top of the throttle was used to cage the gyro properly. When it had stabilized the pilot released this button, uncaging the gyro. Next, SPECIAL STORES was selected on the ARMAMENT SELECTOR switch. During the loading process, the pylon load panel was set.

Next, the release lock was unlocked. When over the target the pilot pushed the bomb release button on top of the stick, selected afterburner and went from 1g to 4g in two seconds. The LABS indicator horizontal needle now registered g-forces and the vertical needle showed yaw and roll (from the yaw/roll gyro). This was held caged by a single pin and the gyro was uncaged at pull-up if the wings were level. The pilot simply had to hold the two needles centred. Another detail was provided to assist the pilot. When he depressed the bomb release in LABS ALT or the timer indicated 'pull up' in LABS, the horizontal needle (if kept cen-

tred) would program one to four 'g' within two seconds At about 145 degrees pitch angle, as determined by the vertical gyro, the horizontal needle indicated a relaxed 'g' command and the pilot continued in an Immelmann, diving to the deck to go like hell. For successive runs he had to cycle the MODE SEL switch in straight and level flight.

Col Tom Germscheid was involved in an early Auto-LABS training initiative while he was with the 429th TFS, 474th TFW:

It was called Project *Randy Boy*, using the autopilot to perform an automatic OTS manoeuvre, release and escape. The autopilot on the F-100D was shaky at best. However, for this project they really had them peaked up. You could approach the target or predicted offset point at 1,000ft in autopilot. Afterburner was selected shortly before the pull-up point. At the pull-up point you would hit and hold the pickle button,

trying not to put any pressure on the stick that might disengage the autopilot. The aircraft entered a 4g loop with the autopilot keeping the wings level and the yaw damper keeping the ball centred. At about 120 degrees of climb the weapon automatically released and at 130 degrees the bird rolled out of the Immelmann and entered a 45-degree dive. It pulled out at 1,000ft, heading back out from the target. Great idea when it worked – which was not too often.

LABS equipment in the early aircraft with sensitive airspeed indicators used a constant release angle. The airspeed was varied to account for temperature, pressure, altitude and aircraft gross weight. Later aircraft, including the F-100 used a constant 500 KIAS run in speed and varied the release angle. This was due to the relatively hard-to-read Mach/speed indicator. LABS was also installed in the F-86H Sabre and in contemporary British aircraft such as the Scimitar and Sea Vixen.

A rare view of a 72nd TFS F-100D-25-NA at Clark AB with its red markings outlined in white. The unit was re-designated the 510th TFS in the spring of 1959.
Lt Col A. L. Olman via David Menard

light, not unusually bright. By the time I was in trail with it, it began a 10-degree climb and accelerated at an unbelievable rate. Startled by the extreme speed I turned my IFF [identification, friend or foe] to EMERGENCY and called the Clark radar station. They replied immediately and I asked if they had an aircraft at my twelve o'clock. They replied that there was nothing on the screen other than my emergency squawk. I had viewed the light through the F-100's canopy and all windshield panels and I have no reason to believe that I was watching a reflection, a star or anything other than a flying object of some kind.

Clark AB became home to the 72nd TFS F-100Ds from July 1958, supervised by the 6200th Air Base Wing. Re-numbering of the squadron as the 510th TFS was effective from April 1959 and it joined the newly activated 405th FW at the Philippines base. The Wing had previously flown F-100Ds at Langley AFB from late 1956 until the summer of 1958 with the 508th, 509th, 510th and 511th FBS Squadrons. Reactivated at Clark in April 1959, it included only one F-100D squadron, the 510th. In due course, this unit joined the 3rd TFW upon leaving PACAF in March 1964. The squadron's stylish and unusual purple nose chequers and bird insignia were among the most attractive F-100 colour schemes.

Roy Moore became the unit's Squadron Maintenance Officer. One of his innovations in this role was to find a non-regulation use for damaged 450gal drop tanks. He rescued one of the large, draggy tanks from the dump and asked the 'tin benders' at Clark to cut a 20×36in (50×90cm) piano-hinged door in its side. They then

the southern tip of Vietnam, but because the distance was too great flying that route we went direct across North Vietnam. I never knew whether this was an intelligence-gathering flight or not, but I suspect there was a 'spook' sitting off-shore recording all the radar activity as we crossed. We had no navaids at Bangkok and on another flight we were below 600lb of fuel when we located the runway. We landed two planes in one direction and two in the opposite direction at the same time. We just kept to the right side of the runway and passed in the middle!

Roy even encountered a UFO on one of his training flights out of Clark.

I was on a flight alone in an F-100D a little before dark at 35,000ft when I noticed a light almost level but slightly below my altitude. It was heading in an easterly direction and if neither of us had changed course it would have passed to my right about half a mile away. Thinking that the light was another F-100 in the area I planned to jump him for a little ACT (air combat tactics) training. I lit the burner and dipped the nose slightly for maximum acceleration. I easily went supersonic and started a shallow turn towards the light, which was now almost north of me and slightly above. As I began my turn the light started a left turn away from me. There was never any visible airframe, just a steady, white

Another rare shot of a 72nd TFS F-100D-25-NA from Clark AB. This Hun has a Mk 7 *Blue Boy* nuclear shape under its left wing. Its crew appear to be re-installing the ejection seat. David Menard Collection

Standard TAC décor on a 354th TFW F-100D085-NH, 56-3383. It was lost in a landing accident at Phan Rang AB in October 1970. A Smith

loaded the modified tank with six 50lb (23kg) bags of rice and test-flew it to supersonic speed and 6.66g. This proved that the tank could 'easily carry all the luggage and souvenir goodies for a flight of four aircraft' during off-base visits! Roy's luggage tank was soon detected during an inspection and consigned once again to the salvage yard. Some F-100 squadrons in Europe produced rather more sinister-looking luggage pods by modifying dummy Mk 7 nuclear 'shapes'.

From Kadena, training sometimes involved some ACM sorties with Chinese Nationalist F-86s from Taiwan and 'shooting the rag' with guns. On gunnery sorties Alex Martin reckoned that 'Most could score more consistently using manual ranging with the A-4 gun sight than by using radar ranging'. Bombing practice also placed him among those who had reservations about the Auto-LABS system and autopilot generally.

Laden with a pair of 450gal tanks, F-100D-90-NA 56-3345 (the penultimate F-100D) winds up for take-off. Two dark blue alar markings on the tail and dark blue nose bands indicate the 416th TFS, 21st TFW at Misawa AB. Lt Col E. V. Wells via David Menard

The autopilot was notoriously terrible. In ten years I can't remember five times I got to use it. To get better accuracy in the nuclear OTS delivery they tied the autopilot with the LABS and the autopilot would do your loop for you, releasing the bomb at a predetermined setting. Thankfully there was a 'paddle' emergency disconnect switch at the front of the control column that kicked it off. On my first trip to the range with it the damn thing pitched down and I found myself at 50ft altitude.

Although the F-100's safety record steadily improved in service there were inevitable losses. On 30 June 1959, F-100D 55-3633 took off from Kadena on a functional check flight when at 1,200ft (365m) the engine compartment fire warning light started to glow on the pilot's front panel. As Alex Martin explained, this required an instant response: 'The F-100 has a fuselage fuel tank that all the others feed into and it is nestled next to and around the engine. With a fire you don't fool around, or ... Boom!' The pilot jettisoned two empty fuel tanks and a practice bomb unit

On your wing, F-100D-50-NH 55-2902 of the 21st TFW, Misawa AB with big 450gal tanks. David Menard Collection

An RF-101C snapped *Little John* (foreground), the 531st TFS commander's jet with other red-and-white marked squadron aircraft over northern Japan in 1961. *Little John* was re-named *Schatze II* the following year. FW-809 and -782 were both to become Vietnam War casualties. David Menard Collection

Susan Constant (54-1753), leader of the London to Jamestown anniversary flight. Type II 450gal tanks are carried. The aircraft was later put on display at the Air Force Museum. USAF via Ron Thurlow

into the sea and pulled back on the throttle. The warning light went out and the Super Sabre turned back towards Kadena, but a large explosion shook the aircraft. After re-directing his aircraft out to sea, the pilot punched out 5 miles (8km) offshore. Tragically, the fighter swung back over the coast, its drag chute released and opened and in a chance in a thousand it smashed into a tiny village and school. Seventeen died and 169 were injured as twenty-seven buildings were destroyed. Alex Martin said 'We were all devastated. No matter how much we tried to do it wasn't enough and it was another barb for use by the politicians who wanted us off the island'.

Also in Japan was the 21st TFW at Misawa AB. Activated in July 1958, the Wing's two squadrons, the 416th and 531st TFS, transitioned from the F-84G as the 80th TFS *Headhunters* had done. Flying the F-100D, the 21st TFW was deactivated only two years later. Its squadrons then became part of the 39th Air Division at Misawa until 1964 when they moved to the control of the 3rd TFW at England AFB, Louisiana with the 90th and 510th TFS. The following year, the squadrons were back in the Far East, shouldering a major share of the air action at the start of the Vietnam War.

During its time at Misawa, the 21st TFW was noted for its 'named' F-100s, with nicknames like *Ooh-Ha*, *The Gambler* and *Little John* on their silver noses. In 1962 a tone-down edict removed all individuality from PACAF markings and a simple PACAF insignia appeared on the jets' tails instead. TAC had already ordered the glorious squadron plumage that adorned most F-100s to be removed. From January 1960 only the TAC patch varied their silver surfaces, though small squadron patches survived in some instances.

While four F-100 Wings and numerous other Detachments flew over a quarter of a million combat sorties in the Vietnam War, continental USA (CONUS)-based Wings continued to perform sentry duty at

54-1823 was another of the 422nd FDS Jamestown anniversary flight F-100C-15-NAs.
Named *Discovery*, it flew the Atlantic with 54-1754 *Godspeed* and 54-1753 *Susan Constant* (all named after the original settlers' ships). It later served with the Arizona ANG. David Menard Collection

other Far Eastern bases. Among them were Air National Guard (ANG) units. F-100Cs of the 127th TFS, Kansas ANG and the 166th TFS, Ohio ANG deployed to Kunsan AB, South Korea on 4 July 1968, remaining there for thirteen months with the 354th TFW. These squadrons

took part in Operation *Combat Fox*, with F-105D, F-4D, F-102A and RF-101G Detachments from other bases after North Korea seized the intelligence-gathering ship USS *Pueblo* and a USN EC-121M from VQ-1 was shot down by North Korean MiG-17s.

Brig Gen Robinson Risner flew 56-3730 to Paris in May 1957 (taking 6 hours 37 minutes) to mark the 50th anniversary of Charles Lindbergh's first, non-stop solo crossing (33 hours 39 minutes). Lindbergh himself was due to fly in the rear seat of *Spirit of St. Louis II* (seen here with a replica of the Ryan original) but fell ill on the day. This F-100F went on to fly with the 20th FBW, 50th TFW, Colorado, New Jersey and Ohio ANG before Risner dedicated it at its display position outside the Air Force Academy. It carried its *Spirit* name throughout most of its career. David Menard

NATO Knights

The first USAF unit to receive the F-100C, the 322nd FDG at Foster AFB, Texas, made one of the earliest F-100 deployments to Europe when it flew to Sidi Slimane, Morocco on 19 September 1956 in Exercise *Mobile Baker*, and thence to Landstuhl in West Germany. It was the first of many such trans-Atlantic deployments. Within a few years these lengthy transit flights became routine for F-100 crews and there were some spectacular public demonstrations of the F-100's long-range capability.

On 13 May 1957, six F-100Cs from the 452nd Fighter (Day) Squadron (FDS), 32nd FDG at Foster AFB, led by 54-1753 *Susan Constant* commemorated the voyage of the Jamestown settlers 350 years previously by flying from London to the site of the first English settlement on North American soil. Three of the Super Sabres went on to Los Angeles, a total flight time of 14 hours 5 minutes, at an average speed of 477mph (767km/h).

A week later Maj Robinson Risner (later to command an F-105 unit in Vietnam) flew one of the USAF's newly accepted F-100Fs from New York to Paris for Project *Europa*, following Charles Lindbergh's route. The aircraft (56-3730) was then delivered to the 20th Fighter-bomber Wing (FBW) at RAF Wethersfield, UK, later serving with the 50th TFW and several ANG squadrons before going on permanent display at the USAF Academy. Robinson Risner, who had meanwhile become a Brigadier General, then dedicated the F-100F, which still bore the name *Spirit of St Louis II* that it had carried for much of its service life.

The first single-engined jet aircraft to cross the North Pole made their flight on 7 August 1957. F-100F-20s 58-1227 and -1232 with lightweight Doppler navigation systems (NAVS) completed this venture in Operation *Julius Caesar*, with Col Titus in '232. All these flights bore the vital underlying message for potential adversaries that TAC could deploy a very significant strike force anywhere in the world and very fast.

Of all the global calls upon the Super Sabre's superior strike power, none was more urgent than the Cold War scenario in Europe. F-100Cs became the first supersonic attack aircraft in Western Europe when the 36th Fighter (Day) Wing (FDW) received its initial deliveries on 12

Blazing Swords

A tight diamond formation of Skyblazers in 1961 led by F-100C-25-NA 54-2009. USAF

Part of the light relief from Cold War duties was the spectacular Skyblazers aerobatic team. Founded by the 36th FG late in 1949, the team had moved to the 86th FBW at Landstuhl in 1952, then to the 48th FBW at Chaumont, flying F-86Fs. In October 1956, the 36th FDW resumed responsibility. Capt (later General) Wilbur 'Bill' Creech who had previously flown F-84s with the Thunderbirds, founded a new team with F-100Cs.

After practice sessions from Sidi Slimane and a change of markings to a 'stars and stripes' tail design, the team put on its first shows in 1957, giving forty displays in Europe. The crowd-pleasing use of afterburner was much emphasized and sonic booms were included in the early displays. These usually involved a 'clover leaf' from a partial loop, a 'fleur-de-lis' from a steep climb, a formation inverted pass, a diamond and a final 'bomb burst' which engaged the burners as the team departed over the crowd. The final manoeuvre was usually a high-speed, low-altitude cross over.

Leadership passed to Capt J. W. Armstrong and then to Capt 'Pat' Kramer from May 1960. The team continued until the 36th TFW converted to the Republic F-105D, which was not thought to be suitable for use by the team. Lt Col Gordon 'Horse' Scharnhorst recalled his days flying on the left wing of the formation:

The team received a couple of modified vertical stabilizers from NAA [North American Aviation]. They were built to withstand the continuous stress from the way a pilot flew in the 'slot' position. He was way up in the 'slot' and very shallow, so that the vertical stabilizer was receiving constant vibration from the leader's exhaust. The whole 'razorback' top of the fuselage from behind the cockpit to the vertical stabilizer was black from that exhaust. Needless to say, we never used the burner while in diamond formation!

Leo van Overschelde, who was one of the Skyblazers' maintainers, noted that the new stabilizers were skinned with stainless steel and that there were other modifications to the F-100Cs:

We had an oil container for the smoke in the ammo bay and a pump for that smoke system in the gun-bay with a toggle switch in the cockpit. We also trimmed the engines 'hot'; about 2 per cent above data plate speed. On tour we didn't carry a spare engine with us but the 36th FBW could fly in engine parts such as fuel control systems, or an afterburner unit. We had a spare F-100C but that was usually the one in 100-hour inspection.

F-100C maintenance involved 50- and 100-hour inspections. At 50 hours we changed fuel and oil filters and did a general inspection. For the 100 hours we took all inspection panels off and went through everything. There was a 1,000-hour limit at which new installations of engine and afterburner would be made and a 5,000-hour inspection at Depot level.

The Skyblazers aircraft were kept very clean and polished and we had a couple of painters, though I helped to paint the aircraft. In the ground crew we helped one another. Almost everyone could pack a drag chute. I was an engine specialist but I could install radios, change a tyre or 'crew' the aircraft. We travelled to all shows, mainly in a C-130 or C-119, taking our own MA-2 starter unit, coloured smoke, extra drag chutes, tyres, etc. The pilots had a routine for getting into their aircraft, though not as elaborate as the Thunderbirds. They trained all the time when we didn't have a show. Sometimes the pilots would stay and help us the night before a show. Occasionally the fuel control system on the engine would fail due to trouble with a bleed-valve governor. Also, a hydraulic pump would give up once in a while. I used to change them from inside the intake, which was faster than 'pulling' an engine though it required some good handwork with the wrenches. We sometimes had trouble with the nose-wheel steering too.

The first concern was safety. Sometimes pilots would pop a rivet but not too often. I remember only two accidents and neither was the pilot's fault.

One of these involved the loss of F-100C 54-2006 when 'Horse' Scharnhorst was returning to Bitburg from the second practice flight of the day on 7 August 1959:

I had no altitude control, but did have aileron and rudder. I had to eject and the helicopter from Spangdahlem picked me up and I did get to beer call. The next morning we departed at 0730 hrs for France to fly several weekend air shows.

F-100C 54-1980 was the Skyblazers' 'slot' aircraft, hence the sooty tail. It was assigned to Capt John Clayton, who is possibly the pilot who has popped the aircraft's drag chute before the tyres hit the runway. David Menard Collection

March 1956. The Commander, Col John A. Brooks, had led his Wing's conversion from the F-86F at Sidi Slimane AB in French Morocco, where the 45th FDS, 316th AD had received F-100Cs earlier that spring, and for around a year it existed to convert United States Air Forces in Europe (USAFE) units to the F-100. Subsequently, transition took place at Wheelus AB, Libya. Curtis Burns was among those pilots:

Several of us who were new to the 36th Fighter Day Wing [TFW after 8 July 1958] took ground school conducted by Air Training Command Flying Training Detachment. All the flying instruction (about 29 hours in the F-100C) was conducted by my Instructor Pilot [IP], 1st Lt Ford Smart, an old head with the 53rd FDS who had initially flown F-86s. All tactical fighter pilots have to maintain proficiency in air-to-ground skills and we would qualify at Wheelus or at the French Air Force base at Cazeau.

Don Schmenk enlarged upon the gunnery aspect. For air-to-ground practice in the 1960s, using a 15-degree dive angle:

We started to fire short bursts about 3,500ft out and had to cease fire about 1,500ft from the target or be 'fouled'. We only carried 100 rounds total and the gun didn't have a lot of disperse-ment. We also had to qualify in air-to-air semi-annually. The only place where we could do this was Wheelus. We launched in staggered flights

of two, just behind the target-tow airplane so that when the first two were done firing the sec-ond two were in place to continue. Again, we carried only 100 rounds per gun. Everyone called off target with a 'hit' whether you thought you had hit it or not. The fourth pilot tried to shoot the dart target off so that it went into the Mediterranean and everyone qualified. If it was not shot off the last two pilots had to escort the tow plane back to Wheelus where the target was dropped parallel with the runway and then 'scored'. The third pilot flew on the wing of the tow aircraft and Number 4 flew formation with the dart to see that it didn't drop too low and get dragged through the trees. Flying for-mation on the dart was interesting as a shot-up dart was not always aerodynamically stable.

At the time of transition to the F-100C, the 36th FDW had no 'special weapons' tasking. Its Zulu Alert air superiority role carried over from the F-86F days and in wartime it would have intercepted enemy intruders or strafed them on their air bases. Essentially, it had to provide air cover for TAC and SAC bombing attacks. Curtis Burns:

We spent almost 100 per cent of our time dur-ing the FDS days making intercepts, initiating 'bounces' and defending against other fighters bouncing us, except during gunnery qualifica-tion where we practised ground-strafing and other air-to-ground skills. I never fired an HVA(R) [high velocity aircraft rocket] or

2.75in rocket from an F-100. Even as a TFS, air-to-air scores entailed the most prestige.

In ACM practice against NATO F-86s, there were glimpses of the problems to be faced in the next decade by US pilots in Vietnam against the similar MiG-17.

The toughest adversaries who hassled regularly were the RCAF Sabre Mk 6s, simply because if they saw us they could turn inside us. We had to use surprise and keep our Mach up, but they were tough to get on gun camera film. If we slowed down and turned with them they could eat our lunch. French Mystères and Super Mys-tères were easy meat as were RCAF CF-100 Canucks. Other USAFE F-100Ds were usually easy mainly because they carried 450gal and didn't do as much air-to-air manoeuvring. I never encountered any RAF Hunters [also rated by some F-100C pilots for their tight turns]. Once I was flying at 35,000ft above overcast when an RAF Gloster Javelin popped out of the cloud-tops about a mile away and 10,000ft below; probably running a radar intercept on me. After a little burner and a 270-degree turn I made a supersonic, six o'clock guns pass on him.

RAF Hunter pilots reckoned they could turn inside the F-100 quite easily but they were severely limited by the early Hunter's fuel capacity, which could easily be expend-ed inside 25 minutes with high-speed flight at low altitude. Hun pilots would merely

A Dart target mounted on an F-100 for take-off. The notch in the Dart was to clear the aileron. An automatic tow reel handled
the armoured cable after release in the air. Both cable and Dart were dropped for recovery before landing. Col Art Johnson

Candy-striped F-100D-30-NA 55-3739 of the 366th TFW attracts an inquisitive crowd. The Wing flew Huns from England
AFB from late 1957 to early 1959. Still with the 366th TFW on 25 July 1966 after it reactivated at Phan Rang AB, this
Hun was lost on one of the 615th TFS's earliest Vietnam missions but its pilot, Capt G. J. Farrell, was rescued. David Menard Collection

Standard TAC décor on a 354th TFW F-100D-85-NH with landing gear and flaps down. On 13 January 1967, this fighter and its pilot, Capt Morvan Turley (352nd TFS) were lost during a napalm strike from Phan Rang AB. David Anderton Collection via David Menard

keep their distance with afterburner and wait for the Hunters to run out of fuel.

Alex Martin recalled this kind of training as:

... mainly WWII tactics; splits, yo-yos, 'up the rear' stuff. The RAF and Canadians were the best, though the RAF Lightnings seemed to have little fuel capacity. All you had to do was keep them at bay and then snap pictures as they went for home. The Germans were stodgy and hard to entice into a few turns.

There was much emphasis, in planning tactics, on the F-100C's supersonic performance, illustrated convincingly when the first arrival for Bitburg's 23rd FDS made a high-speed run across the base, smashing US$30,000 of windows and radar tubes. There was even discussion of using the supersonic boom as a weapon against sensitive enemy installations, and in peacetime pilots regularly flew supersonic over land. Curtis Burns:

In Western Europe in the 1950s there were no restrictions other than the common-sense guide 'Don't boom close to the ground since it breaks out many windows and the authorities start questioning the usual suspects'. There was an occasional briefing that such-and-such an area had a mink farm and the owner would appreciate it if we didn't overfly it at 50ft or, of course, 'boom' them intentionally. During my tour at Landstuhl in the late 1950s, as well as my post-Vietnam tour at Ramstein and Spangdhalem we heard almost daily at least one supersonic boom, or 'boom boom' as most fighters drag two shock waves over the ground.

In one demonstration of the F-100C's powers as an interceptor, two Bitburg aircraft were on the tails of four F-86Fs at 32,000ft (9,750m) only four minutes from wheels rolling. The F-86s took off fifteen minutes ahead of the Super Sabres. However, without afterburners, the F-100s' climb would have taken more like fourteen minutes. Each F-100 consequently used four times as much fuel as an F-86 for the flight.

Victor Alert

The change for F-100C/D units including the 36th Wing to 'TFW' status occurred in July 1958 at a time when nuclear deterrence was the basis of all military strategy towards the Soviet bloc. It added another nuclear-capable Wing to the arsenal and brought about a change of tactics for the pilots.

In fact, they had adopted a nuclear role slightly earlier. The Lebanon Crisis in mid-June 1958 took four squadrons of 354th TFW F-100Ds to Incirlik AB from 20 July to late October 1958 as part of a composite Air Strike Bravo force. It had also triggered a full SAC alert condition for USAFE Wings including the 36th, so preparations for the nuclear mission were well in hand. Curtis Burns:

Several months before the change-over we started ground training and bomb delivery training, with OTS and dive bombing at the postage-stamp sized range at Siegenburg, Bavaria. At the same time we started practising low-level navigation at about 50ft above the highest obstacle, flying at 360kt IAS. We made up strip-maps with a tick marked for every 6 miles (or each minute of flight). This made for easy navigation and adjustment of ground-track for an assigned time-over-target [TOT].

Missions were planned against simulated targets, often in the South of France and

Crouching tigers. A group of 457th FBS pilots at NAA's Columbus, Ohio plant to collect their first batch of F-100Ds in 1957. That year the parent 506th FBW transitioned from F-84Fs as a SAC unit to become a TAC Wing and the 457th was the first of its three squadrons to get Huns. Left to right: Capts Ronald X. Sollis, Robert Butler, unknown, Lts C. E. A. van Duren, Max Templin and Allen T. Lamb. USAF via Allen T. Lamb

usually 'on the deck'. Pilots often had a 'shepherd' pilot in another F-100, flying at higher altitude slightly ahead of them to warn them of buildings or other obstacles in the flight path or changes in terrain.

Curtis Burns:

We had no established routes for the 'Lo-Lo' missions. We would pick a typical tactical target, such as a railroad yard, airfield or bridge at about the same range as our targets 'in the East', plan a route avoiding all likely defended areas and fly it. After a while the squadron built up a number of planned routes, but we usually planned our own because that is what we had to do on NATO exercises and ORIs. I distinctly remember three practice routes. One of the first I planned was from Landstuhl pretty well straight to Bremen airport. Without contacting their tower or anyone else I came in over the middle of the airport at 500kt, pulled up into an Immelmann and quickly departed the area. In those days we could do almost anything we wanted in Western Europe.

One amusing aspect of these low-level training missions was that the TFWs based in Germany mostly plotted and flew Lo-Lo routes in France and the French-based Wings (before de Gaulle pulled out of NATO) mostly flew routes in Germany. The beneficial effect of this was that when a 'buzzing' report on, say a yellow-tailed airplane came into USAFE HQ from a location in France USAFE ops would send the report down to all the bases in France and if the alleged buzzing incident happened in Germany it was sent to the Wings there for investigation.

F-100D-85-NH 56-3439 during a 31st TFW visit to Incirlik AB for Exercise *Quick Span* in 1959. USAF via David Menard

Precise formation-keeping by the 35th FBS on 31 January 1957 soon after transition to the F-100D at Itazuke AB. Nose stripes were added later. USAF via David Menard

When the reports came back with a negative response it was assumed that the guilty pilot was French, Belgian, Dutch or RAF and the matter was dropped.

On another Lo-Lo mission my Squadron Commander gave me a bridge target in Southern France. I planned the route to avoid all features on the ground that were likely to be defended. We liked to use the old castles on the map as turning points, figuring they wouldn't be defended by anti-aircraft fire, so I made a turn over a castle somewhere near Avignon. I hit the 'target' exactly on time and thought I had flown

The full 493rd TFS yellow and white markings on F-100D-45-NH 55-2822. Some wear and tear is apparent, a reminder of the hard work that these elaborate schemes created for maintainers. The nose 'vee' was added in 1959. Wing-tips were painted in yellow/white/yellow stripes. M/Sgt Mike Bilcik

F-100D-55-NH 55-2934 in 81st TFS markings at Toul-Rosieres AB in 1959 after a 30-day TDY to Wheelus AB. Markings were yellow with black stars and include the squadron patch and a yellow 'wrench' on the nose to show the crew chief's name. Pilots' names appeared on the other side. David Menard

F-100C-20-NA 54-1922 of the 36th TFW (probably 22nd TFS) at Memmingen AB. This Hun went on to fight in Vietnam with the 136th TFS, New York ANG until it was shot down close to the Cambodian border during a napalm attack.
David Menard Collection

F-100D-70-NA 56-3025 in the red markings of the 417th TFS during a 1959 visit to Wheelus AB.
David Menard Collection

a model profile. When we got back my Commander chewed me out for thirty minutes because I had flown at 50ft directly over the Pope's summer palace. I was dumbfounded. Hell, I didn't know the Pope had a palace in France, let alone where it was. But the Commander did because he was a Catholic!

Huns on the Run

Another F-100 deployment had arrived at Landstuhl earlier in 1958. On March 22, the 457th FBS departed Tinker AFB, Oklahoma with twenty 'red tail' F-100Ds and headed for Langley AFB. Col Mike Kulczyk gave an idea of the logistics involved in these whole-squadron transfers to European bases:

The basic package was eighteen airplanes; seventeen F-100Ds and one F-100F with two spares. Saturday evening and Sunday were devoted to 'crew rest' and briefing. Everyone was so keyed up that damn little crew rest was generated. The gaggle launched at 0600 on Monday in flights of four, with a single flight of two. The first inflight-refuelling took place over Bermuda and the second at 500 miles east of Bermuda, both from KB-50J tankers. Since the F-100Ds were equipped with non-refuellable drop tanks these tanks could not be pressurized for fuel transfer until after the second refuelling. This caused some consternation for a couple of the guys when the external tanks didn't begin to feed initially when turned on, but all the tanks eventually did feed. All aircraft landed safely at Lajes Field in the Azores, 4^1/$_2$ hours after take-off.

Their transatlantic migration continued with a 2^1/$_2$ hour flight, without refuelling, to Nouasseur AB in Morocco and from there to West Germany. At Landstuhl they established four F-100Ds on Victor Alert in the south-west dispersal area with four aircraft from the 'host' 50th TFW from Toul-Rosieres in France. The 50th TFW had converted to the F-100D a year previously and flew F-100Ds until 1966. In September the 457th FBS personnel were replaced by others from the 458th FBS at Tinker AFB and the Super Sabres' squadron markings were changed from red to yellow for the rest of the TDY, which ended in March 1959 with the de-activation of the 506th FBW.

Among the F-100 units deployed for the Lebanon Crisis was the 474th TFW which, like the 354th TFW, made the long flight to Incirlik. The Cannon-

494th TFS red stripes extend from the nose, along the spine and across the tail of Super Sabre 56-3250. This 1958 scheme also included red/white/red wing-tips. M/Sgt Mike Bilcik

In typical German weather, a yellow-tail 53rd TFS F-100C-20-NA sits ready on Zulu Alert with the 36th TFW. via Mike Benolkin

based Wing rotated its four squadrons through the Turkish base on three-month TDYs, sitting alert with Mk 7 nuclear weapons. Alex Martin was among those at Incirlik:

We deployed as a squadron and set up the same quick-strike area as elsewhere with the same rules but just different targets to memorize. We were in place when President Kennedy was shot and went up to a higher DEFCON state.

At Incirlik there were still the 'boxes to fill' to keep up the training requirements, including air-to-air gunnery. On one of these Roy Moore discovered an unusual psychological phenomenon in simulated combat:

I was Flight Lead with Capt Lukers on my wing. Flying 'combat spread' formation he would be in a position to roll in on the dart target as I cleared from the first pass. Our aircraft were

USAFE F-100s made extensive use of the range facilities at Wheelus AB. This trio was photographed over north Africa in 1958. David Menard Collection

configured with 275gal external tanks and it was normal to use external fuel before attempting to fire on a dart. With a heavy aircraft it was extremely difficult to score a hit. I rolled in on the target and then time seemed to slow almost to a stop. I seemed to have minutes to bring the 'pipper' to bear on the target. I doubt if I fired more than twenty rounds before seeing flakes of aluminium flying from the dart. The actual time between rolling in and breaking away over the dart was probably not more than eight or ten seconds. I was so impressed with this illusion that I reported it to the USAF R&D Center.

Among the pleasures of TDY was the Clovis (Cannon AFB) Wing's liberal policy on weekend cross-country flights for 'R&R'. Crews at Incirlik could extend these as far as UK bases for 'training' purposes. Prior to its departure, the 354th TFW had been asked to display its skill on the ranges rather more publicly in a demonstration for President J. F. Kennedy in Florida. Alex Martin was one of the pilots selected for this:

Our wing had a hand-picked flight of four responsible for dive-delivery of 500lb GP [general purpose] bombs and strafing. It was wonderful; every target timed to the second with a narrative script. President Kennedy talked to us in the hangar afterwards. Every Washington dignitary, military and Congressional, filled the spectator stands. I remember rolling into final approach, arming my guns and bombs and thinking, 'Wow!'

Prestigious assignments like this could lead to some embarrassing situations too, as Roy Moore found when he became IP for the 16th AF Commander while he was with the 401st TFW at Torrejon AB in Spain. The General always liked to fly in the front seat of an F-100F while Roy, in the back, acted as navigator, radio operator and 'General's Aide':

On one flight we were returning to Torrejon at night after a long day of visits to other installations. The General was flying the F-100F through the letdown and was on final approach when he drifted far below the flight path. I let him know he was getting dangerously low and he acknowledged but continued to go low. As an IP I had always given a pilot every opportunity, short of crashing the aircraft, to correct his own mistakes, but as the scrub vegetation was almost touching the underside of the aircraft I told him I would take control. He replied sharply, 'I've got it!' To avoid landing short of the runway I physically overcame the General and took over the airplane, added power and made a safe landing. He was silent throughout the taxi, parking and shut-down and I was furious but there isn't any way for a young major to chastise a two-star general.

Later, Gen Le Bailley apologized and the two men became long-term friends.

Another crisis took Cannon F-100Ds to Chambley in France when construction of the Berlin Wall began in summer 1961 and re-supply aircraft in the Berlin Corridor

were harassed. Roy Moore was in the first aircraft to land:

For some reason the Number 1 and 2 in our flight didn't land at Chambley so our F-100F was the first plane to land. The airfield had not been used in years and weeds had grown up through the cracks in the runway. Our aircraft was knocking down tall weeds as we landed.

Alex Martin pointed out that during this tense period the rules of engagement were simple:

If anything pointed its nose at you or any of our aircraft they were fair game. What a letdown when Intelligence said that nothing had moved on any of the opposition's airfields since the arrival of the F-100s! Sidewinders were loaded on our birds at Chambley. I can still remember the distinctive hum they made when they were checked on the ground with a flashlight to see if their tracking [seeker heads] worked.

This standoff with the Soviets continued for three months until ANG F-84F units relieved the F-100Ds in October 1961.

Peacetime deployments of this kind were not without risk. The technology of inflight-refuelling was still fairly young and the distances involved were vast for single-seat fighters, as Tom Germscheid recalled:

One of our biggest challenges for refuelling in the early days was finding the tanker. With no search radar we relied on ADF [automatic direction finding]. We just transmitted a radio signal by holding down our UHF button. The tankers had an ADF receiver and it would give us a heading to fly and join them. There was no way of telling distances and often we would fly past each other without visual contact, especially if weather was involved. When that happened there was always a lot of floundering around, trying to manoeuvre your flight of four to find the tanker. Sometimes it would turn back towards the flight and again we'd pass with no visual contact. We always had a couple of thousand feet altitude separation. The pucker factor goes up exponentially when you're over the Atlantic and the gauge is nearing, or past minimum divert fuel and you still haven't seen the gas station! On the first deployment of F-100s to Turkey from Myrtle Beach in July 1958 only four birds out of a squadron of twenty-four arrived [at the right base] safely. Several aircraft and crews were lost.

When contact was made with a tanker there was still the physical challenge of

Yellow and black stripes distinguish this Bitburg 53rd TFS F-100C. David Menard Collection

taking JP-4 aboard from a KB-50 or KC-97. Alex Martin:

> That 2ft-funnel on a 50ft hose would play 'crack the whip' while you were flying at a slow, sloppy speed trying to stick your probe into it before you ran out of fuel. Then there was no guarantee that the fuel would transfer. They changed the 'basket' from a solid can to metal mesh in an attempt to stabilize it more. On my test flight I stuck the probe through the mesh

and couldn't get it out: the hose would stretch like a rubber band. After my fuel level started to drop and no one had a better idea I took a deep breath and pulled back on the power. The hose broke loose from the tanker and I flew back with it beating up the tail of my F-100.

Cracked canopies or windshields were also possible consequences of contact with a 'wild' basket.

Booms at Bitburg

As it changed from FDW (and Zulu Alert) to nuclear TFW (Victor Alert) status, the 36th TFW was reduced to three squadrons. The 22nd and 23rd TFS were at Bitburg and the 53rd TFS remained at Landstuhl, across the autobahn from Ramstein with which it was combined at that stage to become Ramstein/Landstuhl AB. Curtis Burns:

> That was quickly abbreviated to Ramstuhl AB, which we fighter pilots quickly referred to as 'Sheepsh*t AB'. I don't know whether higher authority got wind of that inglorious nickname but the base was soon re-named Ramstein. The Wing's fourth squadron, the 461st FDS, based at Hahn AB was disbanded with many of the pilots transferring to other squadrons within the 36th TFW.

The 461st FDS CO's F-100C was 54-2000 and the tradition of a Triple Zilch aircraft for the wing commander was continued by the 20th TFW with 56-3000.

A fifth squadron, the 32nd FDS/TFS flew its F-100Cs from Soesterberg AB, 200 miles away in Holland, from 15 August 1956 until it came under Dutch control in 1959. The squadron had arrived with the insignia red 'Arctic' markings used in transit from the USA, but green and white trim soon appeared on the noses and fins followed by red, white and blue stripes on the vertical stabilizers of its F-100Cs when the squadron was controlled by the 86th Wing. Early in 1960, Soesterberg began to

A USAF test pilot goes over F-100 spin recovery techniques with Lt Allen T. Lamb (right) of the 506th FBW. USAF via Allen T. Lamb

Legendary NAA test pilot Bob Hoover demonstrating how to fly an F-100C low,
slow and safely in October 1958. This 'max performance' demo was for the benefit
of pilots at the world's first all-supersonic USAF Tactical Fighter Weapons Meet. USAF
via Ron Thurlow

F-100F-10-NA 56-3826 in full 50th TFW markings on 26 March 1962. Perched on the
wing is Dave Menard, who had joined the 'Mach Busters' club in this aircraft the
previous day. David Menard Collection

transition to the F-102A Delta Dagger.

Although the squadrons were so dispersed and there was very little transfer of personnel between its far-flung bases, the 36th TFW still had its periodic 'wing dings'. At one of these the 53rd TFS share of glass and furniture breakages was US$195,

'which would have bought a hell of a lot of glass and furniture in West Germany in 1957' according to Curtis Burns. Each squadron was responsible for its own maintenance before the SAC-inspired, Wing-based maintenance procedures were introduced in 1960 – 'a bad system when applied

to fighter outfits', in Curtis' opinion.

Col Walter B. Putnam succeeded Col John Brooks as the Wing's commander. Curtis Burns remembered him as:

A legend and a hard-crusted commander who didn't take any sh*t from anybody. He was nicknamed 'Boom Boom' but not to his face. Many of the 53rd TFS pilots alleged that he got his nickname from his habit of always having an F-100C scheduled for him late afternoon on Fridays. He would drag a sonic boom over the 36th TFW HQ at Bitburg just as retreat was being played and the flag was being lowered at 1800 hrs.

At that time the loss rate in F-100s was still very high and test pilot Bob Hoover came over to USAFE to show all the pilots that the Hun was easy and safe to fly. Hoover did things with the F-100C that I didn't think possible, let alone safe. 'Boom Boom' was livid. He said that the Wing pilots had too many dangerous tricks already without learning some more from a company test pilot!

When the 36th TFW 'went nuclear', Col Putnam drew up a plan based on a 24-hour alert, with armed F-100Cs and pilots briefed for up to 100 targets behind the Iron Curtain. Frederick 'Boots' Blesse (later a USAF Major General) objected to the idea of single-seat aircraft with the ever-present possibility of engine failure or other mechanical deficiencies flying around with nuclear weapons aboard in all weathers. He displeased his 'Wing King' by sharing these thoughts with him. Despite this, he was eventually given command of the 32nd TFS and threw himself into the task of improving its unimpressive readiness rates. Blesse even resurrected the distinctive, Disney-based wolf's head insignia (from the squadron's WWII past) that the Soesterberg unit carried for the rest of its existence.

As members of a TFS, pilots had to focus increasingly on the grim business of LABS nuclear delivery. Curtis Burns elaborated on the way those Armageddon tactics were applied in the European scenario:

Whenever the assigned target was within the fuel/range capabilities of the F-100C with three drop tanks and the 1800lb weight of a Mk 7 we preferred to plan and fly a low-level profile to be under their radar coverage. We would fly at 360kt until we reached the IP and then push up the speed to 500kt at about 50ft altitude. Over the target impact point we would plug in the burner and start a 4g Immelmann. LABS gave a display, very much like an ILS display. If we kept the vertical and horizontal needles crossed in

This shot shows how the F-100D/F's modified airbrake cutaway fitted around an MN-1 store with the 'speedboard' extended. M/Sgt Ray Petrusch via David Menard

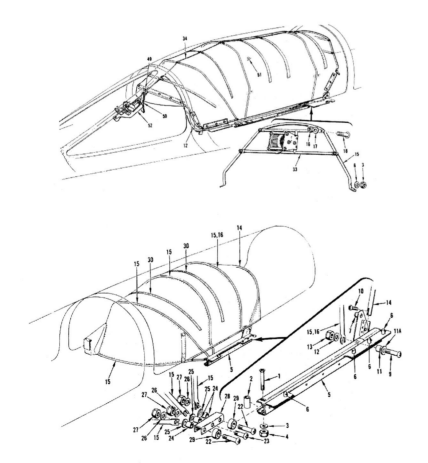

The nuclear radiation shield in the F-100F cockpit. USAF

the middle our flight trajectory was perfect (except for wind correction, for which we had to adjust our pull-up point).

LABS then released the weapon in the usual way, allowing it to rise to about 20,000ft (6,000m) before plummeting to its detonation as the F-100C sped away. Bombs were usually fused so that an internal radar fuse detonated them at about 1,500ft (450m), exploding with the bottom of the fireball just above ground level.

The required effects of the bomb were heat, blast and radiation, but not fall-out from picking up a lot of dirt that reduced the other three effects. We could also set the bomb fusing in the F-100C's cockpit for a ground detonation, which most of us expected would be used if we got shot down at altitude over enemy territory. Our procedure was to arm the bomb after crossing into Communist territory. I was targeted on a couple of targets that were too distant to be reached at low altitude and I had to plan a cruise-climb flight to the target, dropping fuel tanks as they emptied. In that case I would have had to deliver the weapon by dive-bombing, with the bomb still fused to explode at the designated height above ground.

LABS training in the USA took many pilots to the Gila Bend gunnery range for a fairly uncomfortable ride. Ron Herrick: 'Doing 500kt at 200ft over the desert in summer gave quite a bumpy ride. One learned to tighten the shoulder straps real good!' Nuclear 15-minute alert required pilots to become surprisingly close to the fearful weapons they carried, even to the extent of inserting the Uranium 235 cores into their own Mk 7s.

The nuclear weapons maintenance specialist in the bomb dump didn't have enough time to load up all the weapons so our squadron maintenance people loaded them on the aircraft and we pilots were responsible for getting the U235 core, which was kept in a 'birdcage' for safety. We installed it into the bomb before we went and took it back to the locked storage room in Squadron Ops after we went off status. Our F-100Cs had no capability to deliver the weapons, or fly the routes, at night so we were not on Victor Alert the whole 24-hour period. The core, a nuclear sphere about the size of a shot put but a lot heavier, was constantly decaying and producing neutrons, but not enough to approach criticality. But if you took two of the spheres and banged them together you would get a blue flash and you would be

Thunderbirds

The Thunderbirds, seen here with F-100Ds, flew Super Sabres from 1956 to 1969 with a brief period on the F-105B in 1964. USAF

To North American Indians the Thunderbird was a gigantic, legendary eagle-like bird that could confer success in battle and a happy life to those it favoured. Lightning streamed from its eyes and huge thunderstorms filled the sky when the creature fought with its enemies.

The USAF flight demonstration team that has borrowed the Thunderbird's name-and image for half a century formed on F-84G Thunderjets in May 1953, progressing to swept-wing F-84Fs in 1955 and then F-100C Super Sabres after the final Thunderstreak show on 19 May 1956. As the world's first supersonic aerobatic team, the 3600th Air Demonstration Flight was a guaranteed showstopper. A move from Luke AFB to Nellis Air Training Command (ATC) base accompanied the change of aircraft and nomenclature to the 3595th Air Demonstration Flight (changed once again to 4520th Air Demonstration Flight when TAC took over Nellis). Sev-

eral of the earlier pilots stayed on, including the leader, Maj Jack Broughton, Capt Ed 'Lucky' Palmgren and Bill Ellis.

Changes were also made to the aircraft and to the show routines. The F-100Cs each lost their autopilot, gun sight, gun camera and radar. The aircraft flying in the 'slot' position had a stainless steel leading edge to its vertical stabilizer and the VHF antenna moved from the fin to a position under the nose. UHF radio was fitted and the rear fuselage tank could carry either 'ferry' fuel or smoke oil for air shows. Gun ports were faired over and the nose radome area was replaced by sheet metal.

As for the show, the opening move became a maximum power take-off together with a solo pass during which Capt Paul Ross cut his engine in and out of afterburner to provide a loud series of pyrotechnics. With the

show organizers' permission he would also do a supersonic pass, until this was banned by the FAA. Liberal use of afterburner in diamond formation passes was a big success with audiences, as was the 5g, 360-degree turn and the vertical bomb-burst.

Maj Robby Robinson replaced Maj Broughton for the 1957 season and the team added Canada, Puerto Rico and Bermuda to the twelve countries already visited, a total that would rise to forty-five by 1966. The F-100Cs gained their distinctive Thunderbird design on the underside of the aircraft the following year and the Outstanding Unit Award decal to add on the aircrafts' noses. Their initial batch of F-100Cs were completed and decorated in record time for the 1956 season. F-100C 55-2724 was first to arrive, followed by 55-2723 (Broughton's *Thunderbird One* lead aircraft) 55-2725, -2727, -2728, -2729. The team also used 53-1718, -1740; 54-1860, -1882, -1969; 55-2717, -2730, -2732, -2733.

For the team's 1959 tour of PACAF bases the 18th TFW hastily repainted six of their F-100D-15-NAs (54-2281, -2285, -2287, -2292, -2295, -2299) for the team's use and modified them as far as was practicable. Maj Bob Fitzgerald led the team in displays at bases in Japan, the Philippines, Taiwan, Korea and Hawaii.

The team also acquired an F-100F to replace its trusty T-33A and it continued to devise innovative stunts such as the 'dual solo' in which two aircraft took off and rolled in opposite directions as soon as their wheels were in the wells. This was followed by an opposition pass in afterburner.

1963 was the last season on F-100Cs but it was marked by the first Thunderbirds visit to Europe, during which displays, led by Maj Ed Palmgren, were given in nine countries. In 1964 the team switched to extensively modified F-105Bs, each around 10,000lb (4,550kg) heavier than the F-100C but offset partly by a better power-to-weight ratio. Six shows into the season, a major accident grounded the team and prompted an immediate return to Super Sabres. A batch of F-100Ds was suitably adapted and painted up by May 1964. The aircraft had the *High Wire* updates including cranked refuelling booms. In all, thirteen aircraft were used from 1964–68 (55-3506, -3507, -3520, -3560, -3561, -3582, -3606, -3708, -3737, -3754, -3776,-3779, -3791) though serials were not displayed after 1965. The practice of polishing alternate afterburner 'eyelids' was also standardized but cannon ports remained open. Lt Col Ralph Maglione led the 1965 team on a Caribbean tour, followed by a second USAFE base tour when twenty-two demonstrations were given in twenty-seven days. A sixteen-day deployment to Latin America completed a total of twenty-three countries visited and 121 shows flown in 1965. The team's 1,000th demonstration took place in Michigan that summer. Maj Neil Eddins, slot pilot in 1959, returned to lead the Thunderbirds in 1967. Operation *Big Wing II* involved another European tour, ending in Paris. From there the team flew 7,000 miles (11,300km) with seven inflight-refuellings to appear at the USAF Academy, Colorado Springs.

The year was marked by a spectacular escape by Tony McPeak when his aircraft (55-3520) suffered a structural failure during the team's show at Laughlin AFB, Texas

on 21 October. During a solo pass with rapid aileron rolls, the main wing box failed and the wings folded upwards. Fuel from the punctured forward fuselage tank deluged through the engine and it exploded, blowing off the nose of the aircraft ahead of the cockpit. With fire entering the cockpit, McPeak made a hasty decision to eject, losing his helmet and getting dragged by his parachute in a 30kt crosswind when he landed close to the crowd. He survived to fly again with the team but the aircraft all needed reinforcement to their wings around bolt-holes near the main landing gear mounts where the fatigue cracks had occurred. Fatigue failure was also responsible for losses in Vietnam at that time and a major programme of wing-box strengthening was begun soon afterwards.

The Thunderbirds flew their last F-100 show, the 471st on the F-100D, at Nellis AFB on 30 November 1968. In 1969 they received eight F-4E Phantoms and after initial training on the F-100Ds they switched to 'regular' camouflaged F-4Es before opening the 1969 season in white Phantoms at the USAF Academy.

One of three F-100Fs used by the Thunderbirds between 1960–68. It has the same rear fuselage pipes for formation smoke as the single-seaters. Author's collection

F-100C 55-2728, one of the original six F-100C-10-NHs used by the Thunderbirds and flown by Maj Ed 'Lucky' Palmgren, the leader in 1963. Gun ports were faired over and the intake painted red for the first 12in of its interior surface. The Thunderbirds image was applied to the undersides of the aircraft towards the end of 1958. USAF

A similar view of the Skyblazers scheme for comparison. F-100C 54-2009 was flown by the team leader, Capt (later, General) Bill Creech in 1959. David Menard Collection

dead in six weeks. The birdcage, made of aluminium tubes with a cradle [cylinder] in the centre to hold the sphere, would physically separate two adjacent spheres of U235 or plutonium by about 2ft, enough to create a safe separation. I always thought it was really nuts for us to handle nuclear spheres because in my previous experience at the Fighter Pilots' Nuclear School at Nellis AFB in 1955 they treated 'nukes' like the Holy Grail. In the 36th Wing at that time it was no big deal though.

Ron Herrick was adamant that different procedures applied in PACAF and TAC squadrons where no pilots would normally have handled the nuclear cores.

French Foils and English Épées

By the summer of 1957, the USAFE build-up of F-100s had almost reached the planned eighteen-squadron level as F-84 and F-86 units transitioned to the new fighter.

In the UK, the 20th FBW at Wethersfield and Woodbridge relinquished its F-84F Thunderstreaks in 1957. The Wing Commander, Col Raymond F. Toliver, called a special 'Sabre Day' to acquaint the local population with the new, noisy F-100D. The 79th TFS at Woodbridge was the first to convert and the base received

an F-100 simulator and a nylon barrier-arresting system. France continued to host several USAF Wings including the 48th FBW Statue of Liberty Wing at Chaumont and the 49th FBW (formerly 388th FBW) at Etain-Rouvres, both of which progressed to the F-100D in 1956–57. At Toul-Rosieres, the 50th TFW traded its F-86Hs for F-100Ds in 1957. This was a time of unusually eye-catching squadron colour schemes as F-100 units adopted markings increasingly reminiscent of medieval knights in armour. At Chaumont, Col Stanton R. Smith led the 48th FBG for over two years in his multi-coloured F-100D 'Wing Ship' 56-3262.

A classic shot of a 20th TFW Hun in post-1961 markings. This aircraft ended its service with the 122nd TFS of the ANG and was then converted into a QF-100D, meeting its end on 12 November 1987 after a hit from an AIM-9M during its second NOLO flight. via Tom Germscheid

The first twelve years of Col Smith's career are a reminder of how rapidly the USAF had moved from the piston era to supersonics. After graduating from West Point he became a flying instructor in 1941, flew P-40s in northern Burma in 1943, P-47s and P-51s up to 1947 and then the P-80 Shooting Star. After a tour with SAC he commanded the 49th FG in Japan, became Director of Operations at FEAF HQ in Tokyo during the Korean War and finally landed the 'Wing King' job at Chaumont on supersonic F-100s via the Imperial Defence College in London.

From mid-1956, the 48th Wing converted to the F-100D at Chaumont with the airfield at Brienne-le Chateau as a *terrain de dispersion* for its 492nd FBS. It had been named *Statue of Liberty Wing* in July 1954 by the residents of Chaumont in recognition of the many Americans who had given their lives in the liberation of France. The distinction of bearing both a number and a name remains unique to the 48th Wing.

As the first USAFE F-100D Wing, the 48th was responsible for evolving strike tactics and procedures for the aircraft in the European theatre. From March 1957 it began training on inflight-refuelling with the KB-50J tankers of the 420th Air Refuelling Squadron (ARS) at RAF Sculthorpe, UK. By September of that year, the technique had become sufficiently familiar to enable a group of eighteen 493rd FBS machines to refuel from KB-50s en route to a Weapons Detachment at Wheelus AB. They replaced the 492nd FBS at Wheelus, where it had completed its qualifications in gunnery and weapons delivery on the ranges.

It was the Wing's role as USAFE representatives at the 1958 William Tell Meet that triggered a blaze of candy-stripe colours on its Super Sabres. The 494th FBS reworked its modest red panels on the vertical stabilizers into unmissable red and white stripes extending to the noses and wingtips of the William Tell jets. On return to Chaumont, Col Smith elected to extend the scheme to the other squadrons in the Wing, using their own colours, during the last few months in France. The revised colours appeared on the *High Wire* F-100Ds that replaced some of the older Super Sabres at Chaumont, although all the Wing's aircraft went through IRAN at Getafe, Spain and some were transferred to the Armee de l'Air in 1958. Among them was 54-2165, which became '11-ML' with Escadron 2/11 and was eventually put on static display at the American Air Museum, Duxford. Michael Bilcik worked on the F-100s at Chaumont in 1959.

It was what I would call a bare necessities base, even by the standards of the day. There were only three smallish hangars for the entire Wing so hangar space was always at a premium. There was no alert area and some portions of the flight line were still covered with [WWII] PSP [pierced steel planking], though we didn't park aircraft on this. The barracks were 'open bay' with approximately fifteen persons to a bay. You definitely had to get along with one another in a situation like that. There wasn't much housing for married personnel and not many 'lower ranks' were allowed to bring families over. There wasn't a lot of interaction with the local community because of the language barrier. The

By 17 September 1960 the 48th TFW had moved to RAF Lakenheath and adopted new markings, as seen on this 492nd TFS F-100D-90-NA. Author's Collection

Trailing sparks and smoke, he ran into his wingman who had landed first and slowed down. Fortunately, the wingman was able to stop his damaged Super Sabre and clamber out but the lead aircraft rolled on further with flames gradually spreading over it. Lt Col Lyell, flying an HH-43 rescue helicopter, used his rotors to fan the flames away from the left side of the F-100D so that its pilot could escape unscathed.

The 401st TFW had reactivated as a TAC Wing on F-86s at England AFB, transitioning to the F-100D in 1957 and deploying to Homestead AFB, Florida during the 1962 Cuban Missile Crisis. One of its squadrons, the 613rd TFS, transferred to Torrejon in spring 1966 taking the Wing's title to the Spanish base. The Wing then picked up the 307th and 353rd TFS with F-100Ds (under 16th AF control) until it transitioned to the F-4 Phantom in 1970.

Red Richard

The F-100D's assumption of a nuclear role soon proved intolerable to General Charles de Gaulle. Six months after he was elected leader of France it became clear that he wanted the removal of all American nuclear-capable aircraft from his country (partly as the first stage in establishing France's own nuclear deterrent force). In practice, the French-based F-100 squadrons would have flown to forward bases in West Germany in an emergency. There, if those bases still had runways, the jets would have been loaded with 'nukes' and launched against their targets. A request by USAFE to establish Victor Alert pads in France was met by a demand from de Gaulle that he should give permission for aircraft to be launched from them.

The consequent decision to relocate the USAFE aircraft entailed the relocation of the three F-100D Wings and affected a total of 225 aircraft and 5,300 personnel from 10 July 1959. Chaumont's re-deployment began five days later when the 48th TFW began its transfer to the former SAC base at Lakenheath, UK. The nearby base at Mildenhall was also considered as a new F-100 location. The 'Liberty Wing' was fully operational at Lakenheath by 15 January 1960, its first aircraft having arrived on 5 January after the construction of alert shelters. Mike Bilcik was among the last to leave Chaumont, which reverted to stand-by status.

base was about 8 miles from Chaumont and few single airmen could afford cars. At weekends many of the guys went to Paris.

On another French base, the 49th TFW entered the fashion stakes with a colour scheme based on a lightning bolt. It was activated at Etain-Rouvres AB on 10 December 1957, absorbing the F-100Ds and markings of the 388th FBW – an F-86 unit (1954–56) that returned to the USA and later flew F-100Cs, then F-105 Thunderchiefs.

At Toul-Rosieres, the three squadrons of the 50th TFW flew F-100Ds for about two years, having moved in from Hahn, West Germany in July 1956 with F-86Hs. In the following year it converted to F-100Ds. Training routines were similar to those established by the Chaumont Wing with periodic visits by whole squadrons to Wheelus for armament practice camps.

It was there that the 388th FBW experienced an unusual air-sea rescue of one of its pilots. 1st Lt Herdis S. Clements took off from Wheelus in F-100D 55-3660 bound for Etain, but engine failure forced him to eject over the sea shortly afterwards. A Malta-based RAF Shackleton crew located him and dropped an inflatable raft. One of the SA-16B Albatross amphibians operated by the 58th ARS at Wheelus landed beside Clements, whose raft had by then been tossed for four hours in an 8ft swell. This heavy sea defeated

three take-off attempts by the SA-16B and the last was aborted when a metal cylinder from the life raft damaged one of the amphibian's elevators. In time-honoured fashion, the SA-16B set course for a sea voyage to the nearest base at Bizerte in Tunisia. After half an hour of seasickness and buffeting, the salt-encrusted aircraft was met by HMS *Birmingham* and Clements was taken aboard together with the 388th FBW Flight Surgeon. The Albatross crew ploughed on for another five hours through the waves, until their aircraft was taken in tow by a French destroyer, arriving at Bizerte early the next day.

SA-16s were on the scene again in March of the following year when another engine failure claimed the 49th TFW's F-100D 54-2250 as it headed back to Wheelus AB from the El Uotia bombing range. This time the pilot was rescued without incident, although a similar attempt in August 1960 was frustrated when F-100F 56-3877 from the 49th TFW crashed offshore. As the Albatross crew moved in for a pick-up, the on-shore breeze carried the parachutes of both F-100 crew members back over the beach and they landed safely ashore.

Wheelus was also the scene of a lucky escape involving two visiting F-100Ds of the 401st TFW at Torrejon. On 29 October 1968, a pair of its F-100Ds arrived back from a mission. The flight leader's brakes failed as he powered down the runway.

F-100D 55-3683 flown by Lt Tic Loitwood in December 1962. Tom Germscheid

assigned to the newest A/3C on the team was to swab out the engine intake with a rag soaked in JP-4 after the engine was removed for maintenance. Nobody wanted to ride next to him on the bus that evening!

The F-100 was a fairly easy aircraft to work on and it gave good service. A good crew could perform an unscheduled engine change and have the aircraft ready for flight in a few hours. The engine and fuselage had quick disconnect points for most of the fluid lines, saving time and effort. The engine was leak-checked and the trim run was completed before the aft fuselage was re-installed. I loved doing those checks from the cockpit, especially lighting the afterburner. This would give you real kick in the pants even with the aircraft tied down at the main gear mounts with cables or chained to the test pad.

John Clarity shared that pleasant recollection:

The infrastructure at Lakenheath was well-suited to our needs and everything, such as maintenance docks and shop equipment from Chaumont was moved there. There were some slight adaptations required but nothing major. When I flew from Chaumont to Lakenheath I rode in a C-124 aircraft that was also carrying a maximum load of 20mm ammunition. It was so heavily loaded that it was unable to climb above 7,000ft for the entire journey. Good thing there aren't any mountains between France and the UK!

The other French-based Wings also had to find new homes. The 49th TFW removed to Spangdahlem in West Germany, displacing the 10th TRW's RB-66s to no less than three UK bases: Alconbury, Bruntingthorpe and Chelveston. At Toul Rosieres, the 50th TFW packed up and returned to Hahn in the German Eifel area. Toul Rosieres was used briefly by F-84 units during the Berlin Crisis and by the 'non-nuclear' RF-4Cs of the 26th TRW for a few months in 1966 before General de Gaulle decided to oust the remaining USAF units from his country under Operation *Freloc*.

Sword Sharpeners

At Spangdahlem the 49th TFW settled down to two more years on F-100s before preparing for the arrival of the mighty F-105 Thunderchief early in 1962. Its distinctive squadron colours were changed soon after the move when, in 1960, the USAF introduced the centralized maintenance

concept, replacing squadron-based arrangements. From then on all aircraft carried the red, yellow and blue colours of the three based squadrons, the 7th, 8th and 9th TFS.

For those who, like Troy Clarke, kept their aircraft flying, the daily routine went on much as it had in France. Trained on F-100s at Amarillo, Clarke specialized in inspection of aircraft under the Periodic Maintenance plan.

I loved working on the F-100D and in Periodic we performed all the required maintenance and checks plus working out inspection write-ups uncovered during maintenance. The first job

There was such a sense of power. The F-100 would pull against those chains and ride up on its wheel chocks. At night the flame from the afterburner would reach out into the darkness and project a fiery tail coloured blue, yellow and orange for about 20–30ft.

Crew chief Bobby Wright added, 'When we went into afterburner it got a little scary because the nose would dip way down with the power thrust and you just hoped like hell the cable wouldn't break!'

At Lakenheath, John Clarity was crew chief on 48th TFW F-100D 55-2834. Fresh from postings in Florida and Texas, he found the English climate a real deterrent.

Start-up time for F-100D 56-3300 from the final production block. Its markings comprise the red nose and tail bands of the 9th TFS, 49th TFW as seen at Toul-Rosiere AB in summer, 1959. David Menard

Lt Tic Loitwood's jet, 55-3683, seen through the rather restrictive windshield of Col Tom Germscheid's aircraft. Tom Germscheid

Most days were overcast, damp and chilly. Obviously these were excellent days to go to a pub and sit by a fire. But if you had to repair something outside or in a hangar, such as a tyre or an engine change at the end of the day it could be miserable. Imagine starting a tyre change with darkness setting in at 3.30pm. when you have already been outside most of the day. Your uniform is probably damp and uncomfortable. When I arrived at Lakenheath the barracks were the same ones used in WWII. The heat was piped from an outside source several blocks away and hot water for showering was limited. For the first month after I arrived in November I would go to bed wearing my entire Air Force issue of clothing including a 'horse-blanket' dress coat and still I shivered myself to sleep!

The aircraft didn't seem to notice the dampness and cold as much as the personnel. When work was needed it seemed to get done quicker than in the southern USA. De-icing the aircraft was sometimes necessary and at times fog cancelled flying so we would find ourselves in the Rod and Gun Club just off the flight line. For me, inspecting and repairing the carbon-darkened inside of the aircraft's tail section was the

The Boss Bird F-100D, 55-3668, in highly polished metal finish, carried a full set of 20th TFW insignia in 1958, as did the oft-illustrated 56-3000 Triple Zilch for an earlier wing commander. David Menard Collection

the cloudless skies around Cannon AFB previously and his eagerly awaited posting to USAFE in April 1961 was at first blessed with pleasant weather.

Flowers were blooming everywhere. I thought I was in paradise and it didn't even rain for my first few days in the UK. I soon discovered that sunny days were not the norm for Essex. Because of the foul weather and low ceilings the 20th TFW had established a special in-theatre training programme to hone the instrument flying skills of newly assigned pilots. Those of us from sunny places like New Mexico really needed this and soon found that it would probably save our lives many times over. Training was conducted in an F-100F, usually in actual weather conditions and culminated in a full-blown annual instrument check.

Ice on the runways was another occupational hazard, and Wethersfield came up with its own attempted solution.

A jet engine was mounted on some type of trailer with its exhaust canted downwards. It was then fired up and towed slowly down the icy runway in an attempt to melt the ice. I think the final result was a runway with ice smooth enough for Olympic skating! One time Lt 'Tick' Loitwood and I launched on a cross-country flight the day after Christmas. We got to Spangdahlem and it started to snow. We were weathered in for several days but finally got airborne to Bitburg, about 25 miles away, where we enjoyed German New Year celebrations. The weather in England was also bad and the runways were coated with ice. It was about ten days before we were able to get back to Wethersfield.

In 1960 there was a little light relief from the climate, at least for the groundcrews. F-100s were usually started on home base with the MA-2 ('Ma Deuce') turbine in a separate piece of ground equipment, using an air hose, rather than the cartridge-start system. The hose was plugged into a receptacle under the fuselage behind the main gear wells. One of the routine jobs for groundcrew was cleaning out insects and other airborne debris from the air intake with a JP-4 impregnated rag held by a maintainer who had to slither deep into the maw leading to the engine. This experience was made more exciting by the prospect of ram-air bleed doors suddenly opening up inside the intake. But there was worse in store for the uninitiated, as John Clarity described:

A 36th TFW F-100F-10-NA on the taxi strip at Husum AB on 12 June 1960. Kropf/Luftwaffe via David Menard

Jim Wilson's 77th TFS F-100D closing in from the darkness in June 1961. Tom Germscheid

worst job. My hands were covered in carbon and working in a dark hangar added to a medical syndrome known as 'seasonal disorder caused by light deprivation leading to depression'. No wonder I found the pubs such a welcome sight!

John would have been delighted to see the 48th FW's spotless Phase Dock hangars

forty years later, with their white-painted floors and well-lit areas for working on F-15 Eagles.

English weather also tended to dominate the lives of 20th TFW pilots at Wethersfield and Woodbridge, where they began to fly F-100s in the summer of 1956. Tom Germscheid had been flying the aircraft in

A 79th TFS *Tiger* squadron F-100D leaves for a training sortie with an under-wing practice bomb dispenser. USAF via Tom Germscheid

Practical jokes on 'newby' maintainers included sending the guy down the intakes and then starting the MA-2 turbine that was already hooked to the plane, giving the illusion of an imminent engine start. The new guy would usually travel backwards out of that 25ft intake at rocket speed.

TDYs sometimes got us out of the cold. We spent a month at Wheelus AFB and four weeks in Turkey. I loved working on aircraft in those places, but we also went to northern Germany and Aviano in the foothills of the Alps in winter.

Other duties could take aircrew off-base for long periods. Tom Germscheid and Lt Bob Edney were sent to Getafe, near Madrid, to collect a couple of F-100Ds and ferry them to the USA. After a week waiting for the aircraft to leave the IRAN process at Getafe, the two pilots were delayed while the weather over the Atlantic settled down. Finally, they managed to join a flight of 48th TFW F-100Ds and successfully deliver the aircraft to Langley AFB. The entire process took almost six weeks.

Among the first pilots with Maj 'Skinny' Innis' 492nd FBS *Mad Hatters* to transfer to Lakenheath was Chuck Horner, later to become the architect of the US air effort in *Desert Storm*. His career was almost ended on his final flight from the base in 1963 after a three-year tour. During a simulated night attack on a French air base his F-100D dumped the fluid from its primary and utility hydraulic systems. He

had sufficient flight control power to return to Lakenheath, only to find the base virtually closed by thick fog and no ground controlled interception (GCI) available. With warning lights glowing in the cockpit and fuel almost gone, Horner managed to find the runway and pulled off a safe landing in fog so dense that the attendant fire truck almost ran into his aircraft.

Lakenheath's primary mission was still nuclear alert, with a Mk 7 on the left pylon until 1966 when the centreline pylon was used with consequent alleviation of the asymmetric flight trim. This pylon was virtually a permanent fixture on F-100Ds (apart from Block 1–15, 35 and 40 aircraft) for a nuclear weapon or practice bomb dispenser.

By 1966 many F-100 units from US bases had deployed to South East Asian bases leaving USAFE Wings without the usual relief on Victor Alert from TDY units from the States. In addition, the 48th TFW was responsible for rotating squadrons to Italy and Turkey for nuclear alert. Range practice in Turkey from Ismir and Incirlik was held on the Konya ranges. While on alert at these bases half of each squadron would go to Wheelus for gunnery camp, swapping places midway through the one-month tour with the half that was standing nuclear alert. For groundcrews, alert often meant:

Long days, usually in rain or snow, lunch from a box on the flight-line and reminders of the real

purpose of our 'club', i.e. nuclear gloom and doom – no one wins. At Lakenheath I usually 'crewed' my own aircraft. Each aircraft had the name of the crew chief on the side and generally the plane and I stayed together including TDYs. I occasionally went TDY with another aircraft if I switched with another crew chief who preferred staying at home in Lakenheath.

Very occasionally, there were back-seat rides in an F-100F. John managed to wangle a flight to Aviano, Italy after 'a long campaign of public relations and nagging'.

The flight was exactly what I expected and the exhilaration began with the engine start and terminated with shut down. I found the flight insightful; all the systems we routinely checked in a robotic fashion suddenly came into service as the airplane sprang to life. Its spirit was impressive; the g-forces, the speed, the vision of the ground below you one minute and above your head the next minute – it was more than my MGB sports car could ever provide for me. My closest experience would be the sheer freedom and joy of movement you get when skiing the steep, deep, light powdery snow high in the Rocky Mountains.

Away on the Range

Don Schmenk flew with the 494th TFS from 1966 and took part in many TDYs from Lakenheath.

We were required to maintain currency in several weapons deliveries every six months, including strafing, low-level skip bombing, dive bombing and rocket firing. Laydown, LADD and OTS nuclear deliveries were also trained. At Wheelus we always carried the SUU-21 dispenser on the centreline pylon containing two BDU-33 and four Mk 106 (simulated high-drag) practice bombs with smoke marking charges.

A typical range sortie would start with a simulated nuclear 'laydown' pass flown at 500kt and 500ft agl with a Mk 106. Next would be a LADD (timer-released nuclear weapon) also using a Mk 106. The last 'nuclear' pass would be an OTS, releasing a BDU-33. This delivery used a 500kt run-in at 500ft minimum altitude pulling up into a 4g Immelmann. Skip bombing was done with Mk 106s at a 15-degree dive angle (the same angle as for strafing) at around 350kt. A 'foul' was called if you descended below 1,500ft. We dive-bombed at a 30-degree angle with bomb release at about 3,500ft. Rocket launching used the same parameters. It wasn't possible to perform all these

F-100D 55-3652 heads a 20th TFW line-up for an early morning range mission from Wheelus AB, June 1961. Tom Germscheid

tasks within one sortie. The sequencing for the SUU-21 was critical. To qualify in the dive-bombing event you had to drop two qualifying bombs. This meant you couldn't do an OTS delivery in that sortie if you needed to dive-bomb for qualification purposes.

UK-based F-100s used range facilities at Holbeach, Wainfleet and Jurby (off the Isle of Man). Training of this kind was not without risks either. On sea ranges like Jurby, pilots ran the risk of bird-strikes, disorientation through poor visibility, unclear horizons or 'target fixation'. Two Lakenheath F-100Ds (55-2844 on 24 July 1969 and 56-3217 on 30 January 1970) crashed into the sea off Jurby, one accident costing the life of one of Don's squadron mates. Eleven of the Wing's aircraft were lost between 1968 and 1971.

The 20th TFW tended to use the Holbeach range in The Wash or Jurby, shared with the RAF. Tom Germsheid took a turn as Range Officer at both locations.

> The targets at Holbeach were a series of towers sitting on pylons. At low tide the pylons were visible and at high tide just the tops of the towers. Missions to the Jurby range often included a low-level route in Scotland where we could go down to 50ft altitude. The wingman would remain higher, looking out for obstacles and other airborne traffic. Birds were always a hazard and we had a few strikes.

One of them may well have cost the life of Capt P. L. Barwick whose F-100D suddenly entered a dive at low altitude over the Jurby range on 30 July 1970, leaving him no time to eject.

Nuclear strike involved extended low-level route flying just as it did for West Germany-based F-100s. Don Schmenk:

> Low level flights were a blast. We flew all over Europe at 500ft agl and 360kt. We trained to fly low-level and deliver a nuclear weapon on the ground within two minutes of a designated time.

If the Cold War had turned 'hot' each F-100 pilot would have flown solo to his allocated target using pure time and distance navigation.

> We carried target folders with tic-marks and lines drawn on them. We had no fancy navigation equipment like today's folks. The biggest threat would have been running into another of your own aircraft. Any air opposition would have been dealt with on an individual basis. If the whistle had blown there would have been so many airplanes headed east that we could have followed each other. I am sure that targets were multi-tasked [more than one strike for each]. There was one contingency plan that I heard about where just one aircraft would have been launched with a 'nuke' to 'get their attention', so to speak! I would not have wanted to be that guy!

Tom Germsheid was impressed by the

sense of 'freedom of the air' over Europe:

> In the late 1950s flying over Europe was largely unrestricted. You could fly almost any place at any altitude or airspeed. Grab a map, draw up a route and go. Air traffic controllers on the Continent often spoke little or no English so there was little communication with them, especially over France. We used a range in France and a typical mission involved departing Wethersfield in a two- or four-ship formation with a climb to about 25,000ft, homing in on the BBC beacon (which could be picked up from almost anywhere in the European area), starting a descent over the Channel and using dead reckoning to level out at 500ft at a point over France. Entering French airspace we would try to contact French air traffic control but usually got no reply or something in French. We would give a position call and press on. If the winds were different than predicted it was often a scramble to find out exactly where you were when you broke out under the usual overcast. We had to meet an assigned TOT (within +/- two minutes) for our first bomb impact so we couldn't waste too much time fumbling around to get orientated. We then approached the IP at 500ft, adjusting airspeed to make the TOT. The first delivery was always a LABS (over the shoulder) and if the ceiling was high enough we would then execute other types of nuclear or conventional delivery.

At 'bingo' fuel, the flight would join up and head for home, using the BBC London 'homing signal' once again.

> No one really considered that the BBC would probably have been off the air in a real war. We usually made an ADF approach to Wethersfield with a radar vector to GCA [ground controlled approach]. We had a couple of old British GCA controllers at Wethersfield who were excellent. They had been in the business since radar was invented! It was always comforting to hear that accent when letting down through the soup, knowing that the ceiling was right at minimum (around 200ft) as they could talk you down to cement in zero-zero conditions with the greatest of ease.

Wethersfield pilots also used the Radio Caroline offshore pirate radio ship as a useful navigation 'beacon'. According to Tom Germscheid, the pilots found it 'great sport to tune our ADF to this station and home in on it for a low pass over the ship. A few times our activities got broadcast over the air'. During the Cuban Missile Crisis of October 1962 a 'covert alert' status was

An AGM-12B Bullpup missile departs from its launch adaptor on an F-100D-25-NA. The encouraging results achieved in test firings such as this one were seldom replicated in combat. David Menard Collection

initiated at Lakenheath and Wethersfield. Crews were called in to duty by telephone and a number of tactical nuclear force (TNF) F-100s were armed and scheduled to co-ordinate with RAF Thor missiles. F-100Ds would have led the attack with nuclear bombs and then Thors would have hit the same targets. Key targets such as East Berlin were targeted with two Thors and an F-100 strike. At the height of the emergency, DEFCON 2 was reached and F-100 pilots were in their cockpits with MA-2s plugged in ready to roll.

During Victor Alert at Wethersfield, each squadron kept four aircraft on alert. Tom Germscheid:

The alert pad was on the north side of the runway, away from the rest of the base. Each bird was in a 'soft' metal shelter that was open at each end. The area was surrounded by high, chain-link fencing and barbed wire and each shelter had an armed guard. During my time all aircraft were loaded with Mk 28 nuclear weapons of various yields, depending on the assigned target. The aircraft usually stayed there about two weeks. They were started up every day and all systems were checked. If a malfunction was

detected a replacement aircraft would be towed into the area and parked next to the shelter. A Mk 28 was brought from the bomb dump and loaded on to its centreline station, then the 'bad' aircraft was downloaded and the 'good' one towed into the shelter.

Aircrews and crew chiefs were required to remain on the pad twenty-four hours a day. We usually stayed on alert for three to five days at a time. We had four flights in each squadron and each flight was responsible for Victor Alert one week per month. Each flight usually had about eight pilots assigned to it and the squadron had to provide four flight members to be on the pad at all times. Married crewmembers liked to get off alert for the weekends and holidays while bachelors liked to have Saturday nights off to head for London. The 55th TFS bachelors maintained a flat in Radcliffe Square, London that was the site of many great festivities. Food on the alert pad was some of the best on the base. The cooks went all out on holidays such as Thanksgiving and really prepared feasts. The only thing lacking on the alert pad table was the wine!

We passed away the time on alert by reading, watching movies, ping-pong, pool and poker or taking naps to get ready for London. We also spent time studying our targets and attack

routes. The Wing or higher HQ would occasionally spring surprise tests on alert crews. If you didn't have the answers you could be decertified and taken off alert. We were also subjected to simulated launches. At any time of the day or night the wing or HQ could sound the alert siren and we would scramble to our aircraft, simulate a start and call in on the UHF radio that we were ready to taxi. This took around 7–8 minutes. We had to be able to get airborne in 15 minutes.

Awakening from a dead sleep, getting into a flight suit, boots, jacket and g-suit from the top bunk bed of a small four-man trailer in the dark was always very challenging and interesting. Our boots had zippers to facilitate the process and it was somewhat comical to watch half-dressed pilots running to their planes while trying to pull up the zippers. A few times we got to perform this drill in several inches of snow.

Don Schmenk was the Target Officer for the 494th TFS:

As such I had to develop low-level practice routes in Turkey. I used a *National Geographic* 'Lands of the Bible' map as a guide and plotted the routes over as many points of interest as I could find. Schmenk's tours! Back in the UK we flew a lot of

20th TFW pilots watch the wing-tips as they close in for this pose. via Tom Germscheid

close air support flights into the buffer zone between East and West Germany against armour and troops in contact, using simulated high-drag bombs, strafing and napalm passes.

Deployments to NATO's northern flank in Norway were also on the menu and Tom Germscheid went with the entire 55th TFS to Flesland AB.

The base is built into the side of a mountain and the aircraft taxi into the mountain and park there. Servicing and maintenance, sleeping quarters and messing facilities are also inside the mountain. It was very impressive. We also took a flight of four up to Boda AB, above the Arctic Circle and stayed a couple of days. It was summer and still light when we headed home from the bar at about 0400.

Don Schmenk's squadron also participated in two *Polar Express* exercises in Norway.

These were NATO exercises in conjunction with Norwegian, Dutch and German pilots. We operated out of Bodo, Norway and flew with F-104s and F-84s on many low-level sorties. On one the 'target' was a battleship in a fjord. Spectacular! On another exercise in the UK I was launched on an air-to-air sortie with two AIM-9 missiles on each inboard pylon and no tanks. I recall it being a very unstable airplane. I'm glad the RAF Lightning fighter I was supposed

to meet didn't show up. Weather was a problem in trying to stay current in weapons delivery in the UK. I remember returning from a night refuelling sortie and being the only one [of the] eight aircraft that landed at Lakenheath. The other seven went to Upper Heyford because of the bad weather.

Also in USAFE from 1959 to 1962 was Korean War veteran Lt Col David O. Williams. After previous experience of the P-40, P-47, P-51, F-80, F-84E/G/F and F-101A/C Voodoo, he had checked out on the F-100 in Chuck Yeager's 306th TFS at George AFB in 1958. In USAFE he was a member of the Tactical Evaluation Team, keeping a close eye on training and readiness by flying the F-100 with virtually all the USAFE F-100 units and those visiting Europe on deployments. The nuclear strike mission was paramount, although, as he recalled:

We did keep some proficiency in conventional weapons delivery such as strafing and dive bombing. Very little aerial refuelling was conducted, unless one could encounter a KB-50 tanker from RAF Sculthorpe over the Channel or over some suitable area of the UK. At that time USAFE F-100s didn't have the 'bent' probe or refuellable 335gal drop tanks which TAC was enjoying. In my view, outside of the *High Wire* modification programme the bent

probe and 335gal tanks were the greatest improvement to the F-100 ever made.

The 20th TFW, based at Upper Heyford but previously at Woodbridge and Wethersfield, had no monopoly on good weather either. Col 'Lanny' Lancaster recalled:

I was at Woodbridge from November 1968, then moved to Heyford in December 1969. At Woodbridge the 79th TFS was a separate unit with the parent 20th Wing and the other two squadrons (55th and 77th TFS) at Wethersfield. I believe we were the last 'separate' TFS, discounting the 32nd TFS at Soesterberg who were pure air defence pukes [pilots]. What I remember most about 'Woody' was the weather. I think I flew five times in four months. Our principal mission was nuclear alert. The three squadrons rotated so that one month in three you pulled alert duty at home. The next month you would be off alert so that you could do continuation training at home, then the third month you would be TDY for nuclear alert and gunnery training. The TDY itself was divided: two weeks at either Aviano or Cigli and two weeks at Wheelus – one of the best gunnery ranges ever because, unless there was a storm, the wind was never more than about 5kt.

For Tom Germscheid, at Wethersfield with the 20th TFW from April 1961, Wheelus was also memorable for its Officers' Club.

The food was good and often first-class entertainment was brought in from the Continent. Spirits could be purchased very cheaply, especially Scotch, though they were rationed in the UK. There always seemed to be plenty of ration coupons to bring a few bottles home to Wethersfield. One night the 20th TFW C-47 landed after a return flight from Wheelus and the Customs Officer (who had been suspicious of this activity but had never caught anyone) was there to greet it. All hell broke loose when he discovered about twenty cases of Scotch on board.

A lot of good-natured rivalry took place between the various TDY units. The Republic F-105s were fairly new to Europe. There was a large, wooden F-105 model displayed from the ceiling behind the bar and somehow a lemon always seemed to get impaled on the pitot tube of this model. Another highlight was the beautiful white beach and clear blue water. All the pale-faces from England would hit the beach as soon as we landed and debriefed. By the time the sun went down most were fried with a good sunburn. The cockpit harness and parachute straps were mighty painful the next day! One unit

This sixteen-ship flypast led by F-100Fs was flown at Misawa AB in November 1963 as a tribute to President J. F. Kennedy, murdered in that month. David Menard Collection

weeks while a maintenance crew from Wethersfield patched it up, though they never did get the magnetic compass to point in the right direction. Col Royal Baker, 20th TFW CO, who had been my Number 3 on the flight into Aviano, authorized me to fly single-ship to Wheelus in VFR conditions. Under normal circumstances we never crossed the 'Med' single-ship.

Tom also recalled that on 23 January 1963, the 20th TFW suffered a loss that also affected many local residents:

The Wing's Deputy Commander, Col Wendell J. Kelley took off in an F-100F to do an instrument checkout for another pilot, 1st Lt Paul Briggs. At 30,000m the aircraft suffered a compressor failure and Col Kelley turned back for Wethersfield with minimal power. As it approached the airfield another explosion caused the engine to seize up. At 4,500ft and 6 miles from the runway [he] abandoned his approach and his attempts to re-start the J57. He then steered the F-100 away from a series of local villages including Gosfield, the community in which he and his family had become popular and active residents. He ordered 1st Lt Briggs to eject as the aircraft reached 1,500ft and very shortly afterwards it crashed with its pilot into a field close to the Kelleys' home. A memorial service in the village later paid tribute to Col Kelley's self-sacrifice for the safety of the community.

In November 1969, the 20th TFW moved to RAF Upper Heyford, replacing the 66th TRW whose RF-4Cs transferred to Zweibrucken (17th TRS) and Shaw AFB (18th TRS). The 79th TFS moved in from Woodbridge first, followed by the two Wethersfield units in May/June 1970. For the first time since 1952, the 20th TFW was consolidated at a single base. The Wing's aircraft had worn camouflage paint since 1966, including 56-3000 *Triple Zilch*, which had previously been the spectacularly-decorated *Wing King* plane. However, the residency was short-lived and the 20th began conversion to the F-111E on 12 September 1970, its last two F-100s departing on 12 February the following year. Wethersfield, relegated to a diversion base, became temporary home (with Mildenhall) to the 48th TFW in 1971 while Lakenheath's runways were improved in anticipation of the arrival of F-4D Phantoms for the Wing. Deliveries of the F-4D began in January 1972 and the last Super Sabres (F-100Fs 0-63850 /876/884), left the base on 15 April 1972, ending USAFE F-100 operations.

commander issued an edict that anyone who got too burned to fly the next day would be sent back to Wethersfield on the next shuttle plane. Missions were short; generally about an hour. Almost everyone got to fly twice a day and occasionally three times – a fighter pilot's paradise. The Libyan Air Force (in which Lt Col Ghadaffi was an F-86 squadron commander) used the same range as the USAFE aircraft for weapons delivery.

The flights from Wethersfield to Wheelus were always enjoyable. We flew in four-ship flights configured with an SUU dispenser on the centreline, 275gal tanks on the intermediate stations and 200gal tanks inboard. If we had a tailwind component of about 65kt we could make the trip non-stop. A 'bingo' fuel point was calculated for coasting out over Monaco. If anyone called 'bingo' the flight would divert into Aviano and usually remain overnight.

On one such diversion Tom was leading a flight of four and hit thunderstorms and a 1,200ft (365m) ceiling.

We decided to break into two-ship elements for a radar vector to the field for a VFR [visual flight rules] landing. About the time I started down with my element Aviano radar went down. I climbed back on top and decided we would

make single-ship ADF let-downs. I started down first and at about 15,000ft my Hun was struck by lightning. It was quite a fireball and I could really smell the ozone. My first thought was that I had an explosion of some kind so I automatically retarded the throttle to idle.

When I managed to open my eyes and look at the instrument panel, several caution lights were on and the engine gauges were unwinding. I was sure the engine had flamed out. After a couple of seconds things stabilized, I advanced the throttle and the engine began to spool up again. I had lost several instruments including my heading indicator, ADF and UHF radio. I went to emergency squawk on the IFF and initiated a climb back above the clouds where I spotted my wingman and jumped on to his wing. He led me down to an uneventful landing though I did notice that it took more than normal power to keep the beast flying. Upon climbing out of the cockpit I could see why. The front ends of both 200gal fuel tanks had blown off and they looked like torpedo tubes. The tanks were empty at the time of the lightning strike but the fumes ignited, causing the explosion. Lightning had also struck the tip of the pitot tube, exiting through the rudder and taking a 3ft section of rudder with it. All along the fuselage there were burn marks as if someone had run an arc-welder along it. I had to stay with my stricken bird at Aviano for two

CHAPTER 4

Vietnam Warhorse

27th TFW F-100D-21-NAs, armed with napalm, head out for a mission over South Vietnam. T/Sgt Albert Doucet via David Menard

Parry and Thrust

When F-100 Super Sabres made their first deployments to a combat area in April 1961 with the movement of six 510th Tactical Fighter Squadron (TFS) aircraft to Thailand, the Super Sabre was still Tactical Air Command's (TAC's) main fighter-bomber. The first operational Republic F-105Ds (its intended successor) had recently entered service with the 4520th Combat Crew Training Wing (CCTW), and in United States Air Forces in Europe (USAFE), the 36th Tactical Fighter Wing (TFW) began to convert to the new Thunderchief in May 1961, followed by the 49th TFW. At that time, the USAF planned to re-equip fourteen TAC Wings with F-105Ds, replacing the majority of F-100Ds with the faster, all-weather jet that had beaten North American Aviation's (NAA's) F-107A for production orders in

1957. Later in 1961, President J. F. Kennedy's administration reduced that number to eight F-105 Wings. The others stayed with the F-100 until October 1964 when F-4C Phantom IIs began to appear on flight-lines. For the four TFWs that were to fight the greater part of the 'in country' air war in Vietnam, the F-100 was to be their steed for up to ten more years. Although, like the F-105, it was a strike aircraft built for an essentially nuclear defence strategy, it would prove to be adaptable to a very different kind of warfare.

As the situation in South East Asia progressively deteriorated from 1960 onwards, there were numerous small 'flag-waving' F-100 deployments to Thailand and Clark AB throughout the early 1960s, including brief periods of Victor Alert in Formosa and short visits to Da Nang in South Vietnam. One of these, Operation *Bell Tone*, took a Detachment of 510th TFS *Buzzards* to Don

The Buzzards of Bien Hoa (510th TFS). Bruce Gold

Muang airport on 16 April 1961 in response to the loss of a 4400CCTS SC-47 electronic intelligence (ELINT) aircraft to Pathet Lao anti-aircraft artillery (AAA). The F-100D/F sextet officially provided air defence for the Thai capital. Thai deployments increased to squadron size in 1962 with: the 428th TFS; the 474th TFW,

This line-up of F-100Ds was at Da Nang from August to November 1964, detached from the 401st TFW at England AFB via Clark Field. F-100D-31-NA 55-3724 has 19-shot LAU-3/A FFAR launchers, each weighing around 500lb (225kg) loaded. White tail caps for these pods stand behind each wing. David Menard Collection

weapons delivery, dart target firing qualification and night air refuelling which we could not accomplish at Takhli.

After a major TAC Operational Readiness Inspection (ORI) in July 1964, which the 27th TFW passed with flying colours, the 522nd TFS was designated as the Wing's 'Alpha' squadron.

This meant that if there was a requirement for the Wing to deploy a fighter squadron for an unscheduled mission anywhere in the world we were 'it' and we had to be fully cocked, loaded and on a short tether.

The next stage in escalation was a response to increased North Vietnamese-inspired insurgency in Laos. In January 1964, the US Joint Chiefs of Staff recommended the bombing of North Vietnam and ground operations in Laos. By May of that year Pathet Lao forces occupied the Plaine des Jarres and on 6 June a VFP-63 RF-8A on a *Yankee Team* recce flight was shot down in that area. An F-8D from VF-111, escorting another RF-8A, was lost on 7 June. The decision was taken to hit back at the Pathet Lao AAA sites responsible for these shoot-downs. Eight F-100Ds of the 615th TFS, 401st TFW re-deployed from Clark AB (where they had just arrived on temporary duty (TDY) to Da Nang in South Vietnam. Col George Laven, formerly commander of the 479th Fighter Day Wing (FDW) ten years previously,

which flew in to Takhli Royal Thai Air Force Base (RTAFB) in mid-May; the 430th TFS in September; and finally the 522nd TFS in December (all from the 832nd AD at Cannon AFB). These three phases of Operation *Saw Buck* gave each squadron's pilots a ninety-day rotation at Takhli but used the same eighteen F-100s. Lt Col David O. Williams commanded the 522nd TFS Detachment at Takhli in the spring of 1964.

During our stay there we participated in SEATO [South East Asia Treaty Organization] flying exercises with Thai Air Force units, the Royal Australian Air Force's 77 Squadron and RAF units from Singapore. During the Exercise the King of Thailand visited our organization and I had the opportunity to present him with a memento of the occasion.

In May 1964 we redeployed with our F-100s to Cannon AFB via air refuelling with stops at Guam and Hickam AFB, Hawaii. Once back at Cannon we made extraordinary efforts to catch up on all our training requirements such as

This F-100D, 55-3559 assigned to Capt Paul Phillips, made a successful barrier engagement after landing without brakes or hydraulics. Peter Vanderhoef

Loading a BLU-1 napalm bomb from an MJ-1 munitions loader on to an F-100D's out-board pylon. The requirement to deliver napalm from straight-and-level flight at only a few hundred feet of altitude caused many combat losses. Norm Taylor Collection

led the first combat mission on 9 June. Each aircraft carried a pair of nineteen-shot 2.75in rocket pods and four 500lb general purpose (GP) bombs. Bad weather and difficulty in finding the KC-135 tankers impeded the mission, but Laven's flight probably succeeded in damaging a Pathet Lao defensible position. A second flight of F-100Ds had inadvertently bombed the jungle some 25 miles (40km) away from the assigned target. The eight fighters returned to Da Nang via Udorn RTAFB, ending the first F-100 combat mission.

The 615th TFS was also the first F-100 unit to respond to the Gulf of Tonkin incident on 2 August 1964. Ten F-100Ds were despatched from Clark AB to Da Nang, followed shortly after by others from the 612th TFS and the 614th TFS *Lucky Devils* commanded by Lt Col Cregg Nolan. David Williams received orders on 4 August to deploy the 522nd TFS to Clark AB the following day, and three cells of six F-100s plus spares launched early on August 5, arriving at Clark in the middle of a local typhoon.

It was the worst weather I have ever encountered during approach and landing in my entire career. We penetrated and landed in formation by pairs under TACAN [tactical air navigation] and GCA [ground controlled approach] control.

Rain was coming down so hard I could not see the runway when I reached minimums, but at the last second I was able to acquire the high intensity yellow approach lights and continue to touch-down. Water on the runway must have been at least 4in deep because when I looked back to ascertain that my wingman had deployed his drag chute I could hardly see him because of the 'rooster tail' of water shooting up over his aircraft from my own landing gear. We remained at Clark AB for about a week and were then directed to deploy six F-100s to Da Nang AB and another six to Takhli. I led the six birds to Da Nang and sent my Ops Officer, Maj Bob Buss with the other six to Takhli.

At Da Nang the 522nd TFS crews operated alongside the 615th TFS Detachment commanded by Maj Dave Ward. As David Williams recalled:

Our mission was to provide armed escort for RF-101 photo reconnaissance aircraft flying over South Vietnam and Laos. We were authorized to expend ordnance only if we, or the RF-101s were fired upon. Our ordnance load for the escort mission was two LAU-3 pods and a full load of 20mm ammo. Occasionally we carried AGM-12 air-to-ground missiles. Our other tasking was to provide BARCAP for ECM [electronic countermeasures] and other types of high-altitude reconnaissance missions up in the far reaches of the Gulf of Tonkin, between

North Vietnam and the Chinese island of Hainan. We had long-duration station times on BARCAP missions and had at least two air refuellings per sortie. Our ordnance was a full load of 20mm and two AIM-9 [air intercept] missiles.

From early September 1964, David Williams opted to deploy the entire 522nd TFS to Da Nang, including the six aircraft that had previously gone to Takhli. They continued to fly recce escort and BAR-CAP missions.

On BARCAP we had good radar coverage and direction from Panama, the GCI [ground controlled interception] site atop Monkey Mountain, north-east of Da Nang. We had very few heads-up calls on bogies [MiGs] and no engagements. Occasionally we would sight contrails over land but they never ventured out over the Gulf.

The detection of MiG-17 Fresco-A fighters at Noi Bai AB near Hanoi on 7 August brought demands from the Pacific Air Force (PACAF) commander for strikes against this new threat by Da Nang F-100s, but this plan failed to get approval from Washington. The 428th TFS *Buccaneers* returned to Takhli RTAFB on a 1964 TDY, and two years after F-100s began operations in the area, the first Super Sabre shoot-down occurred. Four F-100Ds were sent to fly combat air control over recovery of downed aircrew (ResCAP) for a Royal Laotian AF T-28 pilot on 18 August after a UH-34 rescue helicopter was also brought down. An F-100D (56-3085) took a hit while strafing enemy AAA sites and the pilot, 1st Lt Arnie Clark of the 522nd TFS, ejected safely over Thailand. It was the first of 242 F-100s (198 combat and 44 operational) to be lost during the Vietnam conflict with the deaths of eighty-seven aircrew. Two were killed over the north of Vietnam, five became prisoners of war (POWs) and five went missing in action (MIA), but fourteen were rescued.

The F-100s held up well under the difficult climatic conditions of South East Asia but there were inevitable technical problems. David Williams:

During the monsoon season the tail-cone 'eyelids' often failed to open properly when afterburners were lit for take off. This resulted in an over-temperature condition for the J57 and a 'hard light'. We called Clark AB to send us a P&W [Pratt and Whitney] technical expert. After his inspections he informed me that gunk from the constant rains

Armourers work on the M39 guns of an F-100D. The F-104 Starfighters in the background indicate Da Nang as the location. Norm Taylor Collection

Da Nang aircraft successfully pounded the defences around an NVA barracks at Chap Le in North Vietnam, backing up six A-1 Skyraider bombers. Although the F-100's 20mm guns were effective against AAA, pilots were to suffer numerous losses in the dangerous business of close-in duelling with flak sites.

After six *Barrel Roll* missions, a review concluded that the operation had been less than effective. The pressure was stepped up with Operation *Flaming Dart*, the first major strikes inside North Vietnam, which began on 7 February 1965. By that time over 150 F-105Ds had been assigned to PACAF Wings. The Republic jet could carry twice the F-100D's bombload 50 per cent faster (particularly at low altitude). It was inevitable that F-105 units would take the burden of strikes against the increasingly heavily defended targets in North Vietnam. F-105s soon displaced F-100Ds on TDYs to Takhli and the 6234th Wing (Provisional) was established with Thunderchiefs at Korat RTAFB. In addition, the 23rd TFW began a two-squadron, eight-month TDY at Tan Son Nhut AB. The F-100 squadrons increasingly supplied fighter cover and flak suppression for F-105 strikes.

After two brief phases of Operation *Flaming Dart*, President L. B. Johnson initiated Operation *Rolling Thunder* on 2 March 1965 with a major attack (*Rolling Thunder 5*) on an ammunition dump and a naval base in North Vietnam. It drew on most of Da Nang's F-100 assets including the 613th TFS and recently deployed 531st TFS. The 428th TFS (which replaced the 522nd TFS at Da Nang from late November 1964) supplied fighter cover for the strike on Quang Khe naval base.

In all, forty Super Sabres accompanied a force of forty-five Korat F-105s. The Huns shared flak suppression with fifteen F-105s, flew MiGCAP with one flight, weather recce and ResCAP. MiGCAP aircraft carried AIM-9B missiles while the flak suppressors were each armed with two pods of 2.75in rockets and a pair of 750lb bombs. No strike F-105s were lost as the flak suppressors were very effective against unexpectedly fierce defences, but five suppressors went down. In three cases they were hit on repeat passes at the same target. Two F-100Ds were lost – one was Takhli-based and its pilot, Lt J. A. Cullen (flying 56-3150), was recovered from the sea by an HU-16. The other, a 613th TFS aircraft (55-2857) was hit during a pass

was forming on the eyelids, causing them to stick together instead of opening properly. He cleaned them all up and used some kind of graphite lubricant, thereby improving the situation but not eliminating it altogether.

In response to the increasing threats to US aircraft, PACAF gradually established a complex search and rescue (SAR) network. It had one of its earliest work-outs on 18 November 1964 when another Da Nang F-100D was fatally damaged while escorting a *Yankee Team* recce flight. Capt W. M. Martin's 613th TFS aircraft took an AAA hit while strafing gun positions that had fired on an RF-101. He ejected, but had died from his injuries by the time rescuers arrived. In all, forty-two aircraft were involved in the attempt, including a flight of newly introduced F-105s that demolished the offending AAA site. In a similar AAA suppression mission in the Mu Gia Pass on 19 February 1965, F-100D 55-3783 was hit and the 613th TFS commanding officer (CO), Lt Col Bob Ronca, was killed. The 613th TFS had been seconded from the 401st TFW (then at England AFB) to Da Nang a few weeks before. It remained at Da Nang until July 1965, losing three more aircraft, another pilot killed and a third captured by the North Vietnamese during the next phase of the war, including Operation *Barrel Roll* and the early stages of *Rolling Thunder*.

Rolling Huns

The first strike in Operation *Barrel Roll* was on 14 December 1964, one of a series of limited strikes aimed at North Vietnamese Army (NVA) forces in Laos near the border with North Vietnam. On this occasion, eight F-100Ds flew combat air patrol to counter enemy air defences (MiGCAP) for F-105Ds carrying 750lb bombs, AGM-12 Bullpups and cluster bomb unit CBU-2A on an armed reconnaissance with an RF-101C for BDA pictures. A vehicle on an 'underwater bridge'was attacked with six bombs, all of which missed. Attacks on secondary targets were frustrated by low cloud, and no enemy opposition was encountered. On a similar mission on 21 December, four 428th TFS Huns were unable to find their targets under dense jungle cover and were lucky to escape some intense AAA fire.

The Da Nang F-100s began to draw the flak suppression mission, attacking a heavily defended bridge at Ban Ken on the crucial Route 7 on 13 January 1965. The main strike was by sixteen F-105s while two flights of Super Sabres flew a 'wall' inline abreast, deluging the thirty AAA positions with CBU-2A canisters. They made repeated strafing passes and Capt Ferguson was shot down while making his fifth run against the guns. In another flak suppression mission on 8 February 1965, twenty

481st TFS four-ship on initial approach to Tan Son Nhut AB. Nearest the camera is Capt Stephen Dvorchak's 56-3063 *The Shadow* (based on a *MAD Magazine* character). '548 was assigned to 1st Lt Tom Tilghman and *Pretty Penny* is flying as Number 2 to the leader's '604. Peter Vanderhoef

against the guns. The pilot, 1st Lt Hayden J. Lockhart evaded capture for a week before becoming the first USAF pilot to be captured in North Vietnam. He remained a POW for eight years.

The campaign resumed on 15 March with *Rolling Thunder 6*, a USN attack. For *Rolling Thunder 7* the tactics changed. Armed reconnaissance of road and rail routes was added to the 'listed' targets. During April 1965 over 1,500 combat sorties were flown over North Vietnam, roughly half by USAF aircraft. *Rolling Thunder 9A* on 3 April brought the first of many assaults on the recently completed Ham Rong (Dragon's Jaw) road and rail

Panels are off this 481st TFS F-100D for periodic inspection, but the extended 335gal tanks remain in place. Peter Vanderhoef

Pete Vanderhoef examines a flak hole in the slat of his aircraft, the only damage he suffered in 130 combat missions. Peter Vanderhoef

A second attack on the bridge took place the next day using forty-eight F-105 bombers (but no Bullpups) and a seven-strong F-100D ResCAP. The 416th TFS *Silver Knights*, newly arrived from Clark AB in a *Sawbuck* Composite Air Strike Force deployment, provided the MiGCAP flight that orbited above the flights of four F-105Ds as they dived to lay their 750lbs bombs on the 'Dragon's Jaw'.

MiG Kill (?)

Green Flight of ResCAP F-100Ds, armed with rocket pods and 20mm included Capt Don Kilgus. They took up station just off the coast to the south-east of the target area, orbiting in case they were needed to cross the coast and cover a rescue attempt. As the F-100s swung north they were met head-on by a pair of MiG-17s, which used their superior turning performance to pull in behind two elements of Green Flight. The Americans took violent evasive action and engaged the MiGs. Don Kilgus (*Green 2*) followed one of them in a near-vertical dive from 20,000ft (6,100m) firing a succession of 20mm bursts at the VPAF jet. He saw a flash on the MiG's right tail-plane and some debris but at 7,000ft (2,140m) he was unable to focus hard on the target as he struggled to haul his plummeting F-100 out

bridge at Than Hoa, only 70 miles (112km) from Hanoi. Lt Col Robinson Risner coordinated a force of twenty-one F-100Ds supporting sixteen F-105s and a pair of RF-101Cs. Ten KC-135As were also required. Sixteen of the Thunderchiefs carried Bullpups and the others had 750lb bombs that, on this occasion, were almost as ineffective as the missiles against such a 'hard' target. Two F-100s flew ahead of the strike force on a weather recce flight, reporting over 5 miles (8km) visibility. In view of the huge and rapid increase in North Vietnamese AAA defences, another seven F-100Ds joined fifteen F-105Ds as flak suppressors. Four Sidewinder-armed F-100Ds formed the MiGCAP flight and eight with 2.75in rockets served as ResCAP. Once again the suppressors kept the defending gunners busy, preventing losses to the bombers but the cost was another aircraft from the 613th TFS. 1st Lt George Craig's F-100D (55-3625) took a hit on its second pass and smashed into the ground before the pilot could eject.

Although the MiGCAP was not challenged by Vietnamese People's Air Force (VPAF) fighters, 3 April also marked the first VPAF combat missions. The F-100D weather recce flight had been detected on North Vietnamese radar and an attack on the Ham Rong bridge was anticipated later in the morning. Two flights of MiG-17s were launched from Noi Bai and

intercepted USN VF-211 F-8E Crusaders attacking another bridge in the Than Hoa area. Lt Cdr Spence Thomas' F-8 was set on fire by Pham Ngoc Lau of the 921st Fighter Regiment but Thomas managed to recover to Da Nang. The MiGs then withdrew without encountering the F-100 MIGCAP over the USAF strike.

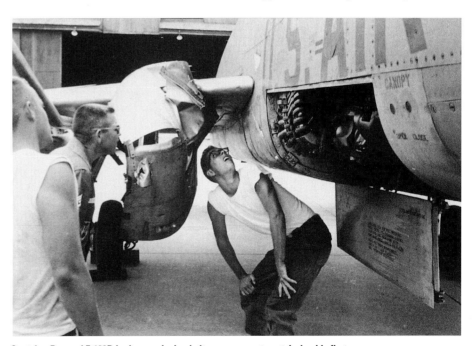

Capt Joe Reynes' F-100D had an explosion in its gun compartment during his first mission after a previous bail-out (on 20 September 1965 from 56-3177 during a CAS mission). Trapped gun gas blew off the gun-bay doors and they impaled themselves on his inboard pylons; one each side. Peter Vanderhoef

of its dive. However, he and other pilots in the flight were pretty sure the MiG had been fatally damaged, though no fire or crash were seen. Don painted a kill marking on his F-100D (55-2894 *Kay Lynn*) but the lack of conclusive evidence meant that he was only credited with a 'probable' kill.

Meanwhile, the four MiGCAP F-100Ds (*Purple* flight) led by the 416th TFS CO Lt Col Emmett L. Hays, orbited 60 miles (95km) to the north, covering the presumed route of any MiGs that might have approached the strike force. Hays' wingman, Capt Keith Connolly, saw four 921st FR MiG-17s led by Capt Tran Hanh diving towards *Zinc* flight of F-105Ds. He called a warning but the Thud drivers didn't receive it and pressed on. Tran Hanh closed to 1,300ft (400m) and fired all three of his heavy cannons at F-105D 59-1764. The blazing Thunderchief crashed, killing Capt James Magnusson of the 355th TFW. Hanh and his wingman, Pham Giang, dived away southwards while a second MiG-17 element led by Le Minh Huan fired at *Zinc* flight leader Maj Frank Bennett's F-105D (59-1754), causing major damage. The wounded Thud got Bennett out to the coast for a bailout, but he drowned before rescuers could be brought in. Hays and Connolly engaged afterburner and closed to within Sidewinder range of the MiGs. Connolly got a good 'growl' from his AIM-9B and fired but the missile passed just above the leading MiG's right wing. *Purple* flight then switched to guns since the alerted F-105 pilots had gone into afterburner and an AIM-9B could easily have found the wrong target. In fact, *Purple* fired another missile later but it failed to find any target. The MiGs managed to evade the less nimble F-100Ds with some strenuous manoeuvring, causing Connolly's bursts of gunfire to miss also. Short of fuel, the MiG pilots headed home. Ironically, three of their number including Le Minh Huan and his wingman Tran Nguyen Nam failed to return. The Vietnamese assumed that they had been shot down by US fighters, giving further credence to Don's claim, but when no USAF claim was made, the VPAF attributed the losses to their own AAA.

In its first and only encounter with MiGs, the F-100D was perceived as inadequate for the air superiority task. In fairness, the skirmish highlighted many of the problems that were to take most of the war years for USAF pilots to solve. Poor communications, unhelpful rules of engagement,

inexperience in handling the rather limited AIM-9B and unfamiliarity with VPAF tactics all put the F-100 pilots at a disadvantage, as did the aircraft's lack of Flying Boom-type air-to-air refuelling capability. However, it was decided that they would not get a second chance to prove their aircraft as a dogfighter, partly because the USAF was keen to put its newest fighter, the F-4C, into action. The first F-4Cs entered the war on April 4 when the 45th TFS detached from McDill's 15th TFW to Ubon RTAFB and flew MiGCAP for all successive *Rolling Thunder* strikes in place of F-100Ds. Its first MiG kills (the first confirmed kills for USAF fighters) did not take place until 10 July 1965 when two MiG-17s were claimed, though the VPAF denied these losses. Although there would be many more F-100 missions over North Vietnam, none encountered MiG opposition and no Super Sabres were lost to enemy fighters.

After a transfer to the 8th TFW as Deputy Wing Commander for Operations flying the F-4D Phantom (and scoring one of the last MiG kills of Operation *Rolling Thunder*) Lt Col David Williams was well placed to provide a telling comparison of the Super Sabre with its successor.

I had experience of flying the F-4D against both the MiG-17 and MiG-21 over North Vietnam. I feel confident that the F-100 would not have fared well in the MiGCAP role against either MiG model. I formed this opinion because I do not believe the F-100 could turn with either of the MiGs, could not climb with them and could not out-dive or out-run the MiG-21. The F-100 suffered from a low thrust-to-weight ratio and in a hard turn the aircraft would shudder, approaching a stall even with the leading edge slats extended. The airspeed would then bleed off quickly, leaving the pilot in a terribly vulnerable position for air-to-air combat. Another problem I noticed in flying ACT [air combat tactics] was that one could experience hard compressor stalls in the J57 when attempting to select afterburner while in a nose-high angle of attack. On one such attempt I experienced a compressor stall so violent that fire exited both the nose intake and tailpipe simultaneously, as verified by my wingman. It shook the rudder pedals so hard that I temporarily lost my foot contact with them. Such an event in air-to-air combat could spoil a pilot's day if he were, for instance attempting to break into a hostile attacker. The F-4 was successful in fighting MiGs largely because of its high thrust from dual J79 engines, its rapid acceleration to supersonic speed, its good radar and its radar

guided AIM-7 Sparrow missiles. The F-100 lacked all of these features.

In Country

Following the initial F-4C deployment to Ubon, PACAF rapidly increased the Phantom presence in the war area. Four squadrons of the 8th TFW *Wolfpack* arrived at Korat from August 1965 and the 12th TFW set up business at Cam Ranh Bay at the end of the year. At Da Nang, the 35th TFW were re-organized in April 1966. The 366th TFW *Gunfighters* transferred from Phan Rang and replaced the 35th TFW, which in turn moved (in name only) to the new base at Phan Rang to control three squadrons of F-100s from 10 October 1966.

In June 1965, Lt Col Hays' 416th TFS had moved out to Bien Hoa for a month before returning to England AFB. In December 1965, the 416th moved permanently to Tan Son Nhut and then rejoined its parent 3rd TFW at Bien Hoa in June 1966.

Of the other squadrons from the pioneering 1964 Composite Air Strike Force, the 614th TFS and 522nd TFS stayed until November 1964 and the 613th TFS until July 1965. This left the 615th TFS, effectively based at Clark Field, which remained at Da Nang until its move to Phan Rang and 366th TFW control on 16 July 1966.

Super Sabre City

Phan Rang was one of the new bases that were rapidly constructed to accommodate the huge increase in the US air campaign in 1966. Like the others at Phu Cat, Tuy Hoa and Bien Hoa it had a 10,000ft (3,000m) concrete runway with parallel taxiways and parking aprons of AM-2 or pierced steel planking (PSP) matting. At the height of the conflict, Phan Rang accommodated 140 Super Sabres.

From 20 March 1966, the 366th TFW under Col George Weart controlled three F-100D/F squadrons: the 614th, 615th and 352nd TFS of which the first two were ex-Da Nang units. The 352nd TFS joined the 366th TFW from 15 August 1966 and remained at Phan Rang until the end of July 1971 when F-100 operations in the area ceased. The 614th TFS returned to action at the base on 18 September 1966 and the 615th TFS arrived on 16 July of

The nose of F-100D-31-NA 55-3797 is already covered in mission markings as it awaits yet another combat sortie
with the 416th TFS from Bien Hoa AB in July 1965. Minimal squadron markings comprise a small green tail-stripe.
Several of the squadron's Huns had crew names displayed in red under the windshield as seen here.
David Menard

that year. These two squadrons also stayed until 31 July 1971. The final unit at Phan Rang was Detachment 1 of the 612th TFS, established to fly the specialist *Misty* F-100F FAC missions from May 1967. From 1 October 1966, a 'nameplate' exchange with the 366th TFW put the 35th TFW in charge of these squadrons and a pair of B-57 Canberra units. Later additions to the crowded base were an RAAF Canberra Squadron, the 8th Special Operations Squadron (SOS) with A-37B Dragonflies and the 120th TFS, Colorado Air National Guard (ANG) which flew F-100Cs with the 35th TFW for a year from April 1968.

South-west of the coastal Phan Rang base and close to Saigon was Bien Hoa, which became home to the 307th TFS from the 31st TFW at Homestead AFB in July 1965. It was joined for a six-month TDY at the base by Cannon AFB's 429th TFS. Both squadrons, under the 6521st

TFW, operated against targets in the south of Vietnam and Laos. The 307th TFS flew over 3,500 sorties without loss. The 429th TFS racked up a similarly massive total but lost two aircraft and their pilots on CAS sorties. It was then decided to transfer the complete 3rd TFW from England AFB to Bien Hoa, and the 307th TFS was then replaced by the 531st TFS, which took over its aircraft. From November 1965, the 3rd TFW, commanded by Col Robert Ackerly, gradually moved its squadrons into the busy base, beginning with the 510th TFS *Buzzards*. By February 1966, it also had the 531st TFS and 90th TFS *Pair o' Dice* in place at Bien Hoa, eventually displacing the 308th TFS *Emerald Knights* to Tuy Hoa after their 1966 TDY. The base rapidly expanded its accommodation and maintenance facilities to deal with over a hundred Super Sabres and their crews. By mid-1966, the Wing had flown 13,000 combat sorties, averaging one a day for

each of the based F-100s.

A third base was sought for the F-100 force that was expanding so rapidly that at the height of the war only five TAC F-100 squadrons remained in the USA. Qui Non was initially earmarked for development, but in February 1966 the *Red Horse* construction teams moved into Phu Cat, a coastal site to the east of Pleiku and the most northerly of the Super Sabre bases. It was only thirty minutes from North Vietnam by F-100. There, the 37th TFW was established on 1 March 1967 with the 416th TFS *Silver Knights* (from Tan Son Nhut via Bien Hoa) and, from February 1968, the 355th TFS, the last F-100 unit to deploy to Vietnam. Phu Cat also hosted the *Misty* FAC Detachment of the 612th TFS between June 1967 and April 1969. The 174th TFS, Iowa ANG deployed to the base for a year from May 1968.

An even bigger concentration of F-100s was assembled at the fourth base, Tuy Hoa,

Crusaders at War

Cartridge start time for this 481st TFS *Crusader* at Tan Son Nhut AB. F-100D 55-3569, assigned to Capt William Carrothers, already bears an impressive tally of mission marks. David Anderton Collection via David Menard

Tan Son Nhut near Saigon became the base for the 481st TFS *Crusaders*, one of the four 27th TFW squadrons. Following one of its regular TDY assignments to Misawa, the unit was put on secondary alert status in response to the Gulf of Tonkin incident. It deployed on 12 June 1965 in Operation *Two Buck 16* with eighteen F-100s via Hickam AFB and Clark AB. The deployment was conducted in such secrecy that staff at Clark were unprepared for the arrival of the F-100s and their attendant KC-135s and C-130s on 14 June. A week later the squadron moved on to Tan Son Nhut, making the last of nine aerial refuellings in the 9,213nm flight from Cannon AFB. However, six aircraft led by David Williams (who had joined the squadron while awaiting a posting to the Air War College) were sent to augment the F-100 units at Da Nang. After a week of MSQ and forward air controlled (FAC) attack missions, these aircraft rejoined the rest of the squadron at Tan son Nhut.

Crusaders were the first tactical jet fighters to fly from the busy base, operating alongside B-57s, RF-101s and A-1E Skyraiders. Of its thirty pilots only four had previous combat experience though their commander, Lt Col Harold 'Hal' Comstock, had flown P-47s with Zemke's *Wolfpack* during WWII. His score of seven German aircraft was featured alongside the copious Vietnam mission scoreboard on the nose of his F-100D (55-3604).

The *Crusaders* began flying close air support (CAS) missions by day and night plus rapid response tactical air strikes, though a number of pilots were not qualified for the *Night Owl* missions. 1st Lt Peter Vanderhoef was among those whose first real night flight was a napalm

attack on road traffic in total darkness. He calculated that his napalm drop was made at about 10ft (3m) above ground level (AGL) since he was suddenly aware of trees on both sides of the road being lit up by flames above his aircraft's altitude.

One particularly successful mission was the relief of a Special Forces Camp at Bu Dop on the night of 19 July 1965. It was the first of many F-100 missions to relieve beleaguered US Special Forces installations. Capt Norm Turner and 1st Lt Don Watson repeatedly attacked Viet Cong (VC) machine-gun positions in dreadful visibility below a 500ft (150m) cloud ceiling. Their FAC, Capt Hal Howbower, was able to steer in a C-123 flare ship to provide some assistance and the two F-100D pilots (flying 56-3613 and 55-3528) were able to repel the VC's attempt to infiltrate the camp. Both men were awarded the Distinguished Flying Cross (DFC) for the mission. Sadly, Don Watson didn't live long enough to receive his medal. His F-100D (55-2837) was shot down on 31 July during a napalm attack on a VC headquarters position.

Five of the squadron's original eighteen Huns were shot down by the end of the deployment on 27 November 1965. Among them was F-100D 56-3177 piloted by Capt Joe Reynes. On 20 September, a day when seven US fighters were lost, Joe was flying on a CAS sortie near the Mekong Delta. The aircraft took a hit and started venting fuel prodigiously. Pete Vanderhoef was on his wing as they climbed to 20,000ft (6,000m) to exit the area.

He was dumping JP-4 in a sheet about a foot wide from the underside split line of his plane and we decided he had best

leave it before it lit off. Everything happened in slow motion just like the book said. Joe floated down as I watched his bird fly way out to sea. His autopilot must have been working, which was unusual. I called in all kinds of cover and stuck around until the company arrived.

A Huey rescue helicopter took Joe back to Tan Son Nhut where he chose to air a grievance to the Base CO. While he had been on the ground, awaiting rescue there had been:

... unidentified folks moving around and Joe was armed with our wonderful Navy reject .38 revolver, six rounds of ammunition and a survival knife. Because we were a 'rotational' squadron, expected to be on base for three months, we were the tailend of the supply chain. There were PCS [permanent change of station] airmen working in the post office at Tan Son Nhut that carried Combat Masterpeice .38s with all the ammunition they wanted.

Joe had been given whisky by the Huey crew and some more was supplied by the C-130 crew who took him back to base. Pete Vanderhoef described the outcome:

The Tan son Nhut Base Commander came out to welcome him home, along with all the 481st guys. Joe seemed sober until he recognized the Base CO and in a rather unsubtle manner he asked why non-combatants were receiving all the survival gear and those of us who were exposed to combat every day couldn't even get a box of .38 calibre shells for our side-arms. I seem to remember two or three of our Squadron members carrying Joe off to the infirmary 'to be checked' (read 'separated from the Base CO'). The next day we were no longer at the end of the survival gear supply line.

For Joe, the next mission almost cost him another bailout when his gun-bay door was blown off in a gun-gas explosion (*see* page 87).

'Hal' Comstock was assigned an unusual mission when he led a four-ship escort for the less-than-popular US Secretary of Defense, Robert McNamara, on a July inspection tour of bases in South Vietnam. During the flight the F-100s were called upon to bomb and strafe a VC command post while McNamara looked on at a safe distance from his T-39 Sabreliner.

1st Lt Thomas E. Lowe was Intelligence Officer with the squadron, organizing the pre-flight briefings that F-100 crews received about ninety minutes before take-off and debriefing them after each mission. Every evening the squadron received a 'frag' order for the following day's operations and began planning for missions against 'suspected VC concentrations' or 'VC headquarters', indicated by map grid references. Aircraft and pilots were assigned by the Squadron Operations Officer while ordnance type, radio frequencies and times-over-target (TOT) were also settled. Tom Lowe commented on the high failure rate in the ordnance supplied to them:

During the first month's combat the M117 750lb GP bombs with M163 fuses were used in quantity and the squadron was plagued with many duds on their missions. Most of these bombs were of Korean War vintage. When the new

Another view of '569 on an earlier four-ship napalm strike before nose art was painted on *Crusaders* aircraft. David Anderton Collection via David Menard

Mk82 streamlined bombs became available the dud rate dropped radically.

There was also a shortage of ordnance, denied officially but evident to the people flying the missions. 'For a short time, flights of 481st TFS F-100Ds were sent out on missions with each airplane carrying only one bomb.'

Pete Vanderhoef flew 130 missions during the deployment, 20 per cent in support of troops under attack, 20 per cent on known VC positions with no 'friendlies' in the area, and the rest were 'toothpick' missions where, 'we dropped bombs in the dense jungle on a spot chosen by a FAC that he thought might contain a VC position. They were called "toothpick" missions because we converted large trees into tooth-picks with 750lb bombs'. Early in

the war, he was among the pilots who began to sense the way in which Washington's micro-management of the war minimized the effect of the combat effort and put airmen in unnecessary danger.

Every mission had to be personally approved by President Johnson and SecDef McNamara. By the time they sent it back to Viet Nam everybody knew what it was so the VC were either gone or ready for us. We had one mission where there was a village on a north–south road with a small river running through from east to west. We were told to hit the north-east quadrant but were explicitly told not to drop anything on the south-west quadrant because there was a meeting of a dozen VC and NVA Generals there! We did as we were told.

In its six-month TDY (extended from three months) the squadron dropped 5,665 bombs including 155 Mk 82 Snakeye retarded weapons. The *Crusaders* were among the first USAF units to use this type of bomb. Over South Vietnam, described by one pilot as 'one big gunnery range', the squadron also fired an incredible 1,597,145 rounds of 20mm high explosive/incendiary (HEI). Each shell cost US$2.45 in 1965 dollars. Of the twenty-nine pilots who originally deployed, twenty-one flew over 100 missions. They logged 1,000 hours of combat flying in their first thirty-four days of battle and 2,000 hours by 6 September, averaging thirty sorties per day.

which was located to the south of Phu Cat and also on the sandy coast. Work began in June 1966 and AM-2 temporary runways were in place for the first F-100Ds of the 308th TFS *Emerald Knights* when they arrived on 15 November. It was the first of five F-100 units to share the base under the auspices of the 31st TFW, which had previously sent some of its squadrons to Bien

Hoa on TDYs. It took up residence at Tuy Hoa from 25 December 1966, bringing its 306th and 309th squadrons to join the 308th. A fourth squadron, the 307th TFS, had returned to the USA at the end of 1965 and eventually joined the 401st TFW at Torrejon, Spain to replace one of its units that had deployed to PACAF. The re-constituted 31st Wing was established

under Col James Jabara, one of twelve Korean War aces who later commanded F-100 squadrons, until his death in a car accident whereupon Col Raymond Lee assumed command. Later additions to the Wing were the 355th TFS (moved from Phu Cat) and the much-travelled 416th TFS *Silver Knights*, both in May 1969. A pair of ANG squadrons, the 136th TFS,

Rolling out of its revetment at Bien Hoa AB, F-100D-61-NA 56-2920 has the 'CE' codes of the 510th TFS *Buzzards* and Snakeye bombs. Some of the squadron's aircraft later received nicknames, such as *Buzzard of Bien Hoa* (56-3087) flown by Capt Ronald Fogleman who later became USAF Chief of Staff. Norm Taylor via David Menard

The SUU-7 dispensed a variety of CBU-1/46 series bombs containing BLU-series sub-munitions for anti-personnel, fragmentation or smoke. The ordnance was ejected rearwards from a combination of the nineteen tubes, with springs and air pressure through the front of the dispenser providing the required force. A fully loaded SUU-7 could weigh up to 900lb (410kg). Peter Vanderhoef

New York ANG and the 188th TFS, New Mexico ANG joined the Wing from May/June 1968 on a one-year TDY.

Life on the Line

Despite every attempt to make the new bases secure, they were inevitably exposed to VC attack, most frequently during the January 1968 Tet offensive when twenty-three US and Vietnamese AF bases were hit. At that time, forty-five missiles were fired at Bien Hoa, destroying F-100D 55-3568. An F-100F (56-3923) was wrecked at the base, three others damaged in a similar raid on 17 February and two more were burned out at Phan Rang in January 1969. F-100 ECM technician Al Neubecker experienced a VC base attack at Tuy Hoa.

I was asleep when the sapper attack started but was awakened by the explosions. That morning we went to see the destruction and I saw in the revetments a lot of

615th TFS armament personnel re-arm F-100D-31-NA 56-3307 at Phu Cat AB on 7 March 1971. A detachment from the 35th TFW at Phan Rang AB was sent to Phu Cat to suppress Viet Cong activity around the base. Norm Taylor

ashes and only landing gears left. Guys told me they shot all seven sappers dead as they headed for the fuel tanks. An autopsy was done and they were all on heavy drugs.

Fuel at the coastal bases was meant to be piped in directly through lines that connected to fuel ships off shore. In practice, these pipes were frequently sabotaged. The Phu Cat pipeline was out of action most of the time and fuel had to be brought in by other means.

Personnel soon got hardened to the almost nightly rocket or mortar assaults on their bases. At Phan Rang, fuel systems mechanic Bob Macavoy quickly learned to tell the difference between the loud bang of a rocket landing and the dull thud of a mortar round, 'The "gooks" never tried to get us, they were always after our equipment so we felt somewhat secure near our tents or barracks'.

For pilots there was the constant threat of small-arms fire on take-off or final approach from a VC sniper hidden in the undergrowth near the base with a rifle or light machine gun. 1st Lt Tomkinson's 510th TFS F-100D (56-3269) was hit on approach to Bien Hoa in March 1968 and he ejected as it crashed a mile from the

base. Maj G. J. Butler of the 615th TFS took a small-arms hit as his F-100D (55-2914) climbed away from Phan Rang in June 1968, forcing him to bale out. The following month another F-100D (55-2900) was hit in the same way and the consequent loss of fuel forced the pilot to make an emergency landing in which the aircraft crashed.

On many occasions F-100 pilots took off and attacked troops or suspected gun positions within sight of their base, almost as soon as they had retracted their landing gear. On one such mission, Capt Roland Obenland was shot down while making a napalm drop on a troop concentration only 5 miles (8km) from Bien Hoa.

Aircraft on the bases were initially protected by 12ft (3.5m) high ARMCO revetments, but after the 1968 offensive most bases received 'wonder arch' shelters of corrugated steel shells with an 18in (45cm) concrete core. Over 370 were constructed by the end of 1969.

For the hundreds of maintainers tasked with keeping up the sortie rates at each F-100 base, the war could get dangerously close. Hank Valentine 'crewed' for the 352nd TFS at Phan Rang in 1967–68. On one occasion he was sitting in the cockpit

of an F-100D as it was towed to the north end of the runway, waiting to cross to the engine trim pad between the runways.

We had no radio. While sitting there, checking for aircraft landing, we looked back up the flight line and noted that the lights were out on the base. Then we started hearing pings and popping noises and we saw some tracer bullets north of us but thought nothing of it. After the Line Chief came and told us to head back we understood the reason for the noises and blackout. On return to the revetment we noticed a hole in the Coleman tow-tractor, another in the F-100's intake and one under the ejection seat that I had been sitting in.

Hank went through the eight-week F-100 maintenance course and joined the 352nd TFS.

My trainer was S/Sgt Edwards and the first day he left me alone with 'his' aircraft I found out how complicated the plane was. I forgot to check the utility reservoir and the plane ended up aborting. I learned a great deal when S/Sgt Edwards got back! Aircrews were the first priority, though we had some crews who thought the aircraft was going to fly itself. I remember one pilot who used to come out to the aircraft and climb in the cockpit without doing a walk-around check. We cured him by strapping him into an F-100 with no engine and only 'four pointed' [the rear fuselage was connected to the rest of the aircraft by four bolts while the engine was removed to be worked on]. A second groundcrew member held the starter APU [auxiliary power unit] hose underneath the aircraft. When the pilot didn't get any rpms he was a little uptight and reported us to the commander. Needless to say, he started doing walk-arounds after that. The F-100 was a plane that a crew chief could ground very easily. If a pilot got too cocky we would crack one of the hydraulic 'B' nuts in the wheel well [aborting the mission]. Fortunately, we didn't have to pull these nasty pranks very often.

Dave Menard recounted the tale of a maintainer who was a:

... sort of 'hippy GI' who wore his squadron patch on the top of his fatigue hat instead of on his shirt. One day, a pilot was pre-flighting a Hun when he noticed a puddle of oil in the afterburner tailpipe. The Number 6.5 bearing was known to leak on this aircraft so the pilot asked the GI where the oil was from. He stuck his finger into the puddle, tasted it and yelled, 'Texas!' Boy, did he get a reaming for that, but it rolled right off him.

Pilot Thad Crooks with his napalm and M117-armed F-100D-56-NH 55-2914 of the 615th TFS at Phan Rang AB. On 18 June 1968, this aircraft was hit by small-arms fire, seconds after it was airborne from Phan Rang, caught fire and crashed. Its pilot, Maj G. J. Butler ejected 10 miles from the base. Joe Vincent Collection

Guns, Bombs and Gas

Among the busiest people on a wartime F-100 base were the armourers, feeding up to 200 rounds of yellow-banded HEP 20mm shells into each of the four magazines for an F-100D's M-39E guns. As Richard Such of the 431st Munitions Squadron put it:

Our F-100s really liked to strafe. I noticed a lot of them that were shot up pretty badly but they still made it in OK and went out again as soon as they were repaired. They weren't the fastest planes around but they did what they were supposed to do; they delivered the goods right on target. The 20mm was sent to us in metal ammo cans. We received delivery from the Army and from huge amphibious vehicles called LARKs that also delivered our napalm. Our Munitions Squadron was asked to attend Commander's Call every month. The pilots showed movies of their attacks and I was quite impressed with the accuracy of their strafing and bombing runs.

We had a great base at Tuy Hoa except in the evening when we got shelled. It seemed like we got hit every night but I never knew of anyone getting hurt. We lived in metal buildings and when a mortar round went off it felt like you were in a tin can. There were hobby shops, a movie theatre, a church and all kinds of sports facilities and the sea was like bath water. The heat was so intense, averaging 155°F on the flight line where the F-100s were. Your boots would literally melt walking on the PSP surfaces. The 20mm group worked their butts off and I'm glad we put in so many hours as the time went by much faster. The bomb crews didn't work half the hours that we did but they had free time to think about home. I couldn't have handled that.

The same armourers' workload was significantly increased by their additional work arming the four GAU-2B/A guns in the hard-worked 71st SOS AC-119G 'Shadow' gunships at the base, each of which took 50,000 rounds on a daylight sortie.

One of the gunners on the jet-assisted AC-119K variant was Everett Sprous who had previously done a tour at Bien Hoa in 1968–69 on an F-100 weapons crew.

I was an MJ-1 'jammer' driver. The MJ-1 held the bomb in a cradle and a good driver could line up the bomb so perfectly that it went right up to the F-100's pylon and clicked into the bomb hooks. Most of the time we were never rushed to load the planes. We had four-man weapons crews and were assigned five aircraft during a twelve-hour shift. Once the planes were gone over by maintenance we would do our thing. The armament electronics had to be checked first to make sure all the systems were functional. We 'prepped' and loaded the cannons, then we loaded the bombs. The 'jammer' was a very stable vehicle, but it could slide on wet pavement if you drove too fast and hit the brakes. We didn't use them to load external fuel tanks. Bomb preparation and loading was as safe as the crews doing the work. The fuses were installed before the bombs were loaded, with nose and tail fuses on almost all bombs. The tail-fuse ensured detonation if the nose failed. A wire ran from the nose-fuse fins to the back of the bomb. When the pilot dropped an armed bomb this wire would pull out of the fuses and stay on the aircraft's pylon, allowing the fuses to arm. If a bomb had to be dropped 'safe' for some reason the bomb would release with the wire attached and it would not detonate.

Once, when loading napalm the bomb dump sent us some outdated WP (white phosphorous igniter). This came in sealed cans that you opened with a key like a can of meat. I opened

An F-100D-51-NH at Tuy Hoa AB with the 31st TFW before the application of tail codes. Joe Vincent

one and it started smoking. We had cans of water always available so I dropped the thing in and called out to the ordnance squad. A guy picked the WP out of the water and said, 'There's nothing wrong with this', as it started smoking again. They didn't doubt our calls after that. On another occasion a maintainer was backing a vehicle and hit a bomb square on the nose. My crew was about fifty feet away and we hit the ground, for all the good that would have done. The bomb flew off its stand and fell on the ground but luckily it wasn't fused. Ordnance dropped this way was a rare event but rather worrying, particularly where CBU was concerned as it was thought to be unstable.

An incident that stuck in Everett's memory involved a scramble by two Bien Hoa alert pad F-100s.

The first F-100 took off but the second got up to take-off speed and didn't leave the ground. The pilot deployed the drag chute with little effect. Next, he dropped his tail hook as he went past

Richard G. Such and his colleague Geno Randolph (seen here in July 1969) filled endless F-100 ammunition cans with yellow-banded 20mm HEI in this 431st MMS building at Tuy Hoa AB. Richard Such

The 416th TFS was allotted 'HE' tail codes as seen in slightly asymmetric format on F-100D-26-NA 55-3620. It also carries a large 'Nite Owl' zap on its nose, a souvenir of a visit to Ubon RTAFB in September 1968. In the background is a 'BE' coded 390th TFS F-4D from the 366th TFW. Al Piccirillo via David Menard

Here, 20mm ammunition cans are being refilled in a Phu Cat AB revetment for VZ-coded F-100D 56-3307. By March 1971 many F-100Ds had the nose-mounted RHAW blister. Norm Taylor

us at about 100mph with only about a hundred feet of runway beyond where we were standing. The hook grabbed the chain arresting gear, dragging each 100lb link out to its limit. The last stopping device was a net barrier across the very end of the runway and that came apart like nothing, but the F-100 stopped anyway. Being the kind of people we were we went running to the aid of the pilot, instead of running for cover since the plane was loaded with napalm. The tyres were smoking and most of the rubber was gone. Apparently, a maintainer had 'lost' a screwdriver that had jammed the aircraft's control column, preventing take-off.

In addition to the ceaseless flow of weaponry (just one squadron, the 120th TFS, dropped 14.3 million pounds of bombs, 5.6 million pounds of napalm, 423,000 rockets, 227,000lb (103,000kg) of CBU and 1.8 million 20mm rounds in a one-year deployment) the F-100 force needed enormous quantities of JP-4 fuel. Managing the aircrafts' fuel systems was the job of specialists like Bob Macavoy

who was at Phan Rang in 1967–68.

Our fuel systems shop was segregated due to the hazardous nature of our work. Our repair pad was covered by AM-2 and when an aircraft was on the pad for repair the area was roped off and no one ever entered the area without our permission. We had two men dedicated to the repair of drop tanks, which were constantly shot up, leaking or had bad filler valves. I worked the midnight to noon shift six days a week. I spent most of my time with an impact screwdriver and hammer, pounding on the upper-surface wing screws, which were notorious for leaking. Alert aircraft were kept filled with fuel and when the sun was high the fuel expanded and leaked out around the screw heads. Sitting on the hot metal skin of an F-100 in 100+ degrees temperature, swinging a three-pound hammer, metal to metal, was not much fun.

The fuel system components on the F-100 were better than most of the aircraft I worked on and there wasn't much trouble-shooting to do. Drop tanks were the biggest pain, followed by the inaccessible wing fuel pump and the main

fuel cell. It was kind of spooky to descend into the air intake to disconnect the supports for this cell. Most of the components such as filler valves, dump valves and probes had long service lives and rarely failed but it seemed that we replaced the forward lower fuel cell most often because it took the brunt of VC bullets. Almost all my 'souvenir' bullets were removed from that section. The lower aft fuel section caused the biggest pain for crew chiefs because for us to replace it they had to remove the tail section, which they hated to do.

Check Engine, Brakes and Tyres

Jay McCarthy was an F-100 crew chief at Tuy Hoa from October 1968. He explained the complexities of rear fuselage removal to tackle engine repairs. It was a characteristic the F-100 inherited from the F-86 Sabre and shared with aircraft like the F-84 and F-105.

F-100A-15-NA 53-1572, used by AFFTC/ARDC.
Peter Schinkelshoek Collection

RIGHT: Flying for the 31st FBW team at the October 1958 Fighter Weapons Meet at Nellis AFB was F-100D-30-NA 55-3722. It carries a Mk 7 *Blue Boy* nuclear shape and a counterbalancing fuel tank on the opposite wing. Practice bombs are hung on its centreline pylon. The *Blue Boy*'s lower fin extended when the weapon was released. Col A. H. Johnson

BELOW LEFT: F-100C-25-NA 54-2076 representing the 435th FBS, 479th FBW at a Fighter Weapons Meet. USAF

BELOW RIGHT: Col Art Johnson took this photo of wingman Capt Walt Bruce's F-100D from his own (FW-146), en route to the Nellis AAFB Meet in 1958. Col A. H. Johnson

A pair of 333rd FDS F-100Fs led by a 336th FDS F-100C, all from the 4th FDW, which flew F-100s from 1957 to 1960. Col D. Elmer via David Menard

F-100F-15-NA 56-3923 in 306th TFS colours with its own version of 'The Firepower Team' marking on its tail. The two-digit number system was unrelated to serial numbers. F. Street via David Menard

Huns from the 474th TFW, displaying the markings of the 478th TFS (F-100D-60-NA 56-2934) and 429th TFS (F-100F-10-NA 56-3911). T. J. Cress via David Menard

ABOVE: **F-100D-50-NH 55-2900 of the 31st TFW refuelling from a KB-50 in February 1961. It has the post-1960 standard TAC markings without distinctive unit markings, but on a bare metal finish.**
T. B. Barnes via David Menard

LEFT: **The 506th FBW flew F-100Ds from 1957 to 1959 and its 457th FBS used the red markings shown on 56-3066.** Lt Col D. Nichols via David Menard

BELOW LEFT: **Thunderbird 3.** Peter Schinkelshoek Collection

BELOW: **With 450-gallon tanks aboard, a 474th TFW F-100F gets some attention from the technicians.**
T. J. Cress via David Menard

Complete with a personal shamrock crew panel, this F-100D-1-NA (54-2130) was aiming for good luck as a Fighter Meet contender. F. Street via David Menard

Early F-100D deliveries to the 18th TFW lacked wing fences, including 55-2837. This aircraft became an early casualty of the Vietnam war when it crashed during a night napalm attack on 31 July 1965 with the loss of its pilot, 1 Lt Don Watson. F. Street via David Menard

The 458th FBS's yellow version of the 506th FBW scheme makes an eye-catching addition to F-100D-45-NH 55-2849. Lt Col D. Nichols via David Menard

ABOVE: At Kadena AB, Okinawa the 18th TFW's 12th TFS flew F-100s from 1957, including F-100F-15-NA 56-4002. F. Street via David Menard

RIGHT: A gleaming 77th TFS F-100D-25-NA (55-3664) piloted by Dale Hughes in July 1961. Col Tom Germscheid

F-100D-46-NH 55-2798 of the 492nd TFS, 48th TFW makes an interesting modelling possibility with its weathered camouflage. Peter Schinkelshoek Collection

F-100D-51-NH 55-2901 *Colleen*, armed and ready to launch with a load of finned napalm. Joe Vincent

Don Schmenk's F-100D-21-NA 55-3580 *Mary Jane/Carol Ann* in a 308th TFS revetment with four 'napes' on its wing pylons. Joe Vincent

ABOVE LEFT: With 180 mission markers covering its nose, this 307th TFS F-100D is armed ready for another CAS sortie from Bien Hoa AB. In six months during 1965 the unit flew 3,502 combat missions without loss. USAF via David Menard

ABOVE: Dale Hughes edges F-100D 55-3652 closer to Tom Germscheid's camera for this August 1961 portrait. Col Tom Germscheid

LEFT: F-100D 56-3264 has the unique purple squadron décor of the 510th TFS, 405th FW, seen here at Clark AB in 1961. USAF via David Menard

ABOVE: A pair of 614th TFS F-100Ds returns to Phan Rang AB from an August 1970 combat mission. Unusually, the nearer F-100D-31-NA carries a triple ejection rack (TER). Sgt P. Seel, USAF via David Menard

LEFT: A 'shotgun' (cartridge) start for a 308th TFS *Emerald Knights* F-100D-86-NA 56-3456 in its revetment at Tuy Hoa AB. Using 'Litter' callsigns, the unit deployed to the base in November 1966 from Bien Hoa AB, remaining at Tuy Hoa until October 1970. T. B. Barnes via David Menard

LEFT: F-100C-2-NA 53-1725 soaks up the Turkish sun as its pilot prepares to taxi out. It has the 'bent' refuelling probe, arresting hook and other *High Wire* updates. Soner Capoglu

BELOW LEFT: F-100D-11-NA 54-2204 in the 1976 markings of EC.2/11 at Toul Rosieres. This aircraft was moved to RAF Woodbridge BDRF after retirement. Author's Collection

BELOW: F-100A-20-NA 53-1697 with others from the RoCAF's 23rd Squadron at Chiayi AB. Clarence Fu

G-782 (F-100D-40-NH 55-2782) spent time with the 405th FBW and 31st TFW before joining Esk. 730 in Denmark in August 1961. It remained with this squadron for most of its Danish career before a further transfer to the Turkish Air Force in 1981, where it completed its thirty years of military service in May 1986. David Menard Collection

Groundcrew at Phan Rang AB check a 'cart start' on 'VZ 923' of the 615th TFS. Cartridge burnout time was 18–20 seconds and only two such attempts could be made within a 60-minute period. Joe Vincent Collection

It would come as no surprise to any of us when arriving to begin our shift to find one or more birds with their ass-ends removed for any number of reasons. The ones that galled me most were those incidents when an over-zealous pilot would hard-land his F-100 and push the tail skid through the aspirator in the tail-pipe. Automatic engine change! That meant aft section removal and a case of beer for the crew chief of the plane from the pilot for causing the damage. So while the crew chief (the guy who got all the day-shift glory, very little maintenance, all the take-off and landing work and his name painted on the canopy below the pilot's) is throwing down the Budweisers back in the hooch, we night owls fix his plane! Taking off the aft section took a few guys and it involved unbolting the fuselage at four points. We had to remove or uncouple hydraulic lines, electric cables [via quick-disconnect cannon plugs] and other assorted wires. Then the engine hoist would be bolted on to the top of the fuselage near the separation point and it would be adjusted to lift or lower the engine when the aft fuselage was removed. Then the engine was worked on.

The aft section was then lowered on to a specially designed trolley fitted with hydraulic jacks to ensure clean separation from the forward fuselage.

Any engine change required the jet to be taken to the trim pad for initial testing after the engine was re-installed. Initial engine run-up was undertaken with the aft end still off the plane in case the engine didn't check out at that stage. If all went well the F-100 would be towed back to the revetment area and the aft section would be re-installed by the same bunch of 'grunts' who removed it. This time the labour was a little more problematic and took longer. Then the aircraft would go back to the trim pad for a final check. We kept our fingers crossed because if it didn't check out – off came the rear section again. We got pretty good at this game to the extent that each of us became a specialist on an area of the aft section. Mine was the right, upper panels.

John Clarity:

... pulling the aft section was fairly straightforward and almost fun because it was impressive to break the plane in two and because it meant working with a group of chums on a light-hearted, predictable job. It could be a laugh. Engine oil leaks could sometimes be stopped by 'chugging' the engine through compressor stalls which might re-seat the bearing seals.

Engine maintenance occasionally involved dealing with afterburner nozzles that didn't open far enough for an effective 'light up'. This caused a regular post-flight check item known as 'keying the eyelids'. Jay McCarthy:

This was done in the fuel pits after the pilot taxied in. Prior to engine shut down we'd pop off a small panel that was part of the huge belly panel beneath the plane and we had to reach up and locate a 'key', several inches long, in the engine bay. Turning this key opened the afterburner eyelids and we did this a few times to ensure proper operation and also after an engine change on the trim pad. With the engine set at 100 per cent military thrust the eyelids would be keyed and what a noise it would make! You could hear the thrust differential both before and after 'keying' and it was always done just seconds before the engine technician hit afterburner.

The large belly panel (panel 48) was attached to the tail-hook mount. 'Installing it', Hank Valentine recalled, 'required what seemed like a thousand screws and it was a pain'. It was also an area where the 'fixers' had to deal with leaks from the aircraft's systems. John Clarity:

The more the aircraft sat idle the worse the insidious leaks became. If you flew the machine every day you would experience fewer of these problems. They appeared near the main belly panel around the gang drain where fluid drains from various systems were grouped for exit from the aircraft. Usually the leaks would stop while the engine was running and seep slowly while it was parked. However, if a leak continued in flight it would develop an ugly series of grey streaks along the underside of the aircraft, which was as about as attractive as a four-year old with a snotty nose. This staining required the crew chief to chase the evidence constantly from the underside of the F-100 with his handy rag and JP-4, a very available solvent on the line. We were quick to call the plane out of service if there was a potential mechanical problem, but prior to this a crew chief would struggle to keep his ship as tidy as possible as a matter of pride.

Apart from attention to its hydraulic systems, maintainers generally found the F-100's brakes and tyres the most persistent cause of furrowed brows. According to Hank Valentine: 'Sometimes you would wonder if the brakes would ever cool enough to handle. They were made of magnesium and felt as if they would ignite if used heavily'. Richard Newell, a crew chief with the 113th TFW ANG, found himself working at Phu Cat on 355th TFS aircraft from July 1968:

... we landed at 3pm, were shown to our barracks and reported for work at 6am the next day. Our activated Guard troops (who had operated F-

A napalm-armed 308th TFS F-100D leaves its revetment at Tuy Hoa AB. 56-3287 crashed on 30 June 1970 after its pilot lost control during a CAS mission and ejected. David Menard Collection

100C/F models with the 121st TFS or 119th TFS) had never been used to the F-100D. It didn't take long for them to figure out the differences: more accumulators, different main landing gear doors, flaps and cockpit, but the aircraft were in pretty bad shape when we got there.

A tyre change was a bear to do on an F-100 as you had to disassemble the anti-skid and take off the brake to get to the tyre. The brake had to be one degree off centre when you re-assembled it and if it wasn't quite right it wouldn't go back together. Many a crew chief cursed the brakes and tyres on the F-100!

John Clarity:

Tyre changes could take a fast mechanic twenty-five minutes but many mere mortals would struggle for almost two hours. The brake required removal and the brake hoses and wiring had to be threaded though the axle. Changing a Boeing 747 tyre was easy when stacked up to an F-100!

Tyre changes in Vietnam were more common because of the frequency of flights; two missions a day for most aircraft. Jay McCarthy:

... changing an F-100 tyre became an art form and one guy could do it with no problem. All you needed was an axle jack to get the tyre off the ground. The toughest part was removing the

brake assembly, which was quite heavy. But we had fun and contests to see who could complete a change in the shortest time. Anything to pass the time!

Nose-gear tyre changes were rare. The main gear tyres had a series of dimples throughout their surface, indented into the rubber about a quarter-inch. When the tyre wore down so the dimple was gone it was close to tyre-changing time. As they really started to wear, red fabric threading would appear in the worn areas. At times, especially at night, you could colour the red fabric over with a black crayon and maybe the pilot would get fooled on his walk-around. This fake-out could get another couple of landings out of the plane but it could also get you a ton of trouble if discovered. I heard that stateside F-100s had main-gear tyre changes after a set number of landings, but not in 'Nam.

No doubt the crew who named 355th TFS F-100D 55-3749 *Blood, Sweat and Tires* did so with feeling! On arrival in Vietnam, Jay was assigned to the night maintenance shift for the 306th TFS, coded 'SD'.

We were picked up at our hooches every night at about 1745 to begin a shift that would take us to 0600 the following morning. Twelve hours on, twelve off, six days a week. Nights on the flight line were normally hot, steamy and often in monsoon conditions. Turning an F-100 around was a breeze. When I first got to Tuy Hoa

I spent about a week on the day shift. After a mission the pilots would taxi their planes directly to the fuel pits; huge JP-4-filled bladders. Having single-point refuelling made the refuelling effort easy. All you had to do was hook up the nozzle and let the fuel flow. The drop tanks had to be topped off by hand.

A post-flight inspection was pretty much the same as a pre-flight and depending on the extent to which the pilot found problems with the plane you'd put her back to bed in the revetments. For maintenance-related engine starts we weren't allowed to use the starter cartridges but were forced to use the 'Ma Deuce' [MA-2 APU]. Engine run-up checks were conducted on a normal basis by the crew chief and pilot and would consist of a series of hand-signals to check nose-wheel steering, landing lights, brakes, flaps, speed-brake, flight controls etc.

Whenever I could I volunteered for Alert duty. Two F-100s were normally 'cocked and hot' in their revetments so that when the Alert horn sounded, all the pilot had to do was jump in the cockpit, start the engine, taxi and take off. They were fully loaded with 'hot' [armed] ordnance. Armed Air Police guarded those planes. Alert status relieved you from the steady, knuckle-busting work done night after night and afforded the opportunity to stay in the air-conditioned Alert shack, pilots on one side and crew chiefs on the other. At midnight a cook came to make us breakfast. There was no doubt that the Alert horn would sound: it was just a question of 'when'.

For Dick Newell, at Phu Cat with the 'HP'-coded 355th TFS, the day usually began with a check on the mission and the name of the pilot.

This was always nice to know as with some pilots you could always guarantee they would find something to 'write up' about your aircraft. You would spend hours trying to find the problem and it ended up being 'between the headset'. But as crew chief you could never say the pilot was wrong! You had to check it out until there was no doubt in your mind that the aircraft was safe for flight.

Next you would check the fuel load required for the mission and the weapons to be loaded. Most of all you would check your take-off times and how many times you would have to turn the aircraft around during the sortie period. Before you could start your pre-flight (PR) you had to get your tool kit, 'intake suit' and tyre gauge, also a cloth to clean the canopy and some cleaner to go with it. Rags were also needed to wipe down the aircraft before flight. The Basic Post-Flight (BPO) and PR were normally completed

A red fin-tip and crew name panel plus 'CP' codes identify this as 531st TFS *Ramrods* F-100D 55-2881, which was assigned to Oleg Kormarnitsky in 1970. David Menard Collection

together. There was servicing to do along with the inspection including oxygen, tyres, accumulators, etc. If there was nothing that needed repair you could expect to spend two hours or more getting the aircraft ready for flight.

Then we had the pilot's walk-around, strapping him in and starting up. The crew chief checked flight controls and take-off trim, looked for leaks and made sure all panels were secure. Before taxi the pilot showed his pins to indicate that the seat and canopy were armed. Then it was off to the 'last chance' inspection at the end of the runway to check again for leaks, loose panels and cuts in the tyres before take-off.

Jack Engler's F-100D (55-3806) gave him little trouble as its crew chief.

This airplane flew two or three combat sorties per day while it had my name under the windscreen. The only time it missed two days was when it was in the paint hangar getting a new camouflage coat. It was unusual for an F-100 to

fly so many 'write-up free' times. Some minor discrepancies came up but the 'gigs' were fixed during post-flight inspection. She was fuelled, loaded with ordnance, cocked and ready for another mission.

One of the items on the pre-flight list for pilots was a thorough check of the wing slats. Maj Dick Garrett:

Those aerodynamically-retracted slats had a nasty habit of developing sticky rollers, causing one wing to have an extended slat and the other wing to have the slat retracted. This usually happened at slow airspeed (or high g's) and high angle of attack and the Hun would snap roll in the direction of the retracted slat.

Battle Dress

One of the more obvious signs of the F-100's assumption of a war role was the adoption

of T. O. 1-1-4 South East Asia camouflage from late 1965 onwards. Some of the first camouflaged aircraft were for the 510th TFS. They arrived at Bien Hoa in early November 1965 and absorbed that unit's silver-finished F-100s as well. Super Sabres had entered battle in the overall silver acrylic lacquer that replaced the bare metal scheme of early F-100A/Cs. The silver scheme was similar to the finish applied to TAC's F-105 fleet in 1962 under Project *Look Alike*. It was mixed from a gallon of clear lacquer to a gallon of thinner and twelve ounces of aluminium paste. The intention was to seal the aircraft's seams, preventing moisture from seeping into electronics or causing corrosion. 'Vietnam camouflage' used two shades of matt green (FS34079 and FS34102) with tan (FS30219) in an upper-surface pattern and light grey (FS36622) on the undersides. Small black serials were carried on the vertical stabilizer as the only distinguishing feature, but from 1967 two-letter codes identified each Wing by a common first letter and a second letter to denote the squadron (for example, 'CE' for the 510th TFS of the 3rd TFW). 12in (30cm) digits showed the 'last three' of the serial.

Many PACAF F-100s also acquired new nicknames on their noses, restoring a little of the colour that was lost with the removal of the original squadron schemes under the TAC regulation 66-12 in 1960 and in USAFE with the introduction of camouflage. At Lakenheath, where the last silver F-100D (55-2807) was camouflaged in March 1968, John Clarity felt that the warpaint was a retrograde step aesthetically:

> When I acquired 'my' aircraft (55-2834) she was metallic with the squadron emblems front and back; a real eyeful. She was pretty flashy. Later they camouflaged her and she lost much of her grandeur. She looked like a piece of GI issue, all business and about as attractive as a jeep.

The prevalent view of nicknames and nose-art varied according to the tastes of the wing commander and 7th AF politics on the subject. Many names had quite complex origins. For example, Jack Engler's *Rotunda Sneaker* derived from a slightly over-weight, sneaker-wearing go-go dancer in a New York club. 'The name bounced around inside my head and somehow got stencilled on the starboard side of the nose of 55-3806. On the port side appeared *Dee's Delight*, derived from the wife of the pilot, Maj 'Kas' Kastilan, but this was replaced by a repeat of *Rotunda Sneaker* after the Kastilans separated during his tour of duty.

Nose-art in Vietnam was actually made possible initially because squadrons on TDY had a degree of self-management denied to them while they were under Wing-based control in the USA. While USAF policy forbade individual markings under this system, once a squadron had aircraft specifically assigned to it for a TDY those aircraft and personnel came under the control of the squadron commander.

One of the first F-100 units to deploy to South Asia was the 481st TFS whose commander, Lt Col 'Hal' Comstock, elected to decorate his F-100 with his wartime kills and skull nose-art. On arrival at Tan Son Nhut in June 1965 he assigned each of his eighteen F-100s to individual pilots (with some of the thirty pilots sharing a Hun) and designed a green triangular marking

The pilot and crew chief of 56-3379 of the 352nd TFS on 10 March 1971 during a brief deployment to Phu Cat AB. Ginny Lee, the crew chief's young lady, could only be honoured in this covert manner within the Wing's 'artwork rules' at the time, exiling personal decoration to wheel wells, panel interiors and other 'invisible' locations.
Norm Taylor

for the aircrafts' tails. Capt 'Chad' Dvorchak then got 1st Lt Jim Kempton to paint *The Shadow* on his F-100's nose, prompting Kempton to name his own aircraft *Lickity Split*. 1st Lt Peter Vanderhoef helped Jim Kempton with the artwork and then named the aircraft he shared with 1st Lt Gerald Salome *Pretty Penny* (after Salome's wife). The two pilots extended their art gallery to other squadron F-100s including *Why Not?*, *The Mormon Meteor*, *The Back Forty*, *Mr. Magoo*, *Hot Stuff*, *Casanova*, *Snoopy*, *My Little Margie* and others. Several other Vietnam-based F-100 units continued the tradition.

Big Guns

While the new paint-scheme was perhaps an aesthetic disappointment in Europe it ideally suited the 'mud moving' role that F-100s were required to perform in Vietnam. Of the 360,283 combat sorties flown by Huns (more than any other type and more than the type's illustrious ancestor, the P-51 in WWII) the majority were very similar 'taxi rank' missions in support of ground troops in South Vietnam or Laos. Pilots were usually guided to their targets

by airborne forward air controllers (FAC-A), often to drive back enemy attacks on troops in contact (TIC).

An FAC would mark the intended target with a smoke rocket and guide in a pair of F-100s for bomb, napalm or CBU passes, possibly requesting only one item of ordnance on each pass so that aiming corrections could be made. Strafing passes were then customarily called in, with the FAC reporting results. Assuming that no damage was sustained by the fighters, the missions would then conclude with a fairly short homeward flight and a debriefing. The return journey occasionally provided the opportunity for a little variety, as Maj Dick Garrett remembered:

> One of the older heads (actually a new major) attached to the 416th TFS took me under his wing and liked to use left-over fuel at the end of a strike mission to teach me some of the Thunderbirds manoeuvres out over the South China Sea. He was a fellow by the name of Tony McPeak [formerly a Thunderbirds solo demonstration pilot and later USAF Chief of Staff].

Similar missions were flown by numerous USMC and USAF F-4 Phantoms but they were considerably outnumbered by the

F-100D-31-NA 55-3806 of the 90th TFS, 3rd TFW ('CB' codes) in 1969, named *Rotunda Sneaker*. On the nose door is a squadron *Pair o' Dice* emblem. Jack Engler

regular airborne artillery provided by the F-100 force. Although the missions were generally over the less well-defended Route Packs they were far from safe. Of the 242 Huns lost, 189 were shot down over South Vietnam or Laos. Of these, 116 went down during 1968–69, the 'bombing pause' years over North Vietnam.

Joe Vincent flew 280 combat sorties with the 309th TFS from October 1969 at Tuy Hoa. The coastal base had its own inherent problems due to a continuous 25kt crosswind over the runway, sometimes from the north-west but veering to the opposite direction.

We had nine or ten Huns run off the side of the runway or get a 'wingtip' on landing. One [1st Lt Roger Disrud's 'SD 392' *Turtle Mountain Express*] had the nose completely torn off when it ran off the runway immediately after touchdown and dug into the sand. Another ['SP 782' flown by Captain Coleman of the 355th TFS] was blown sideways off the runway as he flared for touch-down. He went round again only to get behind the power curve and into the classic 'Sabre dance', but pan-caked in on its belly.

Pretty Penny **was shared by 1st Lt Jerry Salome (left), husband of the real Penny, and Pete Vanderhoef, seen here with their crew chief. Sharing a plane was quite usual for junior officers. Pete recalled doing the artwork with some 'black spray paint, 3in masking tape and a 2in pocket knife to cut the outlines'. This Hun survived until 21 May 1967 when it was hit during a fifth napalm pass on a 531st TFS mission near Bien Hoa AB.** Peter Vanderhoef

Another example of artwork by Pete Vanderhoef (left) was the leprechaun painted on an F-100D flown by Capt Paul Cohagan, the 481st TFS Maintenance Officer. Peter Vanderhoef

Lt Col Harold Comstock fires 2.75in FFARs at a target in the Mekong Delta. This aircraft, 55-3603, was lost in a strafing attack on 6 November 1966 after passing to the 416th TFS at Bien Hoa AB. USAF via Peter Vanderhoef

'Hal' Comstock's 55-3603 with the skull nose art and seven Luftwaffe kills, as displayed on his P-47D during WWII, plus 117 Vietnam war mission marks. Pete Vanderhoef painted the skull and groundcrew added the iron crosses on this former Thunderbirds F-100D. Peter Vanderhoef

Joe watched the Hun 'dancing' down Runway 3L for 4,000ft (1,220m) 'with his afterburner blowing a plume of sand high in the air. It was slaloming back and forth like an Everglades water skier'. Capt Don Coleman was lucky in that his tail-hook lodged in a hole in the PSP matting and dragged the aircraft down on to the ground before it could crash into the sea. 'He squeezed the control stick so hard that he depressed the trigger and got gun-camera film of the last 150ft of the slide.' Joe and other pilots watched the wild ride on film later, noticing the F-100's pitot boom 'flopping about like a wet noodle'.

Although both pilots and their aircraft were recovered, the 'Sabre dance' was a hazard associated with the F-100's sensitivity to control inputs at low airspeed that was by no means confined to less experienced pilots and it occurred from the earliest stages of F-100 flying. Lee Howard witnessed one 'classic Sabre dance' from a

Pete Vanderhoef's 'own' F-100D-91-NA 56-3285 *Pretty Penny*, armed with a pair of Bullpup missiles.
Peter Vanderhoef

distance of 200–300ft (60–90m) while in training at Luke AFB that resulted in the death of an Instructor Pilot (IP) with 5,000 hours experience. The phenomenon could be accidentally induced by over-rotation on take-off causing a stall, or by inadequate power on final approach resulting in an inability to accelerate without losing height. In either case, the aircraft's angle of attack suddenly increased and it oscillated from side to side in a macabre, balletic motion before stalling and crashing. At least two other losses were attributed to pilot error on landing: F-100D 56-3377 at Tuy Hoa and 56-3283 at Bien Hoa, killing the pilot. Experienced pilots could be caught out by the aircraft's challenging low-speed handling, perhaps at the end of an exhausting mission. Capt James V. Dawson was returning from a morning strike on 16 July 1969 and executed a 'go around' at Tuy Hoa while his wingman landed first. All was well as he began his turn into final approach with landing gear down but he

had to increase his bank to a steep angle to avoid overshooting the runway. The mobile control officers advised him to 'take it around again' as they watched heavy exhaust smoke appear from his aircraft, indicating a sharp power advance. At the same time the aircraft's right wing dropped as the aircraft stalled, the canopy was jettisoned and the F-100 plunged into the sea a mile off the end of the runway before Dawson could eject.

Weather was a factor in some accidents and consequently in shaping tactics for pilots like Joe Vincent:

We flew almost exclusively two-ship missions during my tour. That was due to a terrible accident recovering a four-ship during a heavy rainstorm and a weather divert. The 'fix' was to fly two 2-ships to targets, ten minutes or so apart. That evolved into sending just two-ships.

The accident cost the lives of two New Mexico ANG F-100C pilots, Maj Bobby

Neeld and Capt Mitchell Lane, who probably collided when diverted from Tuy Hoa to Camh Ranh Bay on 4 January 1969.

In Maj Dick Garrett's estimation, the best missions were from the alert pad in support of troops in contact. These were very often with a 'soft' load of 'snake and nape' (Snakeye MK 82 SE and napalm).

Usually some of our grunts were calling for CAS because they were taking fire, so the task was to get a good ID on the bad guys' position, separate the good from the bad and roll in with your 'shake 'n bake' ordnance combo with as many passes as fuel and ordnance would support. I've seen times when helicopter FAC would fly right over the enemy position, getting the sh*t shot out of himself, just to drop a smoke grenade on their craniums so that we could have a good 'mark'. The O-2 and O-1 Bird Dog FACs were no less resourceful and daring when it came to a TIC situation. I'd use every drop of gas I had to stay on station as long as I could in order to help these guys out, then divert to the nearest US airfield. The opportunity didn't present itself often, but when it did you knew that your plane ticket over to 'Nam had just paid for itself.

Inevitably, the nature of the war meant that many of the targets were imprecise 'suspected' arms dumps, supply concentrations or vehicle parks and the real results of F-100 strikes were often impossible to confirm on the ground. In many cases the main damage may well have been to trees (F-100D 55-3681 received the ironic nickname *Tree Surgeon*) but for pilots the aim was professionalism in delivering their ordnance exactly where required.

After his tour with USAFE, Don Schmenk joined the 308th TFS *Emerald Knights*, usually flying 55-3580 named *Mary Jane* (after his wife) on one side and *Carol Anne* on the other. He flew 215 missions without taking a single hit from the opposition, though there were some near misses. On one mission over Laos, Don was giving another pilot a Flight Lead check:

After we came off the target the FAC asked if we had time to check out a truck that he had spotted. Now, we were told that any truck that you found in the clear in daylight was probably put there to sucker you into a trap. I didn't say anything as the Flight Lead accepted the request. On his first pass, sure enough a quad 50 AAA site opened up on him. I looked back to where I thought the gun would be, and there it was. The truck was indeed a trap and we used the rest of our ammunition on the gun.

On another mission over Laos we arrived over the target, a barge that was anchored in the Mekong at a bend in the river. As we arrived another flight of F-100s were still on the target so we went into an orbit to allow them to finish. I noticed what appeared to be puffy clouds in the area. After the FAC briefed us I asked him for the altitude of the clouds that I had observed. He replied, 'Do you mean the flak bursts?' I was so flustered that I forgot to arm the proper switches and the bomb didn't release on my first pass. I saw the gunfire on that pass: streaks of white coming up from the gun, going right past the canopy. This didn't make the second pass any easier and I saw the white streaks again. I learned that several days later another F-100 was shot down in the area. The pilot described the tactics that he had used and it was exactly what I had done. You might say that the gunners went to school on me.

Guns could be hidden in the most inaccessible places. On an August 1966 mission, four 612th TFS F-100Ds from Phan Rang were directed by a FAC to hit a position in a tree-line near a Vietnamese village. As the first two Huns dived to lay CBU-2A in the trees they came under heavy fire from the village into which the VC had retreated when they sighted the fighters. While the second element of F-100s dropped 750lb napalm canisters on the position, the FAC asked permission to strike the village and in particular a solidly built church from which most of the AAA was seen to rise. Despite continued failure to get permission from the local Province Chief to attack this unusual AAA emplacement, the FAC reluctantly cleared the Huns for strafing passes that finally silenced the gunners. Don Schmenk explained that in these relatively low-risk areas:

... tactics were at the discretion of the Flight Lead, depending on the threat. We could do pretty much what we wanted, based on the situation at the target, most of which were 'suspected enemy locations'. To spread out the impact we made multiple passes. 'Out of country', which in our case was usually Laos, we usually limited ourselves to two passes and only strafed if there were troops in contact. 'In country' (South Vietnam) we used 30-degree dive bomb passes; 'out country' we used 45-degree dives. Most of us considered Cambodia the same as Vietnam for tactics.

Cambodian Incursion

On one of the earliest missions into Cambodia, attacking an ammunition dump, Don discovered that the defences were unexpectedly formidable:

The FAC told us that there were no bad guys in the area so we flew pretty much a 'gunnery pattern', dropping a bomb at a time and making several passes with the guns. On this particular day my aircraft was carrying an aft-looking camera, the sort that took movie pictures of where you had been. It was the only time I carried such a camera. Several days later when the film was being put on to my personal roll of film the technician stopped me and asked me what were those streaks that he kept seeing on the film. I looked at it and could see nothing so he sent the film over to Intelligence. They returned it later and said the streaks were B-40 rockets, one of which passed between the trailing edge of my wing and the leading edge of the horizontal stabilizer, a distance of about 8ft. They also counted some thirty to forty other rockets that were shot at me on that pass. I can't help wondering how many other times this sort of thing happened and I never knew about it.

Lee Howard arrived in Vietnam in September 1970, just after President Nixon authorized clandestine bombing of Cambodia to attack the enemy's 'safe haven and massive storehouse, all secure from US air attack'. He was impressed by the opportunities this offered:

We got some great targets over there and the old heads were ecstatic. They finally got to hit something of substance instead of busting trees. There were no big guns over there, it was mostly small-arms fire which, of course, could cook your goose with the 'golden BB' but by and large the AAA threat didn't create a problem early on.

Our normal loads were napalm and high-drag [Snakeye] Mk 82s. The most interesting and demanding mission I flew (other than hauling slick Mk 82s at night, working under flares) was one with a CBU load, flown in conjunction with the *Ranch Hands*. We laid CBU down ahead of the C-123Bs that were de-foliating [spraying herbicide]. The obvious purpose was to keep the small-arms fire at bay while the '123s lumbered through, low and slow. The timing and co-ordination of the CBU was extremely important.

We strafed on almost every mission, especially in Cambodia and the Hun was an excellent platform if the guns didn't jam. When working the trail up in Laos and 'bad guy country' we seldom used the guns as we were specifically cutting roads. Only on a SAR mission or an unusual event would we get 'down and dirty' up there. It was generally 'one pass and haul ass'.

CBU offered the chance of wide ordnance coverage against an imprecisely located target and delayed action munitions to keep heads down while the F-100s continued to work a target. Joe Vincent:

We usually delivered the CBU-49 just like a Mk 117 (750lb) bomb, using a 30–40-degree dive bomb pass. It had radar fusing and the clamshell casing would open well above the ground, scattering the bomblets out in a 'doughnut' pattern. Sometimes we would deliver two in ripple pairs mode with a half-second between them so that the doughnut patterns would overlap for complete coverage of the target.

By that stage of the war an increasing number of CAS sorties were being allotted to F-4 Phantoms but FACs often preferred

Bien Hoa AB, with F-100Ds in open revetments and shelters under construction to protect them from VC rocket and mortar attacks. Bruce Gold

F-100 pilots for tackling precision strikes because they were able to drop from lower altitudes for greater accuracy. Lee Howard recalled how 'We prided ourselves on being far more accurate than the F-4 "station wagon" folks. We often worked within 50 metres of "friendlies" and occasionally closer'. The F-4's prodigious appetite for fuel, however, was a disadvantage.

> On one mission we were about 285 miles from our Phan Rang base and holding to get on a target 60 miles off the end of the runway at Da Nang, home of the 366th TFW *Gunfighters* F-4Es. We were about third in line for the strike, patiently waiting and watching our fuel gauges when a flight of *Gunfighters* checked in demanding to be put on the same strike because they were 'Texaco' [short of fuel]. After all, they had all of 60 miles to go to get home! That same flight featured a four-ship of VNAF [516th FS] A-37B Dragonflies which came over the target and did a 'mini B-52 sky puke' right through our holding pattern. Four sticks of Mk 82s through our formation definitely got our attention!

Flares and Flames

In the ceaseless war against the movement of troops and materials along the labyrinthine Ho Chi Minh Trail complex, 7th AF attempted to devise better ways of interdicting those routes at night when most movement took place. While electronic sensors and infra-red (IR) imaging were rapidly evolving, the standard method used by USAF, USN and USMC pilots was to illuminate potential targets with flares. Using the SUU-25 series, a 500lb (225kg) dispenser holding eight Mk 24 flares, F-100 'day attack' pilots would release the 25lb flares over the target area. Each flare burned for 3–4 minutes at 2 million candlepower, illuminating a large area but also revealing the attacking aircraft to ground defences. The lighter-weight SUU-40 was also used.

Don Schmenk described a flare and napalm two-ship mission over a target south of Saigon:

> I dropped two flares over the target, did a tight circle and put a napalm bomb on the ground to make it easier for my wingman. We were a long way from Tuy Hoa and were getting short of gas so I told him to drop all four of his un-finned napalm canisters on one pass. [BLU-27 and -32 series fire bombs were available with or without stabilizing fins.] I followed him down to drop my last napalm when the sky lit up! I just knew I had lost my wingman! Napalm was dropped in a 15-degree dive at 400kt, about 1,000–1,500ft above the ground, leaving little time for mistakes at that speed so close to the ground. This was particularly true at night. I gave a call to my wingman and, much to my relief, he answered. When the un-

finned napalm came off his aircraft the bombs collided with each other, detonating on contact and causing the explosion I had witnessed. It was a spectacular sight but nothing to compare with the relief that I felt upon hearing his voice!

We were acutely aware of the potential for vertigo when working under flares so we took care not to get complacent at night. We used flares that we dropped ourselves or from other aircraft such as the C-119, C-47 or C-130. We also used aircraft with large searchlights that illuminated the ground and sometimes they, or FACs, would drop 'log markers' that burned on the ground with a high intensity to mark the target. A scary aspect was the possibility of running into a flare that had failed to ignite or burned out before reaching the ground.

Vertigo caught Joe Vincent out on his flare-dropping checkout flight.

> I dropped a flare and then a 'nape' that exploded brightly in my rear-view mirror during my pull-off. This was the first night-time weapon detonation I'd seen. As I watched the pretty fireball I inadvertently rolled almost inverted. My IP, Dick Rung, told me to 'recover'. Imagine my surprise when I looked back inside the cockpit to see 150 degrees of bank. The nose was still above the horizon, but not for long. It wasn't so much not knowing which way was up as being deprived of the normal day-time inputs that keep you situation-aware.

The alternative to flares was to bomb in total darkness. On one mission Joe made a dive attack without illumination, even from moonlight.

> It was more disorienting, rolling in for a 30-degree pass from 8,000ft above the target and releasing from 3,000ft in complete darkness than the low-angle passes I made under flares. It was almost an instrument manoeuvre. With no discernible horizon you had to devote more time inside the cockpit, paying attention to bank angle (a critical input to the bomb release parameters), dive angles, airspeed, etc. than you did in daylight or with flares. Most of my night missions were Skyspot; straight-and-level at 20,000ft like a B-52 with a good controller guiding you and calling for bomb release.

These missions were directed from one of seven MSQ-77 *Combat Skyspot* sites that were established in the area by June 1967. Designed to guide B-52 *Arc Light* missions via a transponder in the bomber, Skyspot was described as 'GCA without the glide-path' in that it gave the pilot an exact

Millie's Moose **with a previous serial presentation showing through its badly worn 'SS' squadron codes.** Joe Vincent

course to his target and a signal to release bombs. For tactical aircraft like the F-100 it allowed reasonably accurate bombing at night or in bad weather, although as Joe pointed out, 'four 750lb bombs don't compare to a BUFF's [B-52 bomber] load but I did get credit for a gun position destroyed one night on a "sky puke" [Skyspot] mission'.

These raids were essentially for harassment rather than pin-point accuracy and 'both the VC and the Hun pilots were harassed by them!' Maj Dick Garrett, who flew F-100 Skyspot missions with 416th TFS recalled:

... bombing monkeys in the trees. What a waste, or at least it seemed that way. It was the big GCA in the sky, straight and level from 18,000ft or so and pickle on the controller's command. Allowing for winds, intel 'lag' and sleep deprivation it was a miracle if the bombs even hit the war zone. Combat Skyspot was common for night alert pad missions when there wasn't much going on in the war and you were an 'asset' just waiting idly by.

The MSQ system was also used by USAFE F-100s in the early 1960s for practice nuclear delivery.

Night missions were flown from the alert pad too in emergencies. Bruce Gold and Larry Peters, flying F-100Ds *Buzzard 01* and *02*, were scrambled from Bien Hoa's 510th TFS pad on 27 September 1968. Bruce Gold (who retired as a USAF Colonel) described the mission:

It was early evening and we were surrounded by large thunderstorms. The weather made flying conditions 'mandatory', i.e. no flying unless it was absolutely necessary to save American lives. We flew into the night, through the storms, to the aid of elements of the First Brigade, fourth Infantry Division who were pinned down under heavy enemy weapons fire on a ridge stretching between two high mountain peaks. The mission was flown without flares or other means to illuminate the target. This required us to 'troll' for enemy fire to help identify friend from foe. We had to deliver ordnance, in very close proximity to friendly forces, from very undesirable axes of attack.

The weapons (napalm and 500lb Snakeye bombs) were delivered precisely on target with devastating effect on the enemy forces, which evidently withdrew, allowing evacuation of wounded US forces and extraction of the remainder. The *Buzzard* F-100Ds recovered at the nearest US base, Phu Cat. Both pilots were awarded the Silver Star for 'outstanding airmanship and conspicuous disregard for their own safety, saving the lives of many US forces on the ground'.

Combat Mods

The F-100 fleet received few updates and modifications during its Vietnam years, though some re-work was needed to compensate for the enormous numbers of

missions flown. After cracks were discovered in the wings of some aircraft, a 4g limit was imposed, limiting dive angles. As F-100s went through inspect and repair as necessary (IRAN) at the Taiwan facility, their wingboxes were inspected and re-built so that the aircraft could pull the maximum 7.33g again. A few jets carried the Combat Documentation Camera Pod on their centreline pylon though it was a very 'draggy' installation. More common was the smaller KB-18 strike camera installed during IRAN under the port fuselage, level with the wing leading edge. This V-shaped fairing enclosed a revolving prism, providing wide-angle images along the aircraft's lateral axis that were recorded by a camera as 70×200mm high-resolution photos. A number of Block 50 NAVS F-100Ds entered combat but most had the Doppler navigation system (NAVS) equipment removed by 1968–69 as it proved unreliable. They were not alone in having the small air scoop in the fin leading edge: this was standard on all PACAF F-100Ds except the earliest models deployed in 1960–61.

A more urgent addition to US tactical aircraft was necessitated by the emergence of the SA-2 Dvina surface-to-air missile (SAM) threat. The first sites were observed around Hanoi and Haiphong in April 1965, though the presumed presence of Russian or Chinese technicians ruled out pre-emptive strikes. Signals from their *Spoon Rest* target acquisition radar and *Fan Song* target-tracking radar were detected and studied from July 1965 onwards by RB-66C ELINT aircraft and Ryan Firebee drones. This data enabled US electronics contractors to develop effective countermeasures equipment, but by then the first of 205 US aircraft to be lost to North Vietnamese SAMs had been destroyed. On 24 July 1965, Capt Roscoe Fobair (a former WWII B-17 crewman) and Capt Richard Keirn (POW and F-100 pilot) were part of a four-ship F-4C CAP F-105 strike when three SA-2s were aimed at them, hitting their aircraft (63-7599) and killing Fobair. Keirn once again became a POW.

Although top priority in fitting ECM equipment went to aircraft operating over North Vietnam, a programme was initiated to re-instate the radar homing and warning (RHAW) system for the F-100 that the Bendix Corporation had proposed earlier in 1965. In fact, the USAF had tested the QRC-253-2 homing system, designed to counter its own Hawk missiles, in F-100Fs

F-100D 56-3048 with a 309th TFS badge on its fin tip and Tuy Hoa AB in the background. Joe Vincent Collection

at Exercise *Goldfire* in 1964. Data from this trial was put alongside proposals from Bendix and Applied Technology Inc. (API) a few days after the first F-4C loss. The eventual outcome was Project *Wild Weasel 1*, using a few RHAW-equipped F-100Fs to 'sniff out' SAM sites. However, the AN/APR-25(V) RHAW and AN/APR-26 launch warning receiver (LWR) developed for that programme were also installed in a number of F-100D airframes. These aircraft were identified by antenna installations beneath the air intake lip and at the rear of the fin above the rudder. Each housing held a pair of small, spiral antennas, each one pointing 45 degrees each side of the nose or tail to give 360-degree coverage. In the cockpit a circular, 3in (7.5cm) cathode ray tube (CRT) scope display was installed above the left of the front coaming (above the drag chute handle) and showed the direction of threat emission sources. A threat-warning light panel below and to the right of this replaced the AIM-9 indicator display. These square lights gave an indication of the type of radar threat: SAM (in three frequency bands), a bright red LAUNCH light warning of an imminent SAM launch, AAA or airborne intercept radar. For the majority of F-100D missions the equipment, if fitted, was reassuring but inessential. No F-100 was hit by a SAM and there were comparatively few radar-controlled AAA sites outside North Vietnam. Joe Vincent kept his RHAW switched on but received no SAM indications, even close to the North Vietnamese border; 'There was an AAA DEFEAT button at the

right of the display for silencing AAA warnings if you were in such a high threat area that the AAA warnings could distract you from the more threatening SAM warnings'. Audio noise warnings could also be relayed to the pilot's headset.

For the groundcrew, the arrival of ECM gear introduced another job: testing the system every time maintenance was done. Al Neubecker counted that among his duties as an ECM tech at Tuy Hoa:

> We had a yellow test box which we set at different frequencies and walked around the aircraft while someone was in the cockpit looking at the CRT scope with the head-set on to see if the correct visual and audio signals appeared in accordance with what we were sending from the box. We could simulate different threat frequencies and a SAM launch. The red LAUNCH light was at the pilot's eye level and he couldn't miss it. I also worked on a couple of C-130 'ferret' aircraft, loaded with electronics, that flew close to enemy positions so that we could update the frequencies.

Wild Weasel 1

API, the Palo Alto-based company that supplied the APR-25/26 were contractors for a programme that was to produce a whole new species – the 'Wild Weasel' suppression of enemy defences (SEAD) aircraft. The company had pioneered lightweight, internally mounted self-protection for the Lockheed U-2 (one of the first SA-2 victims in May 1960). As

well as providing similar equipment for tactical fighters like the F-100 (which had limited carriage space for QRC-series 'add-on' jamming pods), their ECM fit was seen as a way to neutralize the missile sites by detecting and attacking them using the same aircraft. Strike aircraft could protect themselves to some extent by using pods like the ALQ-71 or ALQ-87 and flying in a set 'pod' formation to maximize the effect, or by relying on jamming aircraft like the Douglas EB-66. Ideally though, the missile sites and radars required bombs to put them permanently off the air.

At the 3 August 1965 meeting in the wake of the first loss to a SAM, a committee led by Brig Gen K. C. Dempster examined ECM proposals from Bendix and ATI. Two weeks later it recommended installing RHAW equipment in several F-100F-20 aircraft under Project *Ferret* (later changed to *Wild Weasel* since *Ferret* had already been used for another project). The Block 20 aircraft were chosen because they had received the AN/ASN-7 dead reckoning computer and PC-212 Doppler radar navigation system specified for PACAF use. This could be removed to provide space for the ECM fit without significant weight change. Project Manager John Paup chose the ATI installation and the firm was given a contract. The rival Bendix system was later adopted by the USAF and USN as the AN/APS-107 and widely used.

Initially known as the Vector IV, the APR-25 gave warning of S-, C- and X-Band radar signals. The second system was introduced as the WR-300 launch warning receiver, developed in forty days from 23 September 1965 and adopted by the USAF as the AN/APR-26. It was a tuned crystal receiver to detect SA-2 guidance signals in the L-Band and measure the increase in intensity as missile launch approached. For the Weasel F-100Fs, another component was added, an IR-133 panoramic receiver to pick up, analyse and identify S-Band emissions at longer range. It also provided direction-finding capability to locate SA-2 sites. Amplitude-based 'spikes' on the rear cockpit CRT gave indication to within a couple of degrees to show whether the threat was to the left or right of the F-100F's track. A larger spike of the left would show a stronger signal on that side and vice versa. The rear-seat electronic warfare officer (EWO) had to direct his pilot so that the two spikes

The pilot of this 615th TFS F-100D is about to de-plane without a ladder at Phu Cat AB after a 28 February 1971 mission. His F-100D-21-NA (55-3508) survived the war, served with the Indiana ANG's 163rd TFS and was finally destroyed on 9 November 1989 on its thirteenth NOLO flight as a QF-100 target. Norm Taylor

appeared equal and the aircraft heading towards the site. The problem was that it didn't show whether the signals came from ahead of the aircraft or behind it. Yawing the aircraft would alter the spike-length so that, for example, yawing right shortened the left spike, showing the site was behind the Hun. EWOs also had to listen for the buzz of missile guidance radars and the low groan of early-warning radars on his headset. Training enabled them to distinguish individual radar identities in this way.

Flush, square IR-133 antennas appeared on the fuselage sides in line with the canopy bow and under the aircraft beneath the front cockpit. One aircraft (58-1221) had a different arrangement of periodic (azimuth/elevation) antennas in place of the IR-133 set similar to those later used on F-105G and F-4Cww aircraft. Additional equipment included a KA-60 panoramic camera to photograph SAM sites and a standard TAC Midgetape 400 recorder to provide tapes of radar emissions for later study. The IR-133 contract

was negotiated from 27 August 1965 on a 30-day production schedule for the first unit and 45 days for the second. ATI received contracts for 500 APR-25 and APR-26 units on 19 September 1965.

During the latter part of 1965, tactics were evolved for what was to become a vital component in US strikes over North Vietnam. Using strobe indications from the IR-133, the F-100F was steered towards a site until it could be visually identified. The Weasel would then make an initial attack with LAU-3 rocket pods, followed up by bombs and rockets from an accompanying *Iron Hand* flight of three or four F-105s.

Four low-hours Dash 20 F-100Fs were modified for the programme; 58-1221, -1226, -1227 (a Project *Julius Caesar*/Harmon Trophy aircraft that flew over the North Pole in 1959) and -1231. Later, three replacement aircraft (58-1206, -1212 and 1232) were similarly converted but also equipped to launch the AGM-45 Shrike anti-radiation missile. They retained the standard F-100F designation

(rather than EF-100F) as part of the thick cloak of secrecy surrounding the project. Aircrew were forbidden to keep their usual diaries. Security was so tight that one trainee pilot was dismissed within hours of mentioning to a girlfriend that he was involved in a classified project.

The first four aircraft were delivered to Eglin AFB in September 1965 after initial testing at Edwards AFB. Five volunteer pilots were drawn from several F-100 units and an initial batch of EWOs came from B-52s, with a later batch from EB-66 units. After initial indoctrination at NAA they trained intensively at the Tactical Air Warfare Center at Eglin, using simulated EW threats. Lt Col James Kropnik was their first CO, but he expressed serious doubts about the project and was replaced by Maj Garry A. Willard, who was dual-qualified in the F-100 and F-105. Crews trained as pairs, initiating a bond that was to become an essential feature of *Wild Weasel* operations for decades. Capt Allen Lamb, one of the first pilots, commented:

309th TFS F-100Ds on the tanker for another *Steel Tiger* CAS mission with M117 ordnance. Joe Vincent Collection

There was no training to speak of for *Wild Weasel 1*. It was 'cut and paste' to see if it would work. We did run against the SADS [surface-to-air defence system] at Eglin to check the accuracy of the equipment. Then we went to war to see if it would really work. Each crew did its own thing.

In combat he used his EWO's IR-133 to provide steering until they were close to the site.

I would off-set so that the site didn't think we were homing in on them. Once I had two rings or more on the scope I would use the Vector IV to look for the site on the ground but I would still get the readings from the EWO as, in some cases, there was more than one site.

Capt Ed Sandelius agreed that there was no real way to train for the Weasel mission at that stage. He was the only TAC EWO assigned to the project at its initiation, the rest coming from SAC, where this special skill was much more in evidence. 'SAC had about 85 per cent of the electronic warfare equipment and EWOs. TAC's 15 per cent was spread between the 9th TRS (RB-66s) and the TAC ELINT cell, with a few scattered around in numbered Air Force HQs and Wing HQs.' Ed was on RB-66Cs, with 2,000 hours of experience on the type, when he received orders from 12th AF dated 25 September 1965, to 'proceed to Long Beach, California; Eglin AFB and places within or without the US ... on a 100-day TDY' (later amended to 160 days) with access to classified material 'up to and including TOP SECRET during the TDY'.

There was no mention of *Wild Weasel* or whether or not I had volunteered for the project. When I got to NAA, Long Beach they showed me a couple of F-100Fs that were stripped down and in the process of being converted to the TAC project configuration, which at that time was called *Mongoose*. They still hadn't decided on the final configuration. In fact they were trying to install an AN/APR-9 unit in the rear cockpit with tuners in a modified fuel tank under the wing. I'm glad that one didn't work out. I arrived at Eglin AFB on 4 October 1965. The other crewmembers and the aircraft arrived shortly thereafter with the equipment configured the way we were going to deploy it in South East Asia (i.e. the APR-25/26 and IR-133). At Eglin we trained against the SADS 1 and 2 systems, flying out over the Gulf and then acquiring the signal to vector the pilot over the target with voice commands. We were all trained EWOs so the receivers were a piece of cake. The acquisition of the signal was built into the equipment, along with the audio computer, generated from the parameters of the SAM or AAA that came into the receiver. 'D/Fing' [establishing the direction of the signal] took a minimum of effort to master. The APR-25/26 provided relative bearings. With practice you could interpret signal amplitude and get quite good at estimating range. When you went right over the site the signal's amplitude would get extremely long and switch from 360 degrees to 180 degrees, giving you a positive indication that you had passed right over the site. At this time you would try to pick up the site visually. EWOs would fly scheduled missions with their selected pilots and then at the debriefing they would share their experiences and techniques amongst the other crewmembers and Eglin staff that were responsible for putting together the tactics we would use in South East Asia. During this period they changed the name of the project to *Wild Weasel*.

On 21 November, the four aircraft flew in great secrecy to Korat RTAFB via Hawaii, arriving at Korat on 25 November, only eighty-four days after the first aircraft was converted. They became a new unit, the 6234th TFW (Wild Weasel Detachment) under the control of the 388th TFW. First to arrive were Capts Ed White and Ed Sandelius. 'We were the advanced party. When we arrived we were kept busy briefing all of the F-105 aircrews and Operations personnel on the equipment in the Weasel aircraft and the tactics we had developed back at Eglin.'

On 1 December 1965, the unit flew its first combat mission, with Maj Willard and Capt Truman Lifsey in 58-1231. Initially, their efforts yielded no direct results as Vietnamese radar operators learned to close down their radars to prevent the Weasels acquiring them. 'We had good ELINT on the SAM sites', recalled Ed Sandelius, 'but with the ability of the SAM units to pick up and move at short notice we had to rely on our own equipment.' Some missions were flown with EB-66Cs to compare the signals they received from the emitters. Much was learned about radar emissions, and effective tactics were devised to keep the F-100F, flying at 400kt from being over-run by the faster F-105s.

Capts John Pitchford (ex-27th TFW) and Bob Trier in 58-1231 were scheduled to lead *Apple* flight on 20 December, a strike by twelve F-105s near Kep airfield. A follow-up attack was led by another F-100F flown by Maj Bob Schwartz, the Ops Officer and Capt Jack Donovan with another eight 'Thuds'. As 58-1231 approached the target over heavy cloud cover it was hit in the rear fuselage by AAA and the hydraulic systems soon failed, putting the jet into a steep dive. Although both men ejected, Bob Trier was shot by NVA militia when he tried to resist capture. Pitchford was hit in the arm but he survived for over seven years as a POW.

After that, the Weasels continued with unchanged tactics, flying *Iron Hand* attacks and carrying their own bombs after unsuccessfully experimenting with timed napalm canisters to mark targets for the F-105s. LAU-3 pods were still carried as a very effective weapon, particularly for snapshot

First SAM Site Kill

Capt Allen Lamb and his EWO,Capt Jack Donovan at Korat RTAFB in December 1965. Allen T. Lamb

The new Weasel tactics yielded their first success on 22 December 1965. Capts Allen Lamb and Jack Donovan flew F-100F 58-1226 as *Spruce 5* with four F-105s for a *Rolling Thunder* attack on Yen Bai railyard. Jack Donovan was the originator of the phrase that became the unofficial motto of Weasels from then on. His response when he first realized the nature of the Weasel mission for which he had volunteered was what Allen Lamb called, 'the natural response of an educated man, a veteran EWO on B-52s, upon learning that he was to fly back-seat to a self-absorbed fighter pilot while acting as flypaper for enemy SAMs'. Abbreviated on many Weasel patches ever since to 'YGBSM' his comment was, 'You gotta be sh**tin' me!' (Capt Ed Sandelius commented that, as far as he knew, Jack said the same thing regarding just about everything!)

On 22 December their mission was to probe enemy defences until they got a response from a SAM site. At around 100 miles (160km) from the target, Donovan's vector IV picked up a *Fan Song* transmission. Allen Lamb pushed his speed up, started homing in on the site and transmitted a 'Tallyho':

I kept the SAM at around 10 o'clock so he wouldn't get the idea I was going after him. When I could, I dropped into shallow valleys to mask our approach. Now and again I'd pop up for Jack to get a 'cut'. This went on for 10 or 15 minutes. After breaking out into the Red River Valley I followed the strobes on the Vector IV and turned with the river alongside. The IR-133 strobes started 'curling off' at 12 o'clock, both to the right and left on the CRT and I knew we were right on top

of him. I started climbing for altitude and Jack kept calling out SAM positions literally left and right. The right one turned out to be a second site. I was passing through 3,000ft, nose high and I rolled inverted while still climbing to look. Jack started calling the first site to the right. I said it was to the left because I could see it below. 'Right', he said. 'Left!' I said. 'Look outside', I said. Jack did and saw that we were inverted so the signals from the left and right antennas were reversed. He agreed! I rolled in to line up on the site but came in way too low.

Art Brattkus, flying F-105D *Spruce 4*, recalled:

We were moving smartly up the Red River on radio silence when up ahead I saw Allen pop up and then roll in, way too close to the ground. I thought to myself that he was going to mark the target with his aircraft and that the Old Man would be pissed. I was Flying Safety Officer!

Lamb opened his attack:

My rockets hit short but as I pulled off there was a bright flash. I must have hit the oxidizer van for the SA-2 liquid fuel motors. I called out the site and the F-105 Lead [*Spruce 1*], Don Langwell said that he had it. He went in and *Spruce 2* (Van Heywood) came after him, firing rockets.

From Donovan's viewpoint:

... when Al and Jack first ID'd the site and got us pointed in I saw that it was covered up to look like part of a village. In

the middle of my first pass I did see a few wheels under what appeared to be brush huts. We fired HEAP [high explosive/armour piercing] rockets that, in retrospect were probably the absolute best ordnance for that site. The vans and other structures appeared to jump in the air when the load of rockets hit. I remember I didn't get any ground fire until the second pass and after that there weren't any significant parts of the target that were not fully exposed and hit. I remember Al calling that the site had gone off the air.

Lamb observed that 'We all broke the cardinal rule: "one pass, haul ass" to assure the kill. I came back around for a second pass in front of Art Brattkus (the F-100s were agile birds!)'. Art added, 'I spotted a structure that wasn't burning yet and threw some rockets at it, pulled off to the right to get out of Al's way and damned near hit another Thud'. Lamb then went down beside *Spruce 3*. Bob Bush (later killed on an armed recce with the 421st TFS) and Art, who were hitting AAA alongside the Red River. 'On this pass I strafed the control van and he went off the air. Each of the Thuds came round again, expending all their 20mm ammunition.' As *Spruce 4*, Art was last man off the target, 'As I pulled out I saw several SAMs under their camouflage and threw all the rest of my rockets in their direction'.

Allen Lamb:

Jack Donovan was now calling out the second SAM site but we had nothing left to hit it with. We really blew away the site we did hit.

There was a USO show with Bob Hope that day at Korat and we made a fly-over with the F-100 leading and two F-105s on each wing. A number of people down there knew that meant we had made a SAM kill and they left the show early to celebrate.

In all, *Spruce* flight fired 304 rockets and 2,900 rounds of 20mm. Although the use of Wild Weasels could not be mentioned in the Press, all six *Spruce* crews received the Distinguished Flying Cross (DFC) for this first SAM site kill. After another twelve missions, Jack Donovan returned to Nellis AFB to help establish the Wild Weasel School.

Allen Lamb was credited with two more kills. The second was with Capt Rick Morgan and the third was on a *Rolling Thunder* strike as Lead Weasel with Capt Frank O'Donnell (who later had a major part in evolving the F-4G Advanced Wild Weasel as Test Project Officer). The mission, Frank's first, included some interesting complications. Allen Lamb:

After the strike I was exiting and a Thud pilot from Takhli had been shot down just 17 miles from Hanoi. The Sandies [SAR cover] were trying to get to him but a SAM site was lobbing missiles at them. I went back in with just three Thuds and homed in on the site. The weather was hazy with only 2–3 miles visibility. We missed the radar van but the Thud pilot on Guard frequency was saying the Vietnamese were coming up the hill to get him. I went back in, solo and strafed the van, taking it off the air. SAR were then able to get he pilot out. I received the Silver Star for this mission three years later.

An F-100F refuelling during a *Wild Weasel* mission to North Vietnam. Ed Sandelius

attacks against softer radar targets. The Weasels flew at altitudes below 500ft (150m), using terrain masking when possible but still exposing their F-100s to AAA and small arms fire. Ed Sandelius explained that they were all daylight sorties; 'Without radar none of the F-100 missions were flown at night. The F-105s had terrain avoidance radar but they only flew the day missions since they wanted to be able to see any missile launches'. Also, missions tended to use two Weasels. Allen Lamb:

Weasels only went in if the strike was in Route Pack VI and we had one Weasel before the strikers and a second about twenty minutes into the strike or when the first Weasel was at 'bingo' fuel or had expended its ordnance. They would let us troll [for radar sites] which was better than being with the strikers. Tactics were different for each Weasel, based on the mind-set of each crew.

Crews tended to 'swap off' pilots and aircraft as Ed recalled, 'We flew whatever was available. There was a standard cockpit set-up with very little difference between birds'.

SAM evasion tactics, developed by these first Weasel pilots, were based on a diving turn into the missile's trajectory, breaking away as late as possible so that the missile could not correct its course. Allen Lamb taught this tactic to the first F-105F/G Weasel classes in 1966 while he

worked on Weasel adaptations of the F-4C Phantom (using an F-4D to test the equipment).

Early in January 1966, Gen Dempster opted to use the more powerful F-105F as the basis of the next phase of Wild Weasel development as the F-100F Detachment ended its evaluative process later that month. However, the Huns remained in place until 11 July 1966 and continued to fly missions over North Vietnam. One of the F-105F/G's main weapons was the Texas Instruments AGM-45 Shrike, an anti-radiation missile developed for the USN between 1958 and 1964. Operating independently of the aircraft's detection systems, the 10ft (3m) long missile guided itself to a hostile radar emitter, destroying it with a 145lb fragmentation warhead.

The F-100F Wild Weasel Det at Korat received Shrikes in March 1966 and Maj Don Fraizer with EWO Marshall Goldberg made the first USAF combat firing (a possible kill) on 18 April against a *Fire Can* AAA tracking radar near Dong Hoi. Further Shrike launches were made, each one in the restricted area around Hanoi known to pilots as 'the Holy Land', which needed specific permission from Washington. Clearance for one of Fraizer's missions involved him in a telephone conversation with President Johnson in person. One reason for this and for the delay in awarding Capt Allen Lamb's Silver Star was the

assumed presence of 'round eyed' (i.e. Soviet) technicians at the SAM sites. Shrike-carrying F-100Fs (the three replacement aircraft received after February 1966) often carried LAU-3 pods on their outboard wing stations as well.

In total, the Weasel Huns destroyed nine SAM sites and forced many others to shut down during *Rolling Thunder* strikes. There was one other combat loss among the sixteen F-100s lost over North Vietnam. F-100F 58-1212 was hit by AAA on an *Iron Hand* near Vinh on 23 March, killing Capts Clyde Dawson and Don Clark. F-100F 58-1221 suffered an engine failure after compressor stalls on a familiarization flight on 13 March. The F-100F crews had rapidly developed pioneering tactics that remained effective for the F-105F/G crews who began to arrive in Thailand on 28 May 1966. The APR-25/26 and IR-133 systems were installed and expanded in the F-105 conversions and in the subsequent F-4C Wild Weasel 4 programmes. In Allen Lamb's opinion the F-100F was not far short of the F-105F/G in its suitability for the Weasel mission. Although it lacked the Thud's raw speed, it was more manoeuvrable and its biggest shortcoming was probably that it didn't fit into the Air Force's inflight-refuelling arrangements. After 1966 it was the only type operating over North Vietnam without the standard boom-type refuelling receptacle and it was too difficult to provide KC-135 tankers modified with drogue attachments. Funds were never provided to convert the F-100 to the boom system.

As they withdrew from battle, half of the original batch of F-100F Weasels had been lost and the returning aircraft had systems that had suffered considerably from humidity, corrosion and wiring problems originating partly from the speed with which the original conversions had to be made. However, ATI's 'yellow box' tester could be used pre-flight to ensure that everything was working. Steve Sopko was one of the two technicians working on the original Weasel systems at Korat in 1965:

The field tester was NiCad battery powered and not only tested the APR-25/26 but we also used it to check the IR-133 panoramic receiver and the later ER-142 version [used in the F-105F]. Ted Phillips and I used it for both pre-flight and post-flight inspections, which was not a requirement but we did both for our own peace of mind. We used it for walk-arounds and for a direct feed (by cable inputs) into the pre-amps

Capt Allen T. Lamb serving with the 353rd TFS at Myrtle Beach AFB in March, 1963. On the 28th of that month he survived a supersonic ejection from an F-100. Allen T. Lamb

popular name was Misty FAC, based on their Misty call-sign which was in turn inspired by Mrs Day's love of the Erroll Garner song. Trial missions were flown over the relatively safe Route Pack 1 and then moved to higher-risk areas. The unit was assigned to the 37th TFW as Det 1 of the 612th TFS, using F-100Fs from other units, notably the 'HE'-coded 416th TFS.

The aircraft received no special modifications for the FAC role. 'It was nice to have operational RHAW gear, but not an abort item', recalled Col 'Lanny' Lancaster. The only 'special equipment' in the rear cockpit was a good set of maps and a 35mm camera with a telephoto lens. Armament was usually two seven-shot pods of 2.75 white phosphorous marker rockets and 110 rounds in each 20mm gun. Both occupants of the FAC F-100 were qualified pilots and in mission planning they exchanged roles, flying the aircraft or locating targets and controlling strike fighters. The pilots were volunteers and initially the 'entry requirement' was twenty-five combat missions and 1,000 flying hours. A number were former O-2 pilots. Among the 142 pilots who went through the programme were two future USAF Chiefs of Staff, Ronald Fogleman and Merrill 'Tony' McPeak, who later commanded the Detachment. On one mission, the two men flew in the same aircraft. Dick Rutan, later to fly the fragile Voyager non-stop around the world, was also a Misty pilot.

By the time Col Lancaster joined the Detachment in 1967, entry required fifty combat missions. The task had expanded from FAC duties to cover ResCAP, photo reconnaissance and contributions to the anti-SAM effort. Hazardous ResCAP missions comprised about 30 per cent of the total in 1967–68 with the F-100F taking charge of the rescue effort on site, keeping the opposition at bay with its guns and managing the SAR resources to the best effect.

I think the basics were well-defined when I arrived and didn't change much. With some coordination with 7th AF we established a priority system for our tasks [and target types]:

1) Search and rescue. During my tour I was fortunate that we successfully recovered every single crewman that made it safely to the ground after an ejection. We did lose three Misty pilots during the tour. One aircraft and both crewmen simply disappeared and were never found. One crew

in the nose or tail for sensitivity checks when trouble-shooting antennas, cables, diodes or pilot/EWO write-ups.

Misty FAC

From 1964 to 1969 FAC-A directed the ordnance of countless strike flights on to targets in South East Asia. Incredibly, only seven of the fragile, low-flying 115mph (185km/h) Cessna O-1 FAC aircraft were lost, though six pilots were killed. From 1968 they were supplemented by the more capable twin-engined Cessna O-2, though ten of these were lost. In an attempt to increase the FAC's survivability over high-risk areas, particularly North Vietnam and the DMZ, 7th AF advocated the use of two-seat fast jets. Although the F-4C was the obvious choice for speed and ordnance-carrying, the F-100F was more easily available at first. F-4Cs were used later for operations over Laos.

Maj George 'Bud' Day, an F-84 pilot in the Korean War, was given responsibility for organizing the F-100F Fast FAC Detachment under the code name *Commando Sabre* at Phu Cat, beginning on 28 June 1967 after an initial trial period at Phan Rang from 15 May. He was given sixteen pilots and four F-100Fs. The more

Ed White and Ed Sandelius with Wild Weasel F-100F 58-1226 at Korat RTAFB.
Ed Sandelius

ejected but the front-seat pilot was a fatality – we're not sure what happened.

2) Active AAA. We became very, very effective at discouraging AAA from shooting at us and we were able to persuade 7th AF to provide the strike assets to get the job done, especially after the bombing halt north of RP II freed the Thailand-based fighters to strike in our areas.

3) Artillery sites: we often searched for them in and above the DMZ but I don't recall finding any. If found, they would have had a very high priority because they were causing the Marines fits.

4) Tanks.

5) Water-borne logistics craft i.e. boats of any kind. Usually these were sampans but the occasional motor-boat was found. We also got several very large barges but were never sure whether these were in fact pontoon bridges or whether they carried stores since we never saw them loaded or in position to act as pontoons.

6) Bridges.

Ideally, the aircraft operated in pairs on road recce sorties with one aircraft searching for targets while the other refuelled on

With plain TAC markings giving no clue to its unit, this rocket-armed F-100F-16-NA refuels over Vietnam in 1965. Maj George 'Bud' Day and Capt Corwin Kippenhan were flying this aircraft on a Misty FAC sortie when they were shot down during a search for a suspected SAM site. David Menard Collection

SS 255, 309th TFS (red/yellow). Joe Vincent Collection

The *Little 1* (red/yellow). Joe Vincent Collection

***Lucky Lindy II*, an F-100F-6-NA of the 309th TFS.** Richard G. Such

SP770, 355th TFS, black outline. Joe Vincent Collection

***Booby's Tub* (*Agnez* in background), 308th TFS (white).** Joe Vincent Collection

***The Rapist*, F-100F-11-NA 56-3827, 309th TFS.** Richard G. Such

306th TFS *Soul Sister* (red/white). Joe Vincent Collection

***Teg o' My Heart*, 306th TFS (white).** Joe Vincent Collection

the tanker. For Lancaster, this was, 'always the desired concept of operations as long as we had sufficient aircraft available. There was nothing "typical" about Misty missions, except when the weather was very poor. Then all you did was troll around looking for holes to poke through'. With up to four tanker 'fills,' a mission could last up to six hours. Pilots learned to 'jink' constantly to avoid ground fire and they kept their speed up to around 450kt. Most missions involved flight time over North Vietnamese defences.

Inevitably, orbiting over small areas at low altitude to identify targets exposed the Misty crews to unusually high risks from ground fire. In all, thirty-four aircraft were lost between August 1967 and May 1970 with seven pilots killed – the Detachment's loss rate was the highest for any F-100 unit. In all cases where the cause was known, shoot-downs were attributed to AAA (usually 37mm) or small-arms, sometimes while aircraft were strafing ground targets. Two aircraft and their crews vanished without trace. Maj Mike McElhanon and Maj John Overlock failed to appear as designator aircraft for a strike on 16 August 1968, and their F-100F

***The Blue Meanie* (blue/white).** Joe Vincent Collection

***Ray's Hell*, 306th TFS (red/white).** Joe Vincent Collection

(56-3865) was presumed shot down. On 1 November 1969, Lt Col Lawrence Whitford and 1st Lt Patrick Carroll never made their planned tanker rendezvous and their F-100F (56-3796) was never seen again. Maj Don Sibson and Capt Snyder had to eject from 56-3878 while controlling an attack on a SAM site near Dong Hoi on 30 December 1967, as did Col Hardy and Capt Dave Jenny who led an attack on a SAM battery on 5 July 1968. All four pilots were recovered.

Of all the Misty FAC casualties, the first and most famous was the heroic survival of Maj George 'Bud' Day. On 26 August 1967, he and Capt Corwin 'Kipp' Kippenhan were leading an F-105 mission ('Bud' Day's 139th) in search of another SAM site near Thon Cam Son. Their F-100F (56-3954) took a hit at 4,500ft (1,370m) over the target and the crew ejected 2 miles (3km) short of the coast. Kippenhan was picked up by an HH-3E helicopter but Day was caught. During the ejection he broke his arm badly, suffered a damaged knee and was virtually blinded in his left eye by his flailing oxygen mask. He was quickly captured and tied up in a hole in the ground. Escaping from his two VC guards, he survived for twelve days in the jungle, sustaining further injuries from a US bomb that fell near him. He evaded thirty-two VC patrols and man-aged to navigate, without a compass, to within half an hour of freedom. Wandering semi-delirious into another VC patrol he was injured by gun shots and re-captured, spending six years of extreme hardship and torture in the 'Hanoi Hilton'. (During all that time S/Sgt Bobby 'Orville' Wright, his former crew chief when Bud flew F-100C 54-1903 with the 136th FIS, and his family of eight all wore POW bracelets until his release. Bobby, known as 'Tiger' by Bud Day, was one of many who prayed for the prisoner's safe return.) Following the end of his ordeal in 1973 (one of four Misty POWs to return from Hanoi) Bud was awarded the Medal of Honor, one of only twelve awarded to US airman during that war.

The Misty FAC Detachment was finally replaced by F-4 units in May 1970 and the Detachment reverted to the 612th TFS as F-100 operations in South East Asia ended on 31 July 1971. It had moved to Tuy Hoa on 14 April 1969 for the final stage of its operations. Use of the F-4 for the missions had gradually evolved beginning with a programme code-named Stormy FAC and managed by the 366th TFW at Da Nang. It was followed by a similar Wolf FAC initiative at Ubon. The 388th TFW began Tiger FAC operations in March 1969, followed by the 432nd TRW which used teams of F-4Ds and RF-4C (Falcon/Atlanta) air-craft. The F-4 suffered from poorer rear-cockpit visibility than the F-100F and shorter loiter time, but F-100Fs were getting scarce as retirement approached. Commando Sabre pilots checked out the first batch of F-4 Stormy FACs at Phu Cat. According to Lancaster, 'It was a mirror of our training programme. One of their guys came to Phu Cat and flew five missions in my back seat, then I flew one in his "pit"'. Once again, the F-100 had pioneered major new combat techniques and then stepped aside to let more modern aircraft develop them further as it returned to the USA for a quieter life in ANG units.

Summing up his impressions of the F-100 in both 'hot' and cold war, Lt Col David O. Williams (later to become a Brigadier General) felt that the aircraft was probably employed in the proper roles:

It was a good, stable weapons delivery platform in the conventional weapons role, as it was employed for air-to-ground attack in South Vietnam. During the height of the Cold War it was the best, most available and most ready tactical nuclear weapons delivery platform we had in the USAF inventory. Thankfully, we never had to prove its prowess in that role, but I'm also thankful that we at least had a well-trained, ready F-100 nuclear strike force to prove a credible deterrent when we needed it.

CHAPTER 5

On Guard

New York ANG F-100Cs replaced their silver finish with camouflage and 'SG' tail codes when they flew with the 31st TFW at Tuy Hoa AB. Author's Collection

Asian Action

Working closely with the thirteen regular USAF F-100 squadrons in Vietnam were four Air National Guard (ANG) units. They won universal praise for their effectiveness including a glowing tribute from Gen George S. Brown, 7th AF Commander, 1968–70. Among the eight ANG squadrons called to active duty after the Pueblo incident in January 1968 was the 120th Tactical Fighter Squadron (TFS), Colorado ANG, the first to take its Super Sabres to Vietnam. An F-100C/F squadron since January 1961, the 120th arrived at Phan Rang AB on 3 May 1968. Five days later, after familiarization flights with the resident 35th Tactical Fighter Wing

(TFW) Instructor Pilots (IPs), the squadron flew the first of 5,905 combat sorties. Many of the squadron's maintainers worked on the F-100Ds of other 35th TFW units. The squadron was the first in the ANG to fly combat as a unit since WWII and the sudden change in lifestyle was a shock for its pilots who were mainly 'week day' airline pilots, called to duty at 24-hours notice. Bob Macavoy recalled that, 'When the 120th TFS arrived at our base in April 1968 I remember them being sh*t scared for the first couple of weeks, specially when we were mortared at night. They ran into the bomb shelters while the rest of us regulars stood outside to watch the mortars hit the flight-line'.

The squadron flew for nearly nine months of combat, averaging twenty-four sorties a day, without loss until Capt J. E. O'Neill had the dubious honour of being in the last of the 569 US aircraft to be shot down in 1968. His F-100C (54-1973) was damaged by ground-fire on a close air support (CAS) mission and he had to eject short of Phan Rang. Almost at the end of the deployment, Maj Clyde Seiler was the 120th's only casualty when he was killed on another CAS mission near Song Be City. Seiler, a former Misty forward air controller (FAC) pilot, was pulling up from a strike attack when the wing of his F-100 sustained a structural failure. Colorado's 'VS'-coded F-100Cs scored the

The New Mexico ANG's spectacular markings appear on this F-100A (53-1737) which has also been updated with a tail hook, inflight-refuelling probe and silver lacquer finish. Peter Schinkelshoek Collection

best statistics in the 35th TFW for operational readiness (86.9 per cent), munitions reliability (98.8 per cent) and for the number of missions flown.

The 174th TFS, Iowa ANG, formerly Republic RF-84F flyers, were also alerted after the Pueblo affair and then deployed to Vietnam on 14 May 1968, arriving at Phu Cat after a 12,000-mile (19,310km) flight. Lt Col Gordon Young's aircrew (also predominantly airline pilots) completed 563 combat missions in the first month of their one-year temporary duty (TDY). Like the Colorado Guardsmen, they lost one pilot in a shootdown; 1st Lt Warren K. Brown (54-2004), downed at the same target as a 612th TFS F-100D only ninety minutes previously. It was also the first F-100C lost in Vietnam. By the end of their tour the airmen from Sioux City, Iowa had completed 6,359 missions, delivering a mountain of ordnance including 154 tons of 2.75in rockets, almost 2 million rounds of 20mm and 3 million pounds of napalm.

Tuy Hoa welcomed the 188th TFS, New Mexico ANG in June 1968, the first overseas deployment for the unit that was also the first ANG F-100 operator. It had traded its original F-100As for F-100C/Fs in spring 1964. The Vietnam deployment involved twenty-two 'SK'-coded aircraft and some very experienced pilots, most of whom had over 1,000 hours on the type. Like many ANG squadrons, their highly experienced maintainers soon found themselves in supervisory positions within the parent Wing's support organization. Their superbly maintained Huns averaged over eighteen sorties daily during their year at war and their pilots earned outstanding reputations for accurate ordnance delivery in support of troops in contact. The 'Enchilada Air Force' flyers with 'Taco' call signs were much in demand for difficult CAS missions. The inevitable cost was five aircraft, two lost in a mid-air collision, two to anti-aircraft artillery (AAA) and another in an operational mishap.

Joining the New Mexico men at Tuy Hoa was the 136th TFS, New York ANG from Niagara Falls, also with F-100C/Fs. *Rocky's Raiders* (later, *New York's Finest*) was part of the largest and longest-established group of ANG aviation units. Its history was rooted in 1943 as a P-51D unit within the 8th Air Force. With the NY ANG it had flown some time-expired F-47Ds, 'They had granular corrosion problems and could only fire the inboard 50 cal guns', crew chief Bobby Wright recalled. 'I think if we had fired all eight guns the damn wings would have fallen off!'

After that, it was back to Mustangs, then Lockheed F-94Bs and F-86H Sabres before the F-100Cs began to arrive in 1961. When the squadron eventually transitioned to the F-101B Voodoo in June 1971 it had logged over 50,000 hours in F-100s including 10,200 combat hours (5,500 missions) over Vietnam. Maj Franklyn McKee flew the squadron's last F-100C (54-1878) to Sioux City on 13 August 1971 for another two years of service.

Rocky's Raiders at War

Flying 'SG'-coded F-100Cs out of Tuy Hoa with the 136th TFS, New York ANG, Van 'Sky King' Hall completed 229 missions with one of the most highly regarded Super Sabre units in South East Asia.

Tuy Hoa was the biggest fighter base since WWII, with 125 Huns from three USAF regular units, the New Mexico ANG and 'New York's Finest'. We were commanded by Lt Col Laverne 'Dusty' Donner for the whole tour (14 June 1968–25 May 1969). There were six months for training before we deployed including a water survival course at Homestead AFB plus live ordnance and 'night owl' training, also in Florida. Then there was 'snake school' (jungle survival) in the Philippines after we deployed. We went non-stop to Hawaii on the way over; nine hours in the cockpit with no auto-pilot, wearing a poopy suit and taking seven air-to-air refuellings including three or four at maximum gross aircraft weight. That was real fun!

All the Air Guard units had the F-100C, the 'sport model', with a final approach airspeed of 183kt. It had no flaps and was faster and more manoeuvrable than the F-100D. While the 'D could carry wall-to-wall napalm, the F-100C could be loaded with two 'napes' outboard and two high-drag bombs inboard. We had to drop the napalm first (both tanks together) and then the bombs. The F-100Ds weapons system allowed one pilot to drop his bombs and open up the jungle before his wingman followed up with some napalm. Cluster bomb units [CBUs] came later in the second part of our deployment but it wasn't popular. If you couldn't find a target CBU was jettisoned into the ocean, never brought home.

Half of the missions were up in the Northern Route Packs, including the Mu Gia Pass and the Ho Chi Minh Trail. There were big guns up there – real flak. We always went as four-ships on those missions, carrying four 750lb bombs each. Very few night missions were flown. They required a FAC, fighters and a C-130 flare-ship all running around in the same sky together. They took forever to sort out and by then any bad guys were long gone, I'm sure.

The only fatality was Capt 'Jake the Snake' L'Huillier, shot down during his second attack pass in 54-1912 on a mid-morning mission against a Viet Cong (VC) storage area near Thon Ba. Jake bailed out but his chute didn't fully deploy and he died in the rescue helicopter on the way to Chu Lai.

1st Lt Mike Laskowski in 54-1775 was hit in similar circumstances on 2 August but rescued by a 37th ARRS helicopter. 1st Lt J. J. Thun was hit and baled out of 54-1922 near the Cambodian border on 23 August. 1st Lt Roberts managed to fly his F-100C (54-1931) some distance to Da

Nang after being hit on climb-out from Tuy Hoa, only to bail out over the sea. The fifth loss involved 53-1713 (the fifth F-100C and an ex-Edwards AFB test aircraft) after engine failure on 8 August. In proportion to the huge number of missions flown these losses were relatively light.

Most of the missions were in support of troops in contact, flown by Alert crews. Each squadron had two birds on five-minute Alert 24 hours a day with 'soft' loads of napalm and small, high-drag bombs. We used LITTER call-signs and had 'Rocky's Raiders' and 'Peace is our Profession, War is our Hobby' on the nose-gear doors. The regular squadrons didn't see the humour in this. We called the regulars 'DARTs' (dumb-ass regular troops) and they called us 'FANGs' (f***ing Air National Guardsmen). The big difference between us was that we made our mistakes together and everyone in the unit got better each day. The regulars were always having to train new guys. We went back to WWII stuff: I had my 'own' aircraft (54-1893) and my crew chief, Bernie and I used that F-100C 95 per cent of the time. This was great for morale. I never really looked at the plane during the pre-flight walk-around, just the weapons. If Bernie said it was ready, then it was! We partied hard with our enlisted men – the regulars couldn't do that. We deployed together and stayed together. The 'Tacos' (New Mexico ANG) were good 'sticks' too and great drinking buddies. We worked six weeks, then ten days off and the leave could be taken anywhere in the world as long as you were back in time for the next two to take theirs. I made it [to] Hawaii three times, Australia once and Taiwan many times. We would go to Cam Ranh Bay and hitch rides on ANG cargo planes. No wonder the DARTs didn't love us!

War, as witnessed on an Air Force base, was the most focused thing I have ever seen except pilot training: thousands of folks doing only one thing and that was putting the pilots in their seats and launching them. The whole thing was about numbers: sorties, bombs, commission rates, etc. For the pilots it really was easy except for that small part where someone was trying to kill you. There was a tremendous sense of detachment from the world. It took ten or twelve days to get a letter, and then we wouldn't want to get any bad news because we couldn't help. Life just consisted of, when do I get up? When do I fly? When can I have my first drink? Vietnam is one of the most beautiful countries in the world.

But on the other hand, I remember talking to a young West Point graduate on a night Alert, half an hour before his night checkout flight. He was married with a kid; had it all. Later, I went out for a cigarette and watched him take off, screw up his join-up with the Flight Lead and kill himself against a mountain. Just another day.

Two of the eight ANG F-100 units that were alerted on 25 January 1968 were sent to Kunsan, Korea instead of South Vietnam. The 127th TFS, Kansas ANG (with F-100Cs since converting from the F-86L in 1961) and the 166th TFS, Ohio ANG (formerly a USAF-gained F-84F unit at Etain) combined to become the nucleus of the regular 354th TFW at the Korean base until June 1969. The Kansas *Jayhawks* briefly

adopted 'BP' tail-codes and one aircraft acquired a spectacular shark mouth. The 166th TFS, one of four F-100 squadrons assigned to the Ohio ANG, flew Super Sabres longer than the other units in the Wing, acquiring F-100Cs in 1962 and replacing them with F-100Ds in 1971 until phase-out in 1974. It too received a tail-code ('BO') at Kunsan. The 354th TFW had been an F-100D Wing at Myrtle Beach

from late 1956 until it was effectively dismantled in mid-1968 and moved 'on paper' to Kunsan to replace the 4th TFW and act as parent wing for the two F-100 squadrons. Tasked with air defence of South Korea, the two squadrons suffered badly from lack of spare parts for their aging F-100Cs (all available spares having been channelled to the Vietnam units) and consequent declining readiness. They also lacked the all-weather capability needed for effective air defence in that environment.

Two other ANG squadrons moved to Myrtle Beach to establish a Replacement Training Unit (RTU) for F-100 crews. The 119th TFS, New Jersey ANG was divided up in March 1968, most personnel going to Myrtle Beach while the rest were dispersed to Korea or Vietnam. Half of its pilots were transferred to the 355th TFS at Tuy Hoa (after moving from Phu Cat in May 1969), which became, in many respects, the fifth Air Guard F-100 unit in South Vietnam. This situation continued until June 1969 when the 119th returned to New Jersey control and began conversion to the Republic F-105B. The other half of the Myrtle Beach RTU came from the 121st TFS, District of Columbia ANG which provided the core of the F-100 Combat Crew Training Squadron, coded 'XB'. Like the New Jersey unit, the 121st TFS completed its role as an F-100 'school' in June 1969 and returned to state control for transition to the F-105 Thunderchief.

Back in the USA

Air Guard F-100 squadrons began to return homeward in the summer of 1969 as part of the initial reduction of US forces in Vietnam. For the 120th TFS, return to Buckley ANGB, Colorado on 30 April 1969 meant two more years on the veteran F-100C before updating to the F-100D and subsequently to the LTV A-7D Corsair in April 1974 after thirteen years on Huns. Their F-100D/Fs wore the prominent red wildcat's head marking that had been painted on the nose-gear doors and vertical stabilizers of their 'VS'-coded F-100Cs in South Vietnam.

An even longer track record could be claimed by the 174th TFS with sixteen years on F-100C/D and F Super Sabres before it too became an A-7D outfit in 1976. As well as the Sioux City Squadron, the Iowa ANG included the 124th TFS at Des Moines, which exchanged its F-84Fs

F-100F 56-3786, newly arrived at AMARC from the Ohio ANG's 166th TFS in 1974. Author's Collection

The 119th TFS New Jersey ANG adopted 'XA' tail codes when called to active duty with the 113th TFW at Myrtle Beach AB in 1968. Ken Buchanan via John Maene

Another immaculate New Jersey ANG F-100C-6-NA. This Hun also passed to the Turkish AF in 1974. David Menard via John Maene

Standard New Jersey ANG markings appear on this F-100C-6-NA, which has the 'swan neck' refuelling probe and 335gal tanks. '782 later joined the Turkish AF. David Menard via John Maene

F-100C-2-NA 53-1747 of the District of Columbia ANG's 121st TFS also has *High Wire* updates. The red 'design' on the nose is actually an intake cover. Peter Schinkelshoek Collection

for F-100Cs in April 1971 and then F-100Ds in 1975 before joining the 'Corsair II Club' in January 1977.

As the first ANG unit to take aboard the F-100, the 188th TFS had long experience of the F-100A/C and F and it stuck with the battle-proven C models through to 1973 before taking on A-7Ds. Towards the end of their careers, several F-100Cs sloughed off their worn camouflage for a smart new coat of Air Defense Command (ADC) grey paint and a revival of the black and yellow chevrons and sunrays that the F-100A 'hot Huns' had once worn. The New York ANG 136th TFS, having received an Outstanding Unit Award in January 1970 for its war service, stayed in F-100Cs until April 1971 and then received its first F-101B/F Voodoos the following month, moving to ADC control as a result.

When the two Korean-deployed squadrons returned, the 127th TFS redeployed to McConnell AFB in June 1969. In the spring of 1971 it traded its F-100Cs for F-105Ds as a Tactical Fighter

A 110th TFS Missouri ANG F-100F attracts viewers in 1966. Some of the unit's F-100s had red nose and tail markings.
Peter Schinkelshoek Collection

Training Squadron (TFTS). Its former partner squadron at Kunsan, the 166th TFS, took on a batch of F-100D/Fs two years after its return to Lockbourne AFB and flew them until the end of 1974 when it became yet another A-7D operator. Ohio was one of the largest ANG F-100 Groups with four of its five flying squadrons having used the F-100. At Toledo airport the 112th TFS flew F-100Ds between October 1970 and summer 1979, absorbing some of the aircraft that were returned from Vietnam-based units as they upgraded to later types. Earlier in 1970, the 162nd TFS at Springfield also got F-100Ds to replace its F-84Fs and then received A-7Ds in April 1978. Their fourth unit, the 164th TFS at Mansfield-Lahm airport flew the F-100D for only three years from February 1972 and then changed completely to C-130s, providing logistical support during *Desert Storm*. Ohio's fifth squadron was a much-needed Air Refuelling Squadron (ARS).

A second F-100 TFTS was established within the Arizona ANG using the 152nd TFS. In 1958, it became one of the three Air Guard units to receive F-100As, the other two being the 188th TFS and the 118th TFS, Connecticut ANG. In 1965–66 both the 152nd TFS and 118th TFS began a period flying the F-102A Delta Dagger as ADC-gained squadrons, but by the summer of 1969 the Arizona squadron had reverted to F-100C/Fs as a TFTS, graduating to F-100Ds in July 1975. It then became the hard-worked RTU for Air Guard A-7D training in 1976 and for a time shared duties on both types until its last F-100Ds were phased out in March 1978. Connecticut pilots gave up their F-102As over the summer of 1971 and began a long period of F-100D/F 'ownership' that ended with the introduction of the A-10A 'Warthog' in mid-1979.

In all, twenty-six ANG squadrons flew Super Sabres. Two other states operated a pair of F-100 squadrons. The Indiana ANG

113th TFS at Terre Haute exchanged F-184Fs for F-100D/Fs in September 1971, shortly after the 163rd TFS *Marksmen* at Baer Field. Indiana Super Sabres deployed to RAF Lakenheath in April 1976 for a two-week exercise. Both units traded up to Phantoms in 1979, receiving some of the F-4C Wild Weasel IV aircraft in de-modified form. Massachusetts was the other state protected by a pair of F-100 squadrons; the 101st TFS from May 1971 and the 131st TFS from June of that year. A rapid change of policy meant re-training the 101st TFS on the F-106A Delta Dart a year later while the 131st continued until July 1979 before 'MA'-coded A-10As took over the flight-lines.

Also, upgrading to F-4Cs at that time was the 184th TFS, Arkansas ANG *Flying Razorbacks*, which had flown F-100D/Fs out of Fort Smith airport since the summer of 1972. Michigan's 107th TFS, previously an RF-101 Voodoo user (like the 184th TFS), got its Super Sabres in June 1972

This neat 1975 line-up of 124th TFS, Iowa ANG Huns has F-100D 56-3034 in the
foreground. Peter Schinkelshoek Collection

Another beautifully kept F-100D. This 131st TFS, Massachusetts ANG Hun returns from
a training mission. Coloured tail bands were applied to many of the unit's aircraft
before and after tail codes were marked up in 1979. Author's Collection

and A-7Ds took over six years later. Further north, in Sioux Falls, the 175th TFS *Lobos* of the South Dakota ANG relinquished an ADC role on F-102As to fly F-100D/Fs from May 1970 until it too acquired A-7Ds in 1977.

In the south, the Georgia, Missouri, Texas, Oklahoma and Louisiana Air Guard units all controlled single F-100D/F units in the late 1970s. Missouri's 110th TFS had previously flown the F-100C, beginning in August 1962 after a long period on F-84Fs. Their F-100Ds appeared from regular USAF units at the end of 1971 and stayed until the start of 1979. Georgia's 128th TFS had six years on F-100Ds from spring 1973 and then took over a batch of F-105Gs, while the Kelly AFB-based Texas ANG Squadron, the 182nd TFS, managed eight years (1971–79) on F-100Ds before a long period on the F-4C. Its easterly neighbour, the Oklahoma ANG took on F-100D/Fs in 1973 in place of lumbering C-124 transports, flying them until July 1978. NAS New Orleans was the base for Louisiana's 122nd TFS F-100D/Fs from late 1970 until April 1979. The *Coonass Militia* later

A challenging model diorama subject. A 163rd TFS, 122nd TFW Indiana ANG F-100D in deep periodic maintenance.
David Menard Collection

A rear view of the same Indiana ANG Super Sabre with the tail section slid off. The engine afterburner section was supported by an interim mount, fitted to the top of the fuselage just forward of the point where aircraft 'split' into two. David Menard Collection

became the first ANG squadron to receive the sophisticated F-15A Eagle.

The last ANG F-100 mission was flown by an Indiana ANG pilot, 1st Lt William Layne of the 113th TFS in 56-2979 *City of Terre Haute*. It was also the final USAF F-100 mission, though Brig Gen Frank Hettlinger, Commander of the 122nd TFW had the honour of flying the 23-year old F-100D to the Military Aircraft Storage and Disposition Center (MASDC), Arizona as 'FE627'. It remained there until its conversion to a QF-100 target drone and destruction by an AIM-7F missile on 21 February 1983 during its third target flight. At that time it had over 5,000

The Indiana ANG Hun's tail on its special handling vehicle. Although this aircraft's ANG badge has worn off, the yellow tail band remains. The Indiana logo was later changed to yellow also. David Menard Collection

Another F-100F, this time from the 182nd TFS, Texas ANG in 1976, with its state name in 'Old Western' script on a red band. Author's Collection

Police all around us. We were told not to leave the aircraft and we had two or three police with weapons drawn surrounding each F-100. Even the Base Commander arrived on the scene. We were told to board a bus and taken off to a hangar. About an hour later some Major told us to take all our A7 and MA2 power units and get the aircraft started for a bunch of officers (not ours) to move the Huns. The 136th TFS was famous immediately and the messes were buzzing for several days with stories of the Bandits of Hickam stealing F-100s.

John Maene and his New Jersey squadron participated in Operation *Gold Rush IV* in May 1967, when a dozen F-100s flew non-stop from Atlantic City to Elmendorf AFB for ten days. Tennessee ANG KC-97s were posted to the Alaskan base to refuel the Huns while they practised air defence and CAS missions. Standard training loads for these missions were two 335gal fuel tanks with either 2.75in rocket pods or practice bombs outboard, or inert 500- or 750lb bombs inboard and outboard.

Once or twice a year a flare rocket and inert AIM-9 were hung on the F-100's left inboard pylon. The pilot fired the rocket, waited a few seconds and then fired the Sidewinder, like shooting fish in a barrel.

Summer camps took the NJ ANG to places like Cape Cod, courtesy of the Massachusetts ANG. We lived in old WWII barracks with the Rhode Island ANG marching band coming through at an ungodly hour after a great party

hours of flight on its service record including several years of USAFE service. A number of F-100 pilots could boast even longer periods of flight time, 5,600 hours being the USAF high-time record held by Dick Salazar. For many other pilots who moved on to more user-friendly jets, the F-100 nevertheless remained a favourite memory: the aircraft on which they really learned to fly fighters.

Air Guard units were quite often asked to deploy over long distances for exercises or TDYs. In August 1963, the New York ANG took part in *Swift Strike III* at McGhee-Tyson AFB in Tennessee. One of the unit's biggest deployments pre-Vietnam was *Tropic Lightning* to Hawaii in August 1965, the first Pacific crossing by an ANG tactical fighter squadron. On arrival, some cultural differences between regular USAF and ANG practices caused a few misunderstandings, as Bobby Wright remembered:

We flew in a C-130 from Niagara Falls to California to ready our birds for the second leg of the journey to Hawaii, and then resumed our own journey to Hickam Field, Hawaii. Upon being assigned to our lovely WWII wooden barracks we were briefed to take our aircraft to a designated site some distance from the main base, as we would be using live ordnance on our missions.

Moving the aircraft was routine to us because we were licensed, as full-time technicians, to run up and taxi the birds. We fired them up and

proceeded to the active runway in single file with the canopies open. The control tower operator spotted us and wanted to know what in hell a bunch of non-commissioned personnel were doing in those birds. Air Force regulations said specifically that only officers could taxi aircraft. Our lead man, a Tech Sergeant, tried to explain that we were licensed to do it but the tower wouldn't buy this and told us to shut down engines immediately. Before we knew it there was a bunch of vehicles and Air Force

District of Columbia ANG F-100Cs were camouflaged by 1970 when this later shot of 53-1747 was taken. Two years later it was in the Turkish AF. Peter Schinkelshoek Collection

125

Keeping Them in The Air

S/Sgt Bobby 'Orville' Wright looked after an F-100C for the 136th TFS from 1963 to 1967. His Hun, 'one hell of a performer', earned him Crew Chief of the Month as it did for two of his successors. He explains the routine for getting the F-100C ready to go.

In winter I would first remove the protective cover over the canopy. Then we'd check the afterburner 'eyelids'. We used to push them into the open position on the flight line and cover them over. This retracted the actuating pistons and protected them from the weather. When a pilot went into afterburner and the eyelids didn't open he got a tremendous engine 'chatter' (I did this once in a simulator and it scared the cr*p out of me!).

Then the in-flight refuelling boom would be checked. On practice missions many came back with this boom sticking straight up in the air. It was made of aluminium and could not stand much abuse. Pilots were very embarrassed when they returned with it in this condition. We didn't straighten them out and I saw several in the boneyard but the rule was 'remove and replace'.

Capt Allen Lamb asserted that accidentally bent booms were the inspiration for the later, cranked boom that pilots could see more easily when refuelling than the original straight model. The probes were made of tapered aluminium pipe with a wall thickness that was greater at the rear of the tube where it attached to the wing.

Next we'd check the pitot static boom and the spring-loaded clasps that held the wing slats in the retracted position. The slats would often extend when the F-100 was in the in-flight refuelling position due to the low speed and high angle of attack. Going under the aircraft we would remove the red-painted, metal landing gear downlocks.

The next chore was to fill the liquid oxygen (LOX) canister from the LOX cart. There was no way of measuring the LOX and it was just fed in until you got a steady stream of overflow. This job required us to wear a rubber apron, face shield and heavy gloves. We put a metal pan on the ground to collect the excess LOX, which boiled off very rapidly. It was a very dangerous chore and one had to be extremely careful.

Refuelling the bird was done through the single-point receptacle on the left side of the fuselage, supplying fuel to the wing cells and the forward and aft fuselage cells. Drop tanks had to be filled by hand. The total capacity for the aircraft was 17,933lb, sufficient for 2 hours 20 minutes (with drop tanks).

The 'wet' wings would weep fuel frequently but that wasn't a serious hazard. We would inject sealant when needed but it wasn't very frequent. We would remove old P2 or P3 screws, inject the sealant and replace the screws. Most of this was done as a routine part of periodic inspection.

Fuel pumps in the wheel wells were checked for proper operation. We had to crawl down the air intake and look at the first-stage turbine blades for any nicks or cracks. If there were cracks over 1/8in deep the aircraft would be grounded for engine removal and inspection at the engine shop. Inside the intake was a shield (called a 'dog pecker') that covered a hydraulic pump

and when the pump failed it was a real bitch to change because of the confined space. I did that chore many times on hot tarmac and that ain't no fun.

All tyre pressures had to be checked and corrected if necessary: 231psi for main gear tyres and 175psi for the nose gear tyres. Landing gear strut pressure had to be 3,000psi. Tyres were checked for 'bull's-eye' chafes caused by too much yaw on landing peeling the tread from the casing and showing the layers of different coloured cord underneath. When red appeared the tyre had to be changed. Young pilots (or hung-over ones) would leave with brand new tyres, make one landing, score a 'bull's-eye' and have to write it up on the form. They knew the crew chief would be annoyed because changing a tyre was a big job. Each tyre change required an anti-skid check by two people and a very rigid inspection. Safety wiring of nuts and bolts was an art and had to be done so that the wires were pulling bolts tight all the time. Wheel assemblies also housed the disc brakes that were as heavy as hell. The number of landings per tyre would be judged by the type of landing-strip surface. In Florida some of the old runways were made of crushed coral and tar, which was highly abrasive.

F-100 tyres could take some abuse, as John Maene, a crew chief with the 177th TFG, New Jersey ANG recollected:

One freezing morning our unit was in the middle of an ORI [Operational Readiness Inspection] and we were doing our final inspections before letting the weapons crews arm the bombs and cannons. The last F-100F (just out of periodic inspection with new tyres) had an Inspector in the back seat observing the mission. Its crew taxied on to the active runway, ran up the engine, checked all systems, released brakes and rolled forward, hitting 'burner as they accelerated to take-off speed. Suddenly, someone announced over the radio that the Hun had blown a tyre and we wondered how this could have happened with new tyres.

By the time the maintenance truck arrived at the point where the aircraft had successfully engaged the arresting cable the firemen were trying to push the still-running bird back off the cable. Finally, the pilot shut down. His brakes and tyres were dangerously close to blowing after the aborted take-off, but the puff of smoke that someone had thought was a tyre blowing out was actually the jettisoned drag chute package hitting the runway. Water had frozen in the F-100F's pitot tube preventing any airspeed indication. The pilot aborted take-off, dropped his tail hook and instead of deploying his drag chute he accidentally jettisoned it. The good news was that the maintenance men were cleared of any wrongdoing. [The pitot system had to be purged with dry compressed air by instrument specialists if any moisture was discovered when the pitot drain plugs were pulled.] The first time you personally installed a drag chute and launched your bird your anxiety level went up several notches when you saw your particular F-100 in the landing pattern. Our base had a small rise partly blocking the view of the active runway and I had to wait to see the aircraft appear the other side of the rise to make sure the chute had deployed.

Bobby Wright's pre-flight continued with a check of the F-100's static fluid leaks.

Aircraft perform better the more they are flown. The F-100C hydraulic system ran at 3,000psi, using 5606 hydraulic fluid (the aircraft's oil was 58508e synthetic grade). When the system wasn't under pressure many static leaks appeared. This wasn't really a problem, but convincing a pilot of this point during his walk-around inspection was a pain. We would wipe up all the evidence under the bird when we saw the pilot approaching and if 'greenhorn' pilots made an issue of it we would say, 'Are you going to fly this thing or pull a Quality Control Inspection on it?'

The preparations continued with unfolding and locking the pitot boom and then installing the drag chute.

This was a hell of a job, especially for short guys like me. You had to lie on your back, balancing the chute on your feet and stuff it into the hopper, close the door with your feet and use a 15in screwdriver to close and lock the fastener. I used to wait until the bird was refuelled before I did this because the landing gear struts would compress, bringing the back end of the Hun closer to the ground so that my short legs could reach the drag chute compartment. A red flagged safety cable was attached to the chute and the pilot had to pull this on his walk-around.

We made a visual inspection of the wheel wells, looking for any chafing of hydraulic lines and cables. If any was detected we separated the lines with a leather chafe-pad. The 'saddle' access door on the upper fuselage, behind the cockpit, was removed to inspect hydraulic fluid levels. Using the A7 external electrical power generator we'd do an instrument test and a radio check with the control tower. Then we would connect the MA 2 air turbine compressor hose to the lower rear fuselage ready to start the engine. The pilot made the walk-around check, removing safety flags from the drop tanks and drag chute. We then helped to strap him into the cockpit.

John Maene:

Normally, pilots would position their helmet and oxygen mask on the top centre of the windshield. I once strapped a pilot in and assumed his helmet was down on the right hand circuit breaker panel, out of my view. After all the straps were tightened he reached for his helmet, realized he had totally forgotten it and asked me to go and get the 'missing flight gear'. Good thing he wasn't scrambling that day.

Communication between pilot and crew chief could provide some semantic problems once they went beyond the normal 'semaphore' routines too. John Maene explained:

A new ruling came down that any F-100 running its engine on the flight line had to have its navigation lights on to warn ramp personnel to stay away. My 'mentor', TSgt Wilfred Hickerson saw that a pilot hadn't done this and tried banging on the aircraft's wingtip to get the pilot's attention while he also pointed at the un-illuminated nav light. The pilot merely looked confused. Next, 'Hick' started rapidly blinking his eyes while he continued to point at the light.

When that too failed he finally climbed up the ladder to the cockpit and yelled at the top of his lungs as he pointed at the pilot's navigation light switch.

Some ground crew initiatives lay well outside the guidelines, as John described:

Before one simulated 'strafing of enemy positions' near 'friendly troops' some smart-ass came up with the brilliant idea of putting several rolls of toilet paper up in the Huns' speed brake wells. As the aircraft approached the friendly troops the pilots deployed their speed brakes, bombing the troops with streaming rolls of toilet tissue. Needless to say, the Army boys really weren't amused.

In the final stages before flight, the engine would be started, using an established series of hand-signals to communicate with the pilot. The crew chief would then clamber on to the fuselage and peer into the 'saddle-back' access area to check that the hydraulic pistons operating the rudder were working properly when the pilot moved the rudder pedals. The saddleback was then replaced and latched down. Bobby Wright explained:

We would then remove all external gear, wind up the static line and secure it into the nose-wheel door. Just before removing the chocks the pilot had to show us the two red safety flags from his ejection seat. Chocks were then pulled, the pilot was guided off his parking position with a salute and he was on his way. When a crew chief signed his name to an aircraft form to say it was safe and ready to fly it was kind of a sacred thing because we took great pride in our job. The F-100 carried the requisite Form 781 (stored in the cockpit or in a vent hole in the 20mm bay when the aircraft wasn't on a combat or gunnery mission) to record all 'write-ups' by pilots or maintainers. A red dash on the form indicated the need for routine mainte-nance. A red diagonal meant non-critical scheduled maintenance and a red 'X' meant the aircraft could not fly until the problem was solved. In the ANG, a dropped pencil in the cockpit or the smallest nut or bolt astray meant a red 'X'. This wasn't always done in regular units.

The 136th TFS inherited its F-100Cs from a Bitburg-based Unites States Air Force in Europe (USAFE) Wing and Bobby was not impressed by the state of the aircraft on arrival. 'As we disassembled the aircraft we removed *bags* of FOD.'

Forms 210 and 211 were used for smaller jobs like tyre changes. Work cards would be available in the unscheduled maintenance docks and for 50 or 100hr or later inspections. In the New York ANG a crew chief could work alongside the programmed maintenance personnel as his aircraft went through deeper mainte-nance. However, his work had to be inspected by a mechanic who was generally a rank above himself.

the night before, waking us up with bad headaches. We got even a few days later when someone strung aircraft safety wire across their route causing the first few rows of band members and their instruments to wind up in a big pile on the ground, cursing and yelling.

There were more serious setbacks too, particularly as pilots trained for their forthcoming South East Asia deployments. In 1965, a New York pilot was lost as a result of 'target fixation' during an air-to-ground delivery, and two collided over Lake Ontario in an air combat manoeuvring (ACM) exercise. No trace of either the pilots or their aircraft was ever found.

An active ANG F-100 squadron was just as busy as a regular unit. John Maene:

We had two rows of F-100s facing each other as Flights A and B, comprising roughly twenty-two F-100Cs and two F-100Fs [the normal complement of two-seaters in an F-100 unit]. Each Hun had a Crew Chief and at least one Assistant. They personally serviced their aircraft except that sometimes a lower-rank maintainer from each flight would have a daily work-list of which birds needed to be 'LOXed'. A couple of trucks constantly patrolled the flight line relaying requests from crew chiefs via radio to the various mainte-nance shops (avionics, engine, hydraulics, sheet metal etc.). At regular hours on a progressive basis the aircraft had preventative maintenance per-formed. For example, the J57-P-21A engine had a time between overhauls (TBO) of 200 hours.

Although the F-100 fleet received few updates during its ANG years there was one very practical modification to the engine in many F-100Ds, Fs and a few F-100Cs that solved its earlier afterburner problems. The Convair F-102A Delta Dagger used the same basic engine in its J57-P-23A form with a more reliable afterburner nozzle arrangement using actuating rods. F-102s equipped twenty-three ANG squadrons from 1960 onwards, but all had been retired to the Aerospace Maintenance and Regeneration Center (AMARC) by October 1976. As David Menard explained:

The original afterburner eyelids on the J57-21 drove our engine troops crazy as they would get out of alignment and this affected the thrust. We built special tools to push them back into the correct shape. On bases with F-102s our engine maintainers asking if they could use the afterburners from them for F-100s and the idea got shot down every time. Then an Arizona ANG NCO got permission from his commanding officer [CO] to fit one and try it out. Getting F-102 afterburners from AMARC was a snap and it worked just great, as predicted by regular USAF troops. The NCO got a US$20,000 bonus for 'his' idea!

F-100s served in ANG squadrons for twenty-one years until November 1979. In that year, ten of the twenty-six ANG units that had used F-100Ds relinquished their aircraft and the Hun entered the final stages of its career in the USA – as a target drone for its more potent fighter successors.

An attractive ADC grey colour scheme and original F-100A-style markings were used in place of camouflage on several 188th TFS F-100Cs in 1972, towards the end of their service. Peter Schinkelshoek Collection

A 103rd TFG, Connecticut ANG F-100F-2-NA (56-3732) on a visit to Ramstein AB, 1975. Two years later, it crossed the
Atlantic again on delivery to Turkey. Author's Collection

An impressively tidy parade of 124th TFS F-100Cs. This unit was one of two within the Iowa ANG to fly F-100s and both
transitioned to the F-100D, 1971–74. Douglas E. Slowiak via David Menard

F-100C 54-1873 of the 4758th DSES from Biggs AFB, landing at Howard AFB in the Canal Zone in July 1969.
S/Sgt D. Rankin USAF via Ron Thurlow

Fiery Final Flights: QF-100

The use of full-scale aerial targets (FSAT) to give pilots realistic missile firing experience had been well established with the conversion, between 1973 and 1981, of 215 QF-102A and PQM-102A/B Delta Daggers in Project *Pave Deuce*. Sperry

Flight Systems had removed the weapons and fire control systems, seat and control columns from the ex-ANG F-102s and installed a self-destruct mechanism and a data link package that fitted on to the ejection seat rails. This system fed information from a ground-based control station to the aircraft's engine and flight con-

trols, enabling it to perform like a piloted fighter, or better (8g turns were possible). The *Pave Deuce* drones were destroyed at a prodigious rate between 1975 and 1982, necessitating a replacement type before the F-106 Delta Dart became available for the purpose in 1986.

Sperry received a contract in March 1982 to carry out similar conversions to ex-ANG F-100s in storage at MASDC. An initial batch of nine trial aircraft was prepared at the company's Litchfield airport facility in Arizona. The first two, F-100Ds 56-3414 '092' and 55-3610 '093', were designated YQF-100Ds and retained cockpit controls so that pilots could evaluate the data link systems. The next three were QF-100Ds, converted to the USAF's standard no live operator onboard (NOLO) configuration, followed by a similarly appointed

JF-100F 56-3744 was used by WADC to fly through thunderstorms during Project *Rough Raider*. Sensor probes extend from modified 275gal tanks. Its orange/red décor needed frequent repair due to weather attrition. David Menard Collection

F-100F 56-3746, delivered to AMARC from the 113th TFS at Hulman Field, Indiana awaits conversion to QF-100F configuration in 1979. It expired on 8 October 1970 on its eighth unmanned drone flight. Author's Collection

QF-100 F (56-3984). This aircraft and the second NOLO conversion (55-3669) crashed on take-off after un-piloted flights began at Tyndall AFB on 19 November 1981. Three QF-100Ds (conversions 098-100) were for a US Army requirement for multi-target missions.

Drone conversion involved the installation by Sperry of a command/telemetry system (C/TS) that could decode signals from a remote control station and convert them into data for a newly installed aircraft flight control system (AFCS) or 'brain'. The AFCS also relayed back information from the QF-100's onboard sensors. Control inputs could be made to operate the arresting hook, braking chute, speed brake and landing gear as well as primary flight, engine and fuel controls. AFCS also relayed a 'command destruct' signal if the mission had to be terminated in an emergency but there was also a back-up UHF receiver for this terminal situation. A smoke-emission system (similar to the one provided for aerobatic demonstration

'231' is from the Flight Systems QF-100D conversion batch, using F-100D 55-3679 ex-Louisiana ANG. This very weathered Hun eventually succumbed to an AIM-9M missile on 23 October 1987. Serial and code application on red/orange bands is typical. Author's Collection

One of the most distinctive F-100 schemes was used by AFLC's F-100D-20-NA 55-3511 at McClellan AFB in 1964. The SMAMA (represented here by a group of its personnel) lettering was in red over a yellow alar while the rest of the aircraft was red and white with black cheat lines. The magnificent '511, used by AFLC as a pattern aircraft, later went to war with the 308th TFS at Tuy Hoa and was shot down on 28 December 1969.
Norm Taylor Collection

aircraft) was installed so that the QF-100 could produce a visual 'ID' if required.

In order to increase the useful life of each expensive drone, AAMs with inert warheads could be fired at it, and a digital Doppler system (DIGIDOPS) with four sensors at the aircraft's nose, tail, and above and below the fuselage measured the 'miss distance' of any missile passing within 200ft (60m) of the QF-100. Pilots could then get a theoretical kill while the QF-100 lived on. Ordnance pylons could also take fuel tanks, electronic countermeasures (ECM) pods and chaff/flare dispensers to make the intercepting fighter jock's job harder. All aircraft could be de-converted to piloted configuration if required, with or without the AFCS engaged. Under remote control, the QF-100 could be flown singly or in a formation of up to six aircraft (in manned configuration) to simulate multiple threats. Not all QF-100s had the drone formation control system (DFCS) needed for this mode and, in practice, the usual number for NOLO formation mode was two aircraft.

In unmanned mode, two controllers were needed for each QF-100, one for pitch and throttle control and the other for ailerons and rudder. A mobile control station near the runway managed launch and recovery but the rest of each mission was 'flown' from a fixed ground station. Controllers relied entirely on data from the QF-100's sensors without an onboard TV camera link like the ones used in the USN QF-4N/S Phantom programme. Following the batch of nine trials aircraft, Sperry converted another 89 QF-100D (conversion numbers 101–189) and two QF-100F (501/2) drones for use by the 82nd Tactical Aerial Targets Squadron (TATS), 475th Weapons Evaluation Group at Tyndall AFB, Florida. Some were used by the 82nd TATS Detachment at Holloman AFB.

The FSAT programme then passed to the Flight Systems Inc. (FSI) division of Tracor at Kern County airport, Mojave. The first (55-2863 '201') of 169 QF-100D (201–369) and forty-one QF-100F

(370–410) conversions was delivered to Holloman AFB on 28 September 1985. The programme continued until December 1990 when Program Manager Larry H. Rectenwald had to terminate the contract for the USAF since McClellan AFB was already gearing up to engage with the QF-4 Phantom drone programme. At that stage, fourteen aircraft were still in various stages of conversion and eleven of them (QF-100F '411–421') were returned to AMARC (six flew, five were trucked), given new MASDC serials and stored as possible display items for USAF or other museums. Other AMARC aircraft provided spares for the FSAT programme.

The life of a 'drone Hun' was usually very brief, most ending in blazing showers of debris over the sea after a hit by an AIM-7 or AIM-9 missile during their first three or four flights. Eighty-eight were destroyed on their first NOLO flight and twenty-four either crashed during a mission or had to be destroyed after a technical failure. However, a few survived up to fifteen flights before being nailed by a missile. Larry Rectenwald noted that towards the end of the programme:

We were averaging fourteen shots at a drone before it was killed. Engines were a problem as J57 parts were scarce. Some engines were rated for very few hours of running time. I was buying parts from countries like Turkey and Germany to put the QFs in flying condition. One item that was real scarce also was vertical stabilizers. After the programme was finished I got a call from Supply at McClellan and I went down to their warehouse where they had found nine brand new stabilizers! All the QF-100s re-built while I was managing them could be flown by a pilot [rather than NOLO] just by flipping a switch. They had to be this way so that they could be delivered to Tyndall or Holloman. The aircraft were accepted by the USAF after they arrived at the bases after being ferried in by Tracor pilots.

QF-100s played a role in the AMRAAM programme. QF-100D 55-2877, ex-110th TFS, fell to an AMRAAM fired head-on from an F-16A over White Sands Missile Range on 17 September 1985.

The drones retained their basic Vietnam camouflage, often severely faded after a decade in AMARC's sun-baked storage lots, with Day-Glo red horizontal and vertical stabilizers and bands in the same colour on the nose and wing-tips. Serial numbers appeared on the vertical stabilizer and conversion numbers on the nose in white. In

N417FS (TF-100F 56-3842), a former Danish AF example, seen in 1997. Author's Collection

some cases the insignia of former ANG owners could still be seen. In action, they continued to demonstrate considerable structural strength, returning on several occasions with shredded tail control surfaces or even missing a horizontal stabilizer.

FSI also flew eight F-100D/Fs for the US Army at Holloman AFB in 1992 in connection with Hawk missile development. Four were ex-QF-100s, though not all had been converted, and the rest came from AMARC F-100F stock. An F-100D and six ex- Royal Danish AF F-100Fs were also operated by FSI, some of them to tow high-speed DART targets for USAFE units. Also, three ex-Turkish AF F-100Cs were obtained in 1989 as possible drone conversions but were sold on to private collectors when that project was dropped. A further batch of F-100Fs was used by the US Army for an undisclosed project for which they retained USAF serials along with their 'Army' marking and some QF-100s were bought by the US Army for Stinger missile development.

F-100A 53-1688, the only civil registered F-100A, owned but never flown by Flight Test Research of Long Beach, California. The N100X registration was actually used by a Learjet at the time. Peter Schinkelshoek Collection

CHAPTER 6

Under Foreign Flags

113 Filo's early yellow *Korsan* (pirate) markings enhance this F-100D-10-NA, delivered to the Turkish AF in 1959.
Turkish Air Force/Soner Capoglu via David Menard

Although the F-100 never came close to the success of its F-86 forebear in the export market, it served for a considerable time with the four foreign air forces that operated it. The first to do so was the Armée de l'Air in France, which flew F-100D/Fs for over twenty years. Many examples of the F-100A went to the Republic of China Air Force (RoCAF). The Royal Danish Air Force (RDAF) also used F-100D/Fs and the largest foreign user of all, the Turkish Air Force (THK), absorbed 270 examples of the F-100C/D and F.

Armée de l'Air

As the first 'foreign' user of the F-100, France received eighty-eight F-100Ds and fourteen F-100Fs (including thirteen F-100s that were bought directly by the French government). The first was received at Luxeil AB in the winter of 1958 and the last F-100 flight was made in December 1978; an Army cooperation flight in the French protectorate of Djibouti.

The 11th Escadre de Chasse, formerly an F-84G unit, was the first to receive Huns, some of them early ex-48th Tactical Fighter Wing (TFW) aircraft already based in France. They came to the unit via inspect and repair as necessary (IRAN) in Spain and the first F-100Fs for squadrons EC 1/11 *Rousillon* and EC 2/11 *Vosges* still wore USAF 'FW' buzz-numbers. A group of 11th Escadre pilots went to Luke AFB at the beginning of January 1958 for F-100 indoctrination, returning in May. They were mightily impressed by the Hun with its 'P.C.' ('post combustion' or afterburner),

capacious cockpit and outstanding interception capability. Conversion of the Escadre at Luxeil-St Sauveur took eighteen months and was completed by the end of 1959.

Next to transition was the 3rd Escadre which, like the 11th, had sent F-84Fs to RAF Akrotiri during the Suez crisis. Its first Super Sabres arrived at Reims-Champagne in January 1959 to begin re-equipping EC 1/3 *Navarre* and then EC 2/3 *Champagne* with twenty-four aircraft in each squadron. They were delivered by USAF ferry pilots and refuelled en route by KC-97 tankers. Transition was complete by the end of January 1960 and EC 1/3 (yellow squadron colour) was in action from late 1959 in the Algerian campaign, flying ground attack sorties against targets in eastern Algeria from Reims and refuelling at Istres on the return leg.

F-100D 54-2212 of EC 1/11 *Rousillon*, which flew F-100s from 1 May 1958 until 10 October 1975. This aircraft became a
gate guard at RAF Sculthorpe, and later at RAF Upper Heyford in the markings of 56-3000 *Triple Zilch.* David Menard

54-2267 of EC 1/11 visits Hahn AB in 1960, before the application of fuselage codes.
This aircraft's entire fourteen-year career was spent with the 11th Escadre de Chasse,
ending in 1977. David Menard

The newly equipped squadrons deployed to the Gunnery Live Training unit at Cazaux, south-west of Bordeaux for armament practice with eleven aircraft from EC 2/3 (red squadron colour) and thirteen from EC 1/11. They gained proficiency in air-to-air and air-to-ground gunnery, napalm, rocket and Mk 25 bomb delivery in a total of 937 sorties.

The 3rd Escadre moved to Lahr in West Germany on 10 June 1961 while the 11th Escadre transferred to NATO Base 136 at Bremgarten, West Germany at the same time. This move coincided with the assumption of nuclear strike status, using Mk 43 atomic weapons, as part of the 4th Allied Tactical Air Force. Aircraft had the same weapons and fuel tank configuration as their USAF Victor Alert counterparts except that French pilots never officially flew with actual nuclear weapons and missions with 'training shapes' were very rare too. Mostly, the F-100s flew with 'simulated' nuclear weapons, i.e. empty pylons on low-altitude bombing system (LABS) and

The EC 1/3 *Navarre* badge is painted on the nose of F-100D-15-NA 54-2247, seen here on a low-altitude strike training sortie in the early 1960s. via J. J. Petit

skip-bombing missions over the Bodensee range at 'TBA' (*très basse altitude* – very low altitude). EC 2/11 was the first to achieve readiness in the strike role on 20 May 1963 and it established a two-aircraft alert, guarded by US personnel.

The French squadrons thus became fully integrated into NATO's nuclear strategy without having to upload US nuclear weapons on French soil. After 1967, EC 3/11 Huns were fitted with inflight-refuelling probes (the cranked or 'swan neck' variant) to practise refuelling from C-135F tankers with hose and drogue extensions to their Flying Boom refuelling systems. Armée de l'Air F-100s took part in AFCENT Tactical Air Meets, flying strike, close support and low-level navigation sorties in 1963 at Rhein Hopsten and in 1964 at Chaumont.

When General de Gaulle took France out of NATO, the F-100s left Lahr and Bremgarten, while USAF units were obliged to leave French bases. The 3rd Escadre relocated to Nancy-Ochey in September 1967 after beginning transition at Lahr to the Mirage IIIE. After a brief extension of their stay at Bremgarten, the 11th Escadre moved to Toul-Rosieres, an American-built base, between July and September 1967. Twenty F-100Ds and four F-100Fs from the 3rd Escadre were absorbed to

form a new squadron, EC 3/11 *Corse*. There was also a change of role, as the F-100s became part of France's FATac (*Force Aérienne Tactique*) with a conventional mission involving close air support (CAS)

and ground attack. Their secondary air defence task included protection of the Berlin air corridor.

EC 3/11 became the F-100 Operational Conversion Unit (OCU) and after 1967 it included training for inflight-refuelling as part of its syllabus and for overseas intervention including 'policing' missions in Djibouti territory from April 1970. Prior to that it had flown successful simulated anti-shipping strikes against the USS *Saratoga* with eight aircraft in December 1969 (during *Lafayette* exercises in Mediterranean airspace) and achieved excellent scores in the 1969 AFCENT Gunnery Competition. In November 1971, three of 3/11's aircraft took part in a three-month evaluation of the type's resistance to the difficult climatic conditions in the French protectorate of Djibouti, bordering the Gulf of Aden.

In 1973, North American Aviation (NAA) proposed a structural strengthening programme for thirty of the Escadre's older F-100Ds, comprising strengthening of the wing box and skins, and main fuselage longerons. The work was carried out at the SNIAS facility at Chateauroux, continuing into 1975. At the same time, a three-tone USAF-style camouflage (using lighter shades of tan and green with blue-grey undersides) was applied to the fleet between 1972 and 1976. Toul received its

The last F-100s assigned to ESC 3 leave their base at Lahr in January 1966. 3-JV (56-4009) was later issued to EC 2/11, then 3/11 and finally 1/11 while the 3-JV code was also used for a time by 56-4008. Here, '009 carries the insignia of 2/3 *Champagne*. It was returned to USAF charge as 11-ES and scrapped by the end of 1977. via J. J. Petit

Still in bare metal finish, an EC 1/11 F-100D-15-NA cuts through some typical European weather. David Menard Collection

F-100D 54-2269, still in its EC 1/11 colours, at RAF Lakenheath on 23 May 1976. It was displayed on the gate there as '54-048'. On the tail is the insignia of GC III/6-5e Escadrille. G. Pennick via David Menard

tinued with F-100s until 25 June 1977, when it too transitioned to Jaguars. At that time, the 11th Escadre had completed 205,000 F-100 hours. Col Boichot, Toul's base commander and one of the original cadre of pilots to convert to the F-100 at Nellis AFB, made the last F-100 flight from the base in 54-2131/11-MJ on 11 May 1977.

EC 4/11 continued on with the remaining Huns in Djibouti, replacing EC 1/21 (flying AD-4 Skyraiders) in January 1973. Missions from Djibouti's Base Aérienne 188 shared a runway with the republic's airport and sought to protect the fledgling state from incursions by communist-inspired insurgents. The squadron's initial strength of seven F-100Ds and an F-100F (for one Flight, SPA 158) was soon increased to fifteen aircraft and a second Flight, SPA 161, was added. Between March and June 1978, the aircraft acquired some of the most spectacular shark-mouth markings ever seen on warplanes and one or two recce pods (on the inner wing position) were decorated with eagle heads based on the nose décor of 498th Bomb Squadron B-25Js in WWII. On 24 May 1978, Lt Col Salmon led eleven F-100s in formation over Djibouti to celebrate the squadron's 10,000 hours of Super Sabre flying. Its final flight was made on 12 December 1978 and EC 4/11 was deactivated at the end of that year, concluding over twenty years of F-100 flying by the Armée de l'Air. Under the terms of MAP, the surviving forty F-100s were returned to USAF charge at RAF Sculthorpe where they were either scrapped or donated to museums. Others stayed as decoys at Djibouti AB. One aircraft, 54-2165/11-ML from EC2/11 had previously served with the 493rd Fighter-bomber Squadron (FBS), 48th Fighter-bomber Wing (FBW) at Chaumont from 1957 to 1959 before being passed to EC 1/3 at Reims as 3-IG. After nearly two years of storage at Sculthorpe it was donated to the Duxford American Air Museum and displayed as an aircraft of the 352nd TFS, 35th TFW during the Vietnam War.

first camouflaged Hun (54-2160/11-ET) on 23 June 1974.

On 1 June 1973, EC 4/11 *Jura* formed in Djibouti, drawing pilots and two aircraft from each of the other units with an extra pair of F-100Ds and an F-100F from 3/11. It took over the name and insignia previously used by EC 3/11 *Jura* and a mission involving air defence and escort for reconnaissance flights that had begun in December 1972.

EC 3/11 began conversion to the SEPECAT Jaguar in February 1975, after 36,704 flying hours on F-100s. EC 1/11 also moved to the Jaguar after its last F-100 flight on 10 October 1975. EC 2/11 con-

Republic of China Air Force

In 1960, the RoCAF on Taiwan became the only operator of the F-100A outside the USA. The aircraft were supplied in response to the sporadic conflict between Communist China and Taiwan, initiated

Pilots from the Republic of China AF walk out for another training mission. Both jets have the original three-digit code and USAF buzz numbers. F-100F-15-NA 56-3968/001 and 56-3987/005 were among the first batch of two-seaters to be delivered. '001' was later displayed at the RoCAF Museum. Clarence Fu

in August 1958 by artillery attacks on the Nationalist-held island of Quemoy. Air battles over the Formosa Straits between RoCAF F-86Fs and Communist MiG-15s and MiG-17s had resulted in losses on both sides, but principally to the mainland MiGs. AIM-9B Sidewinder missiles were fired by the Sabres on 24 September 1958, the first use of air-to-air missiles in combat. Communist China then proclaimed the imminent invasion of Quemoy, moving large forces into position opposite the island, as a prelude to the 'liberation' of Taiwan.

The RoCAF's three Wings of F-86F Sabres and two Wings of F-84Gs were thought to be inadequate for a potential conflict of that magnitude, despite the presence of USN aircraft carriers and USAF F-100Ds of the 511th TFS and 354th TFW at Ching Chuan, Taiwan and at Kadena AB respectively, plus other USAF units in the area.

Between February and May of 1960, the USA supplied eighty F-100As to equip three squadrons: the 21st (red), 22nd (yellow) and 23rd (blue) of the 4th Group. Of these the 23rd was later reassigned to the 11th Group at Hsinchu AB, which had already received thirty-five aircraft for its 17th Squadron. The latter unit transitioned at Chiayi AB with the 4th Group and returned to Hsinchu as the 41st FBS. There it was joined by the 42nd FBS, with its distinctive red flash markings and a squadron of F-104A Starfighters. The third Hsinchu-based unit was the 48th FBS that used nose-markings similar to those of the USAF Thunderbirds team. A display at Sung Shan airport, Taipei on 6 December 1959 included a fifteen-aircraft 'anchor' formation with the RoCAF Thundertigers F-86 aerobatic team. The 48th FBS was the last unit in the world to fly the F-100A when it finally phased out its aircraft on 5 September 1984.

The first RoCAF Super Sabres to arrive were six F-100F-15-NAs (56-3968, -77,

-78, -79, -87, -88, numbered 001–006 after delivery) in August 1958 for the 4th FBW. USAF Capts Max Jesperson and Robert Preciado with 1st Lts Duane Mill, Robert Cameron, Steve Braswell and Bob Johnston made the ferry flight from California and trained the first batch of nine RoCAF instructors. Meanwhile, maintainers learned the subtle arts of tending the birds, including the unique trick of lying on their backs to push the drag chute compartment door shut with their feet. They also added their own techniques including a new device for towing an F-100 with a flat tyre.

From this first batch of F-100Fs, three were lost in fatal accidents by 1976, one was scrapped and two lived on as museum exhibits. Another eight two-seaters (F-100F-5-NA, -10-NA and -15-NA variants) were delivered including 56-3808, which arrived in USAF camouflage rather than the silver lacquer of the other aircraft.

When the first four F-100As from the initial batch of fifteen were flown into

F-100F-15-NA 56-3979 with an early serial/code presentation incorporating the original USAF buzz number and the designation 'F-100004' above the serial. It served the Republic of China AF until 4 August 1960 when both its crew had to eject. David Menard Collection

23rd Squadron F-100As with blue trim. 53-1539 was one of the JF-100A-10-NAs used by ARDC until its transfer to the Republic of China AF where it flew with the 48th Squadron as '0104'. David Menard Collection

Chiayi AB, Maj Roy Moore was selected as Flight Commander for the delivery flight.

When we took the planes on from Clark AB to Chiayi, the Chinese pilots were delighted and as excited as we had been when we upgraded from the old F-84Gs to F-100s at Kadena. Their squadron commander was a slightly over-weight major who felt compelled to say 'Thank you' and threw a party for the delivery pilots. Since I was the Flight Commander I was the ranking American and was seated at the VIP table beside the major. The entire squadron was in attendance; something over 200 enlisted men and officers. I learned that it was a custom for each individual to salute both the Commander and the Honoured Guest (me). Throughout the evening, at rather short intervals, a squadron member would approach the Commander, bow slightly and say 'Gombay!' He would then drink about an ounce of rice wine. The Commander responded similarly and then the man would bow to me and repeat the performance. The rice wine glass was the size of an ordinary shot glass. I emptied mine for the first lot of salutes before the Major informed me that it was not necessary for me to consume the entire drink at each salute. The warning came too late and by the end of the evening I had definitely consumed a lot of wine. Whatever the amount, I was in desperate shape the next morning with the worst hangover I've ever had in my life. Fortunately we were returned to Clark AB in a C-46 Base Support Flight aircraft.

The other sixty-five F-100As from the first batch of eighty were transferred to the RoCAF in 1960. Inevitably, attrition of these 'hot' early Huns necessitated another delivery of aircraft, and thirty-eight more were supplied in 1970–71, pushing the total to 118. This attrition batch came from Air National Guard (ANG) units including the 118th TFS Connecticut ANG, 152nd TFTS Arizona ANG and a single example (53-1582) from the 188th TFS New Mexico ANG. They were 'cocooned' at McClellan AFB and shipped to Taiwan. All ex-ANG F-100As passed to the RoCAF received *High Wire* updates, pushing their Block numbers up by one digit, for example: 53-1606 was an F-100A-16-NA.

All RoCAF Huns received extensive updates of which the most obvious externally was the replacement of the original vertical stabilizer with the later F-100D model including AN/APS-54 tail-warning radar. This change applied to all but four aircraft (53-1569, -1581, -1651, -1662) that kept their original tails on delivery from the Aerospace Maintenance and Regeneration Center (AMARC). One of these (53-1581 '0302') was eventually put on display at the Chung Cheng Institute of Science and Technology. The aircraft received Sidewinder capability including the twin AIM-9B launcher adapter. GAM-83A (AGM-12B) Bullpup missile launch controls and equipment were also installed for carriage on the inboard

Red lightning flashes and the 2nd Wing insignia decorate this F-100A-11-NA 53-155 of the 41st Squadron. Its previous owner was the 118th TFS, Connecticut ANG.
Clarence Fu

pylons. These pylons had 'stub' adapters attached under the wing that made them different in appearance from the standard F-100D variant. They could also carry AIM-9s, bombs, SUU-21 practice bomb dispensers or napalm. Outboard pylons were not fitted but tail hooks (with a triangular guard fairing to avoid accidental engagement of the hook) and a radio compass were installed. The 'flapless' F-100A wing was retained and it continued to demonstrate its basic strength though some aircraft eventually needed external structural strengthening of their fuselages. One F-100A (53-1610 '0113') managed to recover with its right wing virtually removed after a mid-air collision to a point just outboard on the mid-wing pylon.

Also supplied to the RoCAF were the four surviving 'Slick Chick' camera-equipped RF-100As: 53-1545, -46, -47, -54, coded '5645, -646, -647, -648 respectively. Codes appeared above the serial on the tail rather than on the fuselage as on

F-100F-5-NA 56-3733/0013 wore USAF camouflage for part of its service career with the Republic of China AF, as did 56-3808/0014 and two others. They operated from Hsinchu AB. Clarence Fu

A 23rd Squadron line-up with F-100A-20-NA 53-1685 (ex-4520th CCTW) to the fore. This aircraft crashed on 25 March 1980 but its pilot ejected safely. Clarence Fu

the F-100As. The first was delivered in December 1958, the others arrived on 1 January 1959 via Yokota. They were operated by the 4th Squadron at Taoyuan AB in full RoCAF markings including six sets of blue/white stripes on the rudder. USAF markings and buzz-numbers were used for the delivery. Their period of RoCAF service was actually little more than one year. Poor readiness rates meant that they allegedly flew no operational reconnaissance missions before being phased out in December 1960 and scrapped. They were replaced by McDonnell RF-101A Voodoos under Operation *Boom Town* and these had a much more active career, overflying mainland China for about six years.

Attrition of the F-100s was generally high with forty-nine aircraft destroyed in accidents and twenty-five pilots killed. By 1970, there were only sufficient operational aircraft to equip two squadrons with eighteen aircraft each, a situation that was improved by delivery of the attrition batch of thirty-eight ex-ANG F-100As. When the type was phased out the remaining aircraft were scrapped although fourteen were retained for gate guard, GIA or museum use including 53-1929 '0101', the first F-100A on the RoCAF roster. It became a gate guardian at Chiayi AB.

An unorthodox proposal for the use of surplus F-100As came from the Chung Shan Institute for Science and Technology, which advocated converting them into explosive-packed 'cruise missiles', aimed at Communist targets from zero length launch (ZEL)-type launchers. Fortunately perhaps, this plan was suppressed by the US Government but it symbolized the determination of an Air Force, some of whose F-100s bore the 'nose art' slogan 'Learn combat skills and kill the Communist bandit!'

Royal Danish Air Force

For the Danes, the F-100 replaced the Republic F-84G that had equipped two Wings, at Karup and Skrydstrup, each with three squadrons of twenty-five aircraft. One squadron, Esk 726, converted to the F-86D in 1958 and Esk 728 went to the RF-84F. The RDAF needed a fighter-bomber for its NATO responsibilities in the Baltic Sea area and was offered twenty F-100D/Fs in 1959 under MAP Project *Centurion*. RDAF pilot K. N. S. Thorkeldsen had already evaluated the F-100 in 1957 and reported favourably on it. In August 1958 a nucleus of Esk 727 pilots and maintainers was sent to Myrtle Beach to train after further demonstrations of the aircraft by the 48th TFW at Chaumont.

The first three F-100F-15-NAs arrived

on 22 May 1959 (56-4015, -18, -19) straight off the production line via Robins AFB, Langley AFB and Chateauroux with USAF pilots in the cockpits. The following year they received 'GT' codes in place of the 'FW' buzz numbers used initially, but retaining the last three of the serials. A distinctive red nose flash was also added over the silver finish. Skrydstrup established a reception unit for USAF Air Materiel Command personnel to introduce the new fighter and establish logistical support.

F-100Ds began to arrive on 30 May when seven flew in, followed by four on 4 June and another quartet a week later. The Huns were fresh from IRAN having served in a variety of USAF units. When the last two F-100Ds in the batch for Esk 727 flew in on 18 June the unit had nine ex-48th TFW F-100D-10 and F-100D-15-NA Super Sabres and three Block 15 aircraft from the 49th TFW plus another aircraft direct from the USA. Twelve Huns were available for the official ceremony at Vaerlose on 12 June when Gen Tage Anderson handed them over to the squadron. Another three ex-49th TFW F-100D-40-NHs followed in September 1959. Of those twenty Huns, eight were eventually passed on to the Turkish AF in the early 1980s. All of the others were lost in accidents, mostly in the 1960s.

Acceptance and work-up of the first RDAF squadron over an eighteen-month period occurred without mishap. The squadron assumed very much the same mission as it had flown in the F-84 days: CAS and anti-shipping with a secondary air defence tasking. The aircraft received some modification for RDAF service, including the installation of the Martin-Baker Mk-DE5A ejector seat. F-100D G-192 (54-2192) was flown to Martin-Baker at Chalgrove via Brize Norton for conversion on 28 April 1960 and all aircraft subsequently received the seats under Mod. /F-100/133. RDAF Huns also had AN/ARN-27 tactical air navigation (TACAN), modified UHF radios and APW-11/APS-54 radar. Later updates from October onwards included AGM-12 Bullpup provision, a Decca Roller Map Type 1664 system and the very accurate SAAB BT-9J bomb sight. Test firing of the Bullpup took place in June 1968 and the missile continued in use well into the 1970s. The RDAF also experimented with triple ejection racks (TERs) on the inboard pylons for either two M117 bombs

F-100D-40-NH 55-2779 flew with the USAF's 405th FBW, 31st FBW and 50th TFW before transfer to Esk 727 on 29 May 1961, then Esk 730 in 1964 with dark blue and white markings. It was supplied to the Turkish AF in 1981 and written off on 26 April 1983. David Menard Collection

leak in the engine compartment. The next batch of F-100Ds arrived on 13 March from IRAN at Getafe and G-283 (ex-8th FBW) was handed over as the first F-100D for Esk 725 on 13 April 1961. This jet served until 1981 when it was transferred to Turkey. As the squadron built up to full strength, three of its F-100Fs were returned to Esk 727 to help with the conversion of the next squadron, Esk 730. F-100Ds G-144 and G-781, delivered on 12 June 1961, completed Esk 725's complement of sixteen single-seaters and three F-100Fs. The majority were Block 15 aircraft from the 8th FBW in Japan with a few more ex-48th FBW too, including 54-2132, a very early Block 1 F-100D.

Esk 730 completed its transition from the F-84G quickly and it was established on the supersonic jet by 3 July 1961. The process was facilitated by the use of the F-100 simulator at RAF Wethersfield, though the generous allocation of F-100Fs helped too. Only one F-100F was lost during the training of the three units: GT-978 sustained a power failure and the Danish pilot and his USAF instructor ejected as the Hun entered a flat spin. The squadron's F-100Ds, with neat green and white trim on their noses and fins, were based at Skrydstrup. Most were ex-United States Air Force in Europe (USAFE) aircraft though six originated

or three LAU-3/A rocket pods. At about the same time, the fleet was sprayed with coats of SM/67 olive green (FS14079) paint in place of the original silver lacquer. National markings were reduced from 900mm to 450mm diameter on the wings and the 700mm fuselage roundels were also halved in diameter. From November 1976, the Huns began to receive the ALR-45D/APR-37D RHAW system mounted in wing-tip pods with the antennas at each end of the pods. ALR-45D was a radar-warning unit and APR-37D gave indication of a hostile missile launch. Wing-tip navigation lights were moved to the outer surfaces of the pods, AN/ARC-159(V)8 UHF radios were added in 1976 and one of the final local 'mods' was the installation of the LINDA 'C' Underwater Locator Beacon.

By that time, there had been a considerable increase in the RDAF F-100 fleet following the decision in 1960 to equip two more squadrons with the type. Esk 725 at Karup was the second unit followed by Esk 730. Their aircrew were sent to the USA for training and thirty-eight new aircraft were ordered, thirty-one F-100Ds and seven two-seaters. The first three F-100Fs (GT-976, -78, -82), all new aircraft, landed at Karup on 26 January 1961 for Esk 727. As usual, USAF ferry pilots made the transatlantic flight but two Danish officers were also aboard. The F-100Fs were used

to convert Esk 725 until it received its own seven F-100Fs on 20 March 1961 and its F-84Gs were then passed to Esk 730. The first loss also occurred in March when G-221 (54-2221, an ex-48th TFW machine) crashed after an explosion following a fuel

Esk 727 used glossy red markings on its silver F-100s including a red flash on the RHAW fairing. This F-100D-5-NA was delivered to the 48th FBW at Chaumont AB in 1957, moving to RAF Lakenheath in 1960. After two years with the Danish AF it was written off in a mid-air collision with 54-2300. It is seen here at Hahn AB on a NATO exchange in April 1961, piloted by the appropriately named Arthur E. Huhn. David Menard Collection

from the 31st TFW at Turner AFB via rework at McClellan AFB.

The three squadrons soon began to participate in NATO competitions. Esk 725 won the 1963 AFNORTH event and the 1965 *Bull's-Eye* competition. However, the heavy attrition that plagued the RDAF F-100 fleet began to mount up, with four losses in 1962, five in 1963 and another three in 1964. From then until 1969, two were lost annually reducing the total to only thirty F-100Ds and seven Fs out of the original complement of fifty-eight aircraft. Four F-100Ds had crashed after mid-air collisions, five as a result of engine failures and four when they hit the ground during low-altitude flight. 54-2199 was lost through an unusual maintenance failure when a loose panel in the air inlet flew off and jammed itself against the front of the engine. Compressor problems grounded the whole fleet in 1966, requiring all Block 40 aircraft with newer, less troublesome J57s to be pooled at Karup for use by all three units. After overcoming these problems through adjustments to the engine and fuel system, the earlier aircraft then faced

F-100F-15-NA has its 'last five' (86978) serial digits beneath the Danish fin flash in its 1961 scheme. In August 1968 it was written off after engine compressor failure caused by a 20mm ricochet during a strafing run. David Menard

On a visit to RAF Coltishall on 19 September 1970, F-100D 54-2222 of Esk 727 (ex-48th FBW) is rapidly losing the gloss from its overall, locally manufactured paint so that it is close to FS 34087 in shade. G. Pennick via David Menard

This TF-100F-11-NA (56-3908) had extensive Vietnam War service with the 416th TFS, 37th TFW at Phu Cat AB, the 35th TFW at Phan Rang AB and the 31st TFW at Tuy Hoa AB after seven years at Cannon AFB. In Esk 727 service it acquired ALR-45D/APR-37D RHAW wing-tip pods. It ended its days as a gate guard for Skrydstrup AB.
Author's Collection

Skrydstrup. Flight safety improved, with no serious mishaps until 1976 which brought three Esk 730 F-100F crashes (two with collapsed nose-gear on landing) and GT-892 of Esk 727 (ex-Iowa ANG) which lasted only five flying hours in RDAF service before crashing after engine failure. A Spectrographic Oil Analysis Programme (SOAP) revealed further engine problems which meant that all J-57s had to go through the analysis before and after every mission. Two further crashes in 1977 were also attributed to mechanical defects (runaway trim in one case and cracks in the fuel control system in another) and lengthy grounding orders were imposed. The decision to order General Dynamics F-16As had been made, but it meant that the Super Sabres had to soldier on until 1982 when deliveries of the new fighter could be completed. Losing thirty-five out of seventy-two F-100s had given the aircraft a poor reputation in the Danish media by 1978 despite the fact that only two more were written off before the type's withdrawal. One of these, GT-961, sustained a collapsed nose-gear on landing but the aircraft was not repaired.

the same fatigue problems that had affected USAF Huns in Vietnam. Aircraft were restricted to 4g manoeuvres and a major rework programme was instigated at Karup from 1970 to 1972 to replace under-wing skins with heavier gauge parts and reinforced wing boxes (Mod/F-100/320).

With a reduced fleet, no prospect of replacements from the USA (due to Vietnam requirements) or from France, the RDAF turned to the SAAB F-35 Draken, ordering forty-six aircraft in 1968. Esk 725 was disbanded and its F-100s distributed to the other two units. The intention was to replace all F-100s with Drakens but funding was insufficient, and in 1971 Denmark elected to keep its remaining Huns flying into the early 1980s. However, continued losses throughout the early 1970s (three in 1970, two more in 1972–73) had reduced F-100F numbers to five, insufficient to maintain effective conversion training at both bases. Fourteen additional F-100F-11-NA and F-100F-16-NAs were ordered, six from MASDC storage in August 1973 and another eight selected from ANG squadrons. They were delivered between March and June 1974, equipped with Martin-Baker seats from redundant RF-84Fs and labelled 'TF-100F' to distinguish them from the non-*High Wire* F-100Fs

received earlier. Some had F-102A type afterburners from the Project *Pacer Transplant* conversions and this applied to a number of F-100Ds from 1978 onwards.

In 1974, all three F-100 units, Esk 727, 730 and the F-100 OCU, were based at

Towards the end of its twenty years of RDAF service the remaining squadrons divided into two sections, one transitioning to the GD F-16A while the other (Esk 730-100) continued to fly Huns. The last flight took place on 11 August 1982 and

Baggage pods on the inboard pylons of F-100F-16-NA 56-4019 suggest a shopping trip abroad. This aircraft had a long career with the Danish AF (1959-1981). Author's Collection

Pilots of Esk 730 line up with TF-100F 56-3826 at the end of its Danish service in summer, 1982. Earlier, it had spent seven years with the 36th and 50th TFWs in USAFE and had combat time with the 31st and 35th TFWs in Vietnam. In October 1982 it became a nicely wrapped 'present' for Flight Systems Inc. before it was written off in July 1994. David Menard Collection

some of the remaining aircraft were returned to US charge via RAF Sculthorpe from 24 March 1981 and many were scrapped there. Twenty-two were transferred to the Turkish Air Force and six F/TF-100Fs went to Flight Systems Inc (FSI) (56-3826, -842, -844, -916 -971, -996). Two (56-3870, -3908) guarded the gates at Skrydstrup in southern Denmark and 56-3927 went to the Danish Aviation Museum. Fifty-eight F-16A/Bs subsequently equipped four RDAF squadrons from January 1980, taking over from F-100s the task of patrolling the North Sea and Baltic where much of the Soviet Fleet would have passed through in the event of a conflict.

Turk Hava Kuvvetleri, the Turkish Air Force

F-100 flying in the Turkish Air Force ended on 1 November 1987 when 132 Filo at

Konya traded in its last Hun and began conversion to the F-4E Phantom II. It was the last squadron anywhere to operate the F-100 as front-line equipment and one of the nine THK squadrons that received Huns between 6 October 1958, when the first F-100F-15-NA (56-3998) arrived, and 27 January 1982. The final batch included ex-Danish AF F-100Ds 54-2222, -2262, 55-2771 and F-100F 56-4019 (via RAF Sculthorpe). THK owned far more F-100s than any other air force outside the USA with 270 deliveries in a total of fourteen MAP programs. Of these, 111 were F-100Cs in two different MAP programs, 106 F-100Ds (three different MAP programs) and 53 F-100Fs (nine MAP programs).

In 1958, nine F-100Fs and fourteen F-100Ds were delivered, beginning service with 111 Filo at Eskisehir, the first F-100 unit. The following year another thirty-two F-100Ds and two F-100Fs arrived, enabling the replacement of 113 Filo's F-84G Thunderjets with Super Sabres

during 1959–60. Very limited deliveries of Huns (only three F-100Ds and a pair of F-100Fs in 1960, with two more two-seaters in 1962) meant that no further squadron transitions could be made until 1962 when 112 Filo was re-formed at Eskisehir, drawing aircraft from the other squadrons. Previously, 112 Filo had flown F-84Gs at Konya AB, having moved there as 192 Filo in 1958. The re-formation of this third squadron meant that 113 Filo could transfer to the newly equipped Erhac AB (established in Malatya from 26 November 1962) in August 1963, where it was renamed 171 Filo in 1972.

Turkish F-100s became involved in combat after the long-running tensions between the Greek and minority Turkish populations in Cyprus flared up in 1964. Greek Cypriot National Guard units and EOKA militants unexpectedly attacked Turkish villages at Mansura and Koccina in the north of the island, causing civilian casualties. The next day, 8 August, Eskisehir-based F-100s of 111

USAF lettering still shows on these newly accepted TUAF F-100D/F Super Sabres. Buzz numbers from former service were also retained for a while. Turkish AF/Soner Capoglu via David Menard

Filo and 112 Filo, with 113 Filo from Adana AB and the F-84Gs of 161 Filo took off in the early morning. They crossed the Mediterranean at 165ft (50m) altitude to evade the British radar site at Dikelia and attacked Greek Cypriot positions in the Koccina area. Capt Cengiz Topel's 111 Filo F-100 crashed while attacking a Greek assault craft off Erenkoy and although he ejected safely over Peristeronori he was captured and killed by Greek Cypriot forces on 12 August.

Because of the shortage of F-100s (at least eight of the sixty-four delivered up to 1962 had crashed by 1965 with the loss of five pilots) 112 Filo had to 're-convert' to F-84Qs (ex-Luftwaffe F-84FQs) by 19 October 1965. The arrival of a batch of sixteen *High Wire* F-100Ds and a pair of F-100Fs in 1969 enabled the squadron to revert to the Hun in December of that year. In the same month, 182 Filo (originally a Diyarbakir-based squadron that had moved to Erhac AB on 25 January

1963) replaced its F/RF-84Fs with F-100s. A further batch of twenty ex-USAF F-100Ds and two F-100Fs arrived for the THK during 1970. In the early 1970s, Turkish F-100 units started to be recognized as being among the best in southern Europe. The F-100s of 111 Filo out-performed the combined talents of Italy, Greece, the USN's CVW-3 A-7 Corsairs and the F-4E Phantoms of the 353rd TFS *Black Panthers* in practice missions on the Osmaniye Range during the 1971 *Best Hit* competition.

In 1972 further deliveries included thirty-six F-100Cs, with another forty-seven in 1973 and more in 1974. They were mostly *High Wire* ex-ANG aircraft equipped to a standard close to the F-100D. As a result of these new deliveries, 113 Filo and 182 Filo at Erhac received new F-100s in 1972, renaming themselves as 171 Filo and 172 Filo respectively. At the same time, a new 113 Filo was formed from 114 Filo at Eskisehir AB to operate fourteen RF-84Fs

and eight F-84Fs, while 182 Filo was created from 183 Filo at Diyarbakir AB and received TF/F-102A Delta Daggers. Then 181 Filo replaced its F-84Qs with some newly arrived F-100C/Fs in 1972. At that point, 111 Filo had eighteen F-100D/Fs on strength while 112 Filo absorbed a batch of F-100Cs to boost its squadron strength. In another round of changes during 1974, 131 Filo and 132 Filo exchanged their F-84F/Qs for F-100C/Fs at Konya AB, which eventually became the last base to use the Hun in the late 1980s. This pair of squadrons also took on the majority of the available F-100Fs and began to serve as a training unit on the type.

July and August 1974 were also times when THK F-100s saw extensive combat following the Greek overthrow of Archbishop Makarios and consequently increased danger for the Turkish residents of Cyprus. In a deteriorating situation many Turkish villages were attacked and the Turkish Government decided to instigate a

113 Filo pilots prepare to taxi out for a mission from Eskisehir AB. The squadron transferred to Erhac AB in August 1963 as 171 Filo. David Menard Collection

Roundels have replaced the square-format national insignia on these F-100Ds, some of which have been camouflaged. Bombs and 2.75in rockets are loaded on '245. Turkish Air Force/Soner Capoglu via David Menard

direct intervention on 20 July. To ease the operation, the squadrons based at Diyarbakir, Erhac, Merzifon, Etimesgut and Konya were placed under the command of the 2nd Tactical Air Force at Diyarbakir. This force included six squadrons of F-100s (111, 112, 131, 132, 171 and 172), two of F-104Gs (141 and 191) plus the RF-84Fs of 184 Filo to support operations over Cyprus. Some of the F-100s from 171 Filo and 172 Filo were moved to Antalya AB and the rest of their aircraft were transferred to Incirlik AB in Adana, together with the Diyarbakir-based 181 Filo.

In the early morning of 20 July 1974, Turkish Army and Marine units went ashore at a beach in Karaoglanoglu, west of Kyrenia, in order to protect the Turkish population. F-100s took off at 0600 hours and were engaged in missions to neutralize Greek Cypriot National Guard positions on the northern Cyprus coast. Between 20–23 July (the first stage of the intervention) the THK completed 733 sorties and lost twelve aircraft, eight of them F-100s. Two F-102As, an RF-84F and an F-104G also failed to return. Although no F-100 pilots were killed, a 184 Filo RF-84F pilot, 1st Lt Ilker Karter, was hit by anti-aircraft artillery (AAA) over Trikoma and killed on July 20. Two F-100 losses (55-3756 of 171 Filo and 55-2825 of 111 Filo) were caused by engine failure, the former crashing at Incirlik on July 20, and the other at Manavgat-Antalya the following day. Two were hit by AAA: F-100C 54-2042 from 132 Filo over Ovacik, Cyprus and F-100D 54-2238 from 172 Filo on 22 July near Nicosia (its pilot, Capt Recai Unhanh, ejecting safely). Another F-100C (54-

Re-arming is in progress on F-100D-56-NA 55-2910 during a visit to RAF Lakenheath in May 1970. The nose undercarriage often made a useful prop for the gun-bay doors. Norm Taylor Collection

F-100F-15-NA 56-3946, one of the Turkish AF's 1969 delivery batch, being prepared for towing. Norm Taylor Collection

2083), crashed into some barriers on take-off at Sivrihisar AB.

In a tragic incident, Turkish jets mistook the Turkish Navy 'Gearing' Class destroyer T. C. G. *Kocatepe* (D-354) for a similar-looking Greek vessel and sank it with 750lb bombs on 21 July. F-100s from 111 Filo and 112 Filo at Eskisehir, others from 181 Filo from Adana with several 141 Filo F-104Gs from Murted AB, Ankara took part in the attacks on the ship in which fifty-four sailors died. In the early morning of 21 July, the vessel T. C. G. *Maresal Fevzi Cakmak* rescued an F-100 pilot, 1st Lt Sadik Dulger, who had been shot down over Cyprus the previous day. Ironically, Lt Dulger had to witness the entire attack on the *Kocatepe* from his position on the *Cakmak* next to the stricken destroyer.

After the invasion, the Greeks were persuaded by US diplomacy not to retaliate. However, Turkish F-100s were in action again during a second phase of the conflict after the northern outskirts of Nicosia were taken by Turkish forces in early August, followed by Famagusta in an operation in which no aircraft are known to

Close communication by hand signals between a 111 Filo crew and the crew chief of F-100F-15-NA 56-3957. Turkish AF/Soner Capoglu

have been lost. An armistice was agreed on 16 August and the island was then partitioned into Greek and Turkish areas, though THK units remained on full alert for several more weeks. By the time tensions increased again in 1987 over disputed oil exploration territory, Turkish F-100s were being retired.

Turkey started to receive F-4Es in late 1974 and on 10 October 1975 the F-100s of 112 Filo were replaced with the newly arrived Phantoms. 171 Filo followed in 1977 with 111 Filo and 172 Filo in 1978. However, deliveries of F-100s also continued with another fifteen ex-USAF aircraft in 1977–78 and twenty F-100Ds, with a pair of F-100Fs from Denmark in 1981 and early 1982. The former Danish Huns retained their Martin Baker DB-5A ejection seats and other RDAF modifications. 182 Filo became the last THK unit to convert to the F-100 when it replaced its delta-wing F-102A fighters in 1980. By 1983 only four THK units had Huns: 181 Filo (15 F-100Ds, 5 F-100Fs); 182 Filo (15 F-100C/Ds, 5 F-100Fs); 131 Filo (15 F-100Ds, 15 F-100Fs) and 132 Filo (20 F-100Ds, 5 F-100Fs). After 181 Filo and 182 Filo completed their re-equipment in March–April 1985 with ex-RCAF CF-

104s, the Konya-based 131 and 132 Filos were the only Super Sabre operators and they retained the type until the end of the F-100 era in 1988. It is known that from 1986 to 1988, thirty-five F-100C/Ds and twenty F-100Fs were used by the two squadrons, both of which had reverted to the role of Weapons (OCU).

Three ex-THK Huns (F-100C 54-2091, F-100D 55-2888 and F-100F 56-3948) were sold to FSI and flown to Mojave, California on 5 August 1989, all three of them remaining airworthy in 2002. However, the final destination for almost all THK Huns was the Ankara junkyards where they were sold to scrap merchants and melted down.

Turkish F-100s generally retained their USAF camouflage, though early examples arrived in bare metal. While some of the former Danish aircraft were repainted in USAF camouflage, most retained their overall faded olive-green scheme and even their Danish buzz numbers (F-100D-40-NH 55-2768 still bore its Danish side-number G-768 when it was scrapped in Ankara in 1990). Colourful unit markings were worn on silver aircraft, with 'FW' buzz numbers and square-format Turkish insignia, which were replaced by roundels

in 1972. Towards the end of the 1970s, codes appeared on the fuselage. The most common practice was in the form of four thin black digits with white outlines, the first denoting the main jet airbase where the aircraft was stationed. The next three numbers were the 'last three' of its serial. Thus, '3-732' on an F-100C denoted 53-1732 from the *3ncu Ana Jet Ussu* (3rd Main Jet Airbase) at that date.

Several Turkish pilots flew more than 1,000 hours on F-100s, with Brig Gen Erol Ozgil clocking up 2,153 hours. During the thirty years of the Turkish F-100 era at least forty-two F-100Cs, thirty-three F-100Ds and twenty F-100Fs are known to have been lost: almost a third of the fleet. A total of forty-nine pilots were killed, most of them young lieutenants. Of the 267 delivered, twenty-four were still preserved in 2002.

[Turkish A. F. section compiled by Batur Avgan © 2002 with reference to:
Ole Nikolajsen, *Turkish Aviation History, Vol II* (2002); Cumhur Erdeniz, *F-100* (2001); Johan van der Wei, Bulent Yilmazer, Lance Barber ('Sabre') and Marco Dijkshoorn, *Marco* (2002)]

F-100 CAS Mission, Danish Style

The following is an account of a 1979 close air support (CAS) mission by an Esk 727 pilot, J. E. T Clausen. One of the squadron's more experienced pilots, he had over 900 hours on the Hun. 'Craven' was the Esk 727 call-sign and 'Mission 3401' was the call-sign used for this mission within an exercise.

'Yes, yes, affirm', I stutter while my eyes are wandering around the landscape.

'From the farm, one nautical mile to the south-west, a small wood. Do you see the small wood?'

'Tally-ho!' I shout as I am pulling the nose over the horizon only to point it downward again at the wood using the correct dive angle. 'Mission 3401 in dummy.'

'You are cleared', shouts the Forward Air Controller (FAC).

The bombsight is lined up on a tank in the fringe of a wood, plus a bit to the west to compensate for the wind. Press the trigger, power and pull off. Whoops, that was a bit low and God, how I sweat behind the oxygen mask. Now it is time for some more info to my wingman who is approaching from the east: 'Number One is off to the west'.

Now the FAC is guiding Number Two towards the target. 'OK, I got you visual. Come 10 degrees to the right. Do you see the red-roofed farm at your 12 o'clock? From the farm, 1nm to the south-west...' etc. as before.

'Mission 3401, nice attacks. Go back to IP3C and I have some new targets for you.' Yeah, yeah, that's easy for him to say. Right now I only know I am somewhere over the western part of Jutland and my wingman is 2 miles (3km) behind.

Before this mud-moving climax is reached, a long period of preparation has passed. We met that morning in the squadron briefing room where I received a time hack at 0800 and a 'Good morning' from the Squadron Duty Operational Officer (Duty-Ops). Today there are no penalties for the moneybox as everyone was in the briefing room on time. According to the briefing, the weather was OK and there were just the usual NOTAMS and active danger areas. Bird intensity was 'One', just perfect for my low-level, FAC-controlled mission in the Army training area at Oksboel for the first pass. After the commanding officer's (CO's) usual words of wisdom it was time to find out who should pay for coffee. Duty-Ops drew a line on the blackboard and each of us, seated in our chairs, attempted to guess how long it was in 1:100,000 scale. Good training for a fighter-bomber pilot. Fingers stretched, eyes squinting, everyone made their guess. Lady Luck (disguised as Duty-Ops) measured the correct distance and the loser, the guy whose guess was farthest off, was found.

Now for mission preparation. We had better hurry so that we can meet our time-over-target (TOT). My Number 2 is given the necessary line-up information: engine start time, aircraft tail numbers, parking, configuration, etc. The Ground Liaison Officer (GLO) is asked to get his briefing ready and assist in planning the mission. We pull out the relevant NATO and national Standard Operational Procedures (SOPs) covering the exercise, study the air task closely, decipher coding to real aircraft frequencies and waypoints, check the pilot qualification table to see if this mission could add some of the necessary check marks, and copy master navigational charts prepared by the pilot responsible for this exercise. Contact Points (CPs) and initial points (IPs) from the air task

are plotted both on the low-level navigational chart (1:500,000) and the target maps (1:100,000) and the highest obstacles are highlighted.

Number Two is putting the finishing touches to the nav charts while I am doing a bit of smart planning: weapons delivery tactics and parameters (we are carrying a simulated weapons load of four Mk 82s and a full load of 20mm), bingo fuel states, formation types, 'silent' take-off procedure, air combat tactics if we are jumped by hostile aircraft, etc. How time is going by! We had better get the briefing started. A quick check with Duty-Ops to see if there are any last-minute changes. Yes, I have to fly another plane that is parked at the other end of the air base. Great! Another five minutes lost.

The briefing. The GLO begins with his situation overview. Then I brief the 'domestic' stuff like parking, silent taxiing (without contact to Air Traffic Control), formation take-off, departure, etc. then on to the essential part: countermeasures if we meet hostile aircraft, tactics in the attack phase and not least, flying safety aspects in the tougher parts of the mission. Questions? Fine. Off we go, but first to the Duty-Ops desk to sign the authorization sheet. Sh*t! Two new pages of information that must be read before the next flight. An ultra-quick scan convinces me that they are not relevant to this mission, but I make a mental note to read them more thoroughly after the mission. Remember to sign out or penalties are due.

Time to change clothes. Luckily there is no need for immersion suits as the water temperature is above 10°C. I grab my helmet and oxygen mask. Oh no! Another delay. The Life Support guys have changed my oxygen mask so I have to check it before flight. I plug it into the 1950s-vintage test box and take a couple of quick breaths: 'shyy-haa, shyy-haa'...yes, it works. Now I need to find the crew chief in a hurry or I will not make it to my agreed silent taxi time. Luckily, he is outside the building, ready with the aircraft log and a set of car keys. Did I remember everything? Helmet, gloves, line-up slip, navigational charts and the secret 'pilot information file' (PIF).

At last we reach the aircraft. A quick walk round and then into the 'office'. My crew chief has already put my helmet on the edge of the windscreen and the ejection seat shoulder straps hang out over the cockpit sides. This is service! A couple of firm kicks on the brake pedals produce the expected howling noise. An enormous black cloud from the auxilliary power unit (APU) indicates that it is time for engine start-up. Taxiing begins at the agreed time – only just – and there on the other side of the runway I can see my wingman appearing. Finally things look right.

After a green light from the tower, we line up and with my circling index finger I give the order to run up the engines. My wingman is nodding to indicate that engine values are in the 'green' and he is ready. I nod deeply to indicate brake release and we are rolling. Well airborne, I 'fishtail' the F-100 a bit, using the rudder to loosen up the formation. Finally, it is time to enjoy all that work we did on the ground.

Heading due north and soon the Jels-lake – our departure point – should appear. Yep, there it is. Is the stopwatch wound up and ready? Yes, we are ready to start timing. I am rocking the wings to indicate to my wingman that the watch should be activated. Hack. The watch is running and the speed is close to 420kt – 7nm per minute. I re-check

using the AN/APN-153 Doppler navigation system (NAVS), the engine pressure ratio (EPR) indication and the airspeed indicator. I also make the necessary corrections for wind at 500ft (150m), as forecast by our meteorologist (the pathological liar). Our altitude is 600ft (180m) indicated. Tactical Air Command (TAC) approved the 500ft and I have added a bit to compensate for the field elevation. At the next waypoint we have agreed to check in on our squadron frequency and thereby we terminate the silent departure procedure. Until now we have been listening in on Channel 14 (local tower) in case Air Training Command (ATC) should want to contact us for flying safety reasons.

Right now we have a few minutes to let our souls catch up because all we have to do is navigate on 'time and heading', just like Charles Lindbergh! In twenty minutes we will go 'feet wet' over the North Sea where, according to the exercise brief, we might meet hostile fighters in the shape of good old Danish F-104 Starfighters.

'Mission 3401. Manual 313. 6. Go.' We change to the common frequency where we have to transmit blind that we are coasting out into the North Sea area with two aircraft at low altitude. What next? Will we be required to say when we reach the next waypoint? Those air defenders only know the date anyway: the rest they will get from the ground controlled interception (GCI) station.

Speed is now increased to 450kt and my wingman is right where he is supposed to be – line abreast at a good distance since the weather is clear. Down to 300ft (90m) and keep scanning 360 degrees for fighters. At intervals we also look upwards because the air defence pilots love to make hit-and-run attacks, diving at high speed, calling 'Fox two' and climbing again as fast as the 'wingless wonder' [F-104] allows.

Aren't those smoke trails at 5 o'clock? 'Craven Red. Break right. Bogies 5 o'clock, slightly high, about 4 miles [6km].'

Plug in the afterburner. Careful not to overstress the aircraft. KA-POW! Great. No compressor stalls this time. Nose over the horizon, not down in the waves. 'Tally ho!' my wingman shouts and the dogfight is on. 'Camera on!' Hopefully, we will be able to shoot some pictures with the sight reticle on an F-104 canopy. In this clear weather we have no problems picking up a smoking J79 engine at long range, so the air defence pilots didn't get the advantage of surprise this time. We manage to meet the enemy head on and at our speed they don't manage to catch us before we have left the fighter engagement zone.

Back in a sensible formation, we set course towards the coast. Now we have to find out where we are. After a bit of dog fighting, the F-100's compass shows whatever takes its fancy until we have flown straight and level for some time. Well, the sun is over there so the coast must be in that general direction. We use the TLAR principle: 'That Looks About Right'. Great. There is the Cheminova factory. Then our next waypoint is slightly to the south near Bovbjerg lighthouse. A masterpiece of navigation!

'Red Two. What is your fuel state?' Now both fuel gauges and compasses should be steady again and as accurate as possible. Good, we have enough fuel for at least two attacks in the Oksboel area. Another time hack: approximately 420kt and a 20kt wind from the right gives us a heading of 165 degrees to match the track on our navigational chart. Now it is time to change to the ALO/FAC

F-100 CAS Mission, Danish Style (*cont.*)

frequency to get a briefing. If we have a 'rear briefer' on this frequency he will already at this early stage be able to give us some overall guidelines before we contact the FAC. If not, we will have to make do with the information from the Air Task and the GLO briefing.

Now it is time to get organized in the 'office'. Pull out the relevant maps and fix them under the clip on one knee. The PIF is wedged in between the canopy and the left-hand rail and the others go on the right side. My right kneeboard is reserved for notes from the FAC briefing (each pilot has his own system, almost with clothes pegs to keep all the papers organized). I am happy that I know my USAF Map Folding Manual by heart.

We are approaching Ringkoebing and it is about time to contact the ALO. 'This is mission 3401, on time, over.' Crackle, crackle. After the mandatory authentication procedure he tells us to contact Whitecliff on one of the coded air task frequencies and fly to IP B4, leaving it asap. 'Red Two. Go offensive.' All he has to do now is hang on and keep a good lookout to warn me of other aircraft or towns we can't fly over because I hide my nose in the low-level chart. IP B4.... IP B4...where is it? Ah, it's a small lake. OK. After the next waypoint we go directly south. Fine, then we don't have to make any stupid 360-degree turns while we set everything up. They aren't too healthy close to hostile territory anyway.

'Red Two. Manual 314. 1. Go.'

'Whitecliff, Whitecliff. Mission 3401. IP B4 in three minutes.' No answer. Typical! We climb a bit to let his advanced walkie-talkie reach us. Contact at last. I am now flying the Hun with my left hand while the right is busy making notes – a sweat-provoking kind of flight that only right-handed CAS pilots get to experience.

'From IP...(crackle crackle)...heading...(buzz crackle)...174. Four minutes 30 seconds...(crackle whine buzz)...target consists of ... column of tanks standing next to a wood, camouflaged.'

At least the footsloggers didn't dig the tanks in. 'Two. Are you ready?' Perfect. Here we go. 'Two, you may take spacing.' Now he has to distance himself from me so that he doesn't fly into the cloud of fragments from the bombs and the target that I will pretend to cause in a short while. The IP is to my right at 1 o'clock; a small lake. A time hack and down to 300ft (90m). The adrenaline is pumping through my body and time flies. Speed: 450kt. How is the camera set? I have to take my oxygen mask off to see anything at all. Who designed this cockpit, where some of the buttons are positioned almost behind your back? After this acrobatic achievement I check airspeed and time: 1 minute 10 seconds.

'After 1 minute 30 seconds you will pass a paved road with a small windmill. From that windmill look to your 2 o'clock about 2nm and you will see a red-roofed farm...' and we are back to the point where the pilot's thumb firmly presses the pickle button and the bomb load leaves the aircraft directly towards the 'hostile' tanks. For the sake of training, we make a second attack, this time from another IP and then it is time to leave Oksboel. Just after the last attack I see the FAC in my peripheral vision. He was risking his life a few kilometres from the tanks – within firing range. But those are the FAC's conditions.

'See you in the Officers' Mess for happy hour?'

'Yes, I'll be there.' I recognize his voice as one of the Reserve Officers flying for Scandinavian Airlines.

After our in-flight report has been submitted to HQ we set course for the Blaavandshuk lighthouse and make a friendly call to the Range Safety Officer at the Roemoe air-to-ground range. We have both fuel and time for an airfield attack. I had better inform Duty-Ops so that he can warn the rest of the squadron over the tannoy. Last time, one of our crew chiefs got pissed off when my afterburner lit exactly over the squadron maintenance hangar when I passed, unannounced, at low altitude.

Inadvertently, he got up and his head hit the airbrake on the aircraft he was servicing. It cost me an apology, coffee and a doughnut. After getting clearance from the tower I call my wingman in close and assign the south-western squadron dispersal area as his aim-point while I 'take out' our own squadron building. Luckily, the guys got some good decibels and the afterburner lit at exactly the right time. That is a bit of an art, garnished with a good helping of luck to make it light at the right time, if at all.

After this team-building exercise we join down-wind directly and manage to touch-down before reaching minimum fuel; 1000lb (450kg). Unfortunately the headwind is too weak to avoid using the drag chute. My crew chief prefers not to install a new chute if it can be helped as it is a cumbersome system and prone to failure in operation.

We taxi in, debrief with the crew chief, sign the manual and get out of sweaty flight gear. Quickly, we have to send a supplementary mission report to Tactical Air Command, Denmark, develop the film with F-104 kills and ground attack results and then debrief with my wingman, the GLO, Duty-Ops and ATC before the next mission: an exercise with the Navy. That means a new Exercise Order, master chart, air task, etc. I grab a sandwich, find my wingmen and it's full speed ahead with the planning.

CHAPTER 7

Son of a Hun: The F-107A

F-107A 55-5118, the first aircraft, with a 500-gal centreline tank containing flight-test recording gear and fire extinguishing equipment. Unlike the other two aircraft it had its 'F-107A' logo behind the cockpit. David Menard Collection

North American Aviation (NAA) proposed a number of improved versions of their outstanding new fighter but only one, the F-107A, proceeded beyond the outline stage. Most versions involved minimum change to the aircraft in order to reduce tooling and production costs. For example, the F-100K would have been an F-100F with the up-rated and more reliable J57-P-55 engine. The F-100L would have given the F-100D the same treatment. NATO air forces, seeking a low-cost, supersonic replacement for their F-84

and F-86s were offered the F-100N with a simplified electronics package.

A more serious proposal involved replacing the J57 with a Rolls-Royce RB-168-25R Spey turbofan, as used with qualified success in the F-4K/M Phantom. The engine could have been produced in its Allison TF-41 variant with afterburner. This change of power-plant was supposed to offer 30 per cent better range with a 50 per cent improvement in ordnance load and up to 10,000ft (3,000m) extra ceiling. Improved take-off distances and rates of

climb were also likely. At this time, Rolls-Royce also suggested 'Speyed' F-8 Crusaders and F-104 Starfighters, but in 1964 the F-100S (for Spey) proposal was thought to have real potential for the European market. The French were seen as customers for up to 200, based on the F-100F and licence-built in France for the Armée de l'Air and then for follow-on customers. Sadly, this suggestion never advanced beyond initial paperwork.

More promising still were projects that sought to increase the F-100's interception

Sharing the ramp with the fifth F-100A (in engineering test flight colours) is the Number 3 aircraft, 55-5120. Its nose logo reads 'North American F-107A'. The F-107A Air Staff Project Officer, Brig Gen Coberly, described the fighter's performance a 'quite incredible for that time period'. David Menard Collection

and all-weather capability. The F-100J would have had a search and track radar installation and might have attracted Japanese interest. Before that, the F-100I was suggested as an interceptor with air-to-air rocket packs replacing its guns. However, the most important of all these projects was the first: the F-100B. This became the foundation for the F-107A, truly a 'Super' Super Sabre.

NAA received USAF requests for studies of an improved version of the F-100 early in 1953, before the F-100A first flew. Around March, the company drafted the NA-211 (F-100B), initially a faster, lighter day-fighter capable of Mach 1.8 with a thinner wing, area-ruled fuselage and a J57 engine up-rated to 16,000lb (7,250kg) thrust with a new convergent/divergent engine nozzle. It might have had dual-wheel 'rough-field' main landing gear and no provision for under-wing fuel tanks. This all had to be modified when Tactical Air Command (TAC) issued new demands featuring a powerful air-to-air radar. In response, NAA designed a pointed nose radome above a bifurcated F-86D-style

'chin' intake, but this caused airflow problems for the release of weapons, 'semi-submerged' in an innovative 'trough' bay under the fuselage. The re-design of June 1953, known internally as the F-100BI, featured a retractable inflight-refuelling probe and a re-appearance of drop tanks.

By October the model number NA-212 had been allotted and a mock-up was commenced together with studies of variable-area air inlets that eventually led to the air intake being positioned above the fuselage. The location was chosen to prevent airflow interference with ordnance dropped from the centreline station, as by November 1953 the company was emphasizing the type's potential as a fighter-bomber with air-superiority capability. Probably NAA had already decided to compete unofficially with Republic's 306A design, the fighter-bomber proposal that eventually became TAC's F-105 Thunderchief. Republic had received a contract dated 25 September 1952 for 199 F-105As, although at that stage the aircraft bore little resemblance to the eventual F-105B production model and NAA

were aware of the type's protracted and troublesome development process. NAA even began studies of a naval NA-212 version, the 'Super Fury' to follow its FJ Fury series. USAF interest in the F-100B/BI at that stage was actually minimal and the interceptor programme was cut back. However, in April 1954 NAA became aware of renewed interest in a fighter-bomber requirement and it began work on beefing up the NA-212 for this mission. On 11 June 1954, NAA received a contract for thirty-three copies of a fighter-bomber that was still called F-100B, although on 8 July the designation was officially changed to F-107A to reflect the aircraft's substantial differences from the basic F-100. Three prototypes were initially ordered (55-5118, -5119, -5120) with nine service test aircraft to follow.

Although it was essentially a new design, the aircraft retained the basic F-100 wing with six hardpoints and leading edge slats, but it was positioned mid-way up the fuselage. Flight control was achieved by spoilers above and below each wing. Inboard flaps, similar to those eventually

The second aircraft has the Sandia 'Shape 27' special store on its centreline saddle tank. Although they are no emphasized in this view, 55-5119 had the same red markings as the other two F-107As. David Menard Collection

installed on the F-100D, were introduced but with boundary layer control to reduce landing speed by up to 25kt. An F-100-type horizontal stabilizer was used but the enlarged vertical stabilizer incorporating the AN/APS-54 RWR rose almost 20ft (6m) from the ground and was 'all moving' above a point roughly 2ft (0.6m) above the rear fuselage. Deflecting 3 degrees left and right (6 degrees with the undercarriage down) it provided powerful 'rudder' control and later appeared in modified form on the company's A3J Vigilante design. A new augmented longitudinal control system (ALCS, nicknamed 'Alice') was included. Essentially, it was an ancestor of fly-by-wire control systems. The F-100's rather inconveniently placed airbrake was replaced by two units extending from the bulky rear fuselage, but the

four-M39A1 gun basic armament was kept and moved further up the fuselage sides. An F-100-style nose landing gear was accompanied by newly designed main landing gear members extending from the fuselage, again like the later A3J.

Crucially, the J57 was replaced by Pratt & Whitney's (P&W) much more powerful J75-P-11 at almost 24,000lb (11,000kg) thrust with afterburning, supplied by around 2,000gal of internal fuel. A new NAA/USAF XMA-12 fire-control system (North American Search and Ranging Radar: NASSR) was specified and installed in the second F-107A although its flight testing under Phase III of the programme was never completed. It provided low-altitude bombing system (LABS) delivery of the electrically fused 10,000lb (4,550kg) of external ordnance and control of gunnery.

A TX-28 (B-28) nuclear store could be carried semi-recessed in the open fuselage bay or on an adapter that doubled as a 250gal fuel tank. This weapons installation was thought to be less troublesome for high-Mach bomb delivery than Republic's standard internal bay.

A large, clamshell cockpit canopy opened vertically, rising 28in (71cm) – only when the engine was turned off! – to allow the pilot to squeeze in and out. Several ejection tests from the first aircraft reassuringly showed that the NAA ejection seat could propel the pilot past the intake at all speeds without being sucked in.

Production design began on 1 May 1955, and the first aircraft flew only eighteen months later on 10 September 1956 with NAA pilot Bob Baker in control. It achieved Mach 1.03 in a dive on the first

F-107A Statistics	
Wingspan	36.58ft (11.15m)
Length	60.81ft (18.53m)
Height	19.54ft (5.95m)
Wing area	367.02sq ft (34.96sq m)
Weights	
empty	25,144lb (11,405kg)
gross	41,537lb (18,841kg)
Internal fuel	1,260gal, supplemented by a 500gal belly tank and drop tanks on the wings.
Armament	Four M-39 20mm guns with 200 rounds per gun.
Power	One P&W YJ75-P-11 turbojet at 15,500lb (7,000kg) military thrust and 23,500lb (10,500kg) thrust in full afterburner.
Fire control system	NAA/Autonetics XMA-12 with air-to-air and air-to-ground modes using an Autonetics R-14 radar. The system was later adapted as the XMA-8 for use in the Republic F-105D.
Cruise speed	588mph (956km/h)
Maximum speed	890mph (1,432km/h) at sea level
	1,295mph (2,083km/h) at 36,000ft (10,970m)
Service ceiling	53,200ft (16,215m)
Maximum rate of climb	39,900ft/min (12,161m/min)
Combat range	788 miles (1,268km)
Ferry range	2,428 miles (3,907km)

flight and would have gone faster but for engine gearbox problems. At the conclusion of the flight, Baker touched down at almost 200kt using half-flaps rather than the usual 45-degree position and had to make a landing roll of no less than 22,000ft (6,700m) when the drag-chute failed to deploy. The aircraft ran on into the dried mud section of Edwards AFB's runway, hit a rut and broke off its nose landing gear. The normal landing run with chute and full flaps was later found to be a more comfortable 3,600ft (1,100m). Repaired by 1 October, 55-5118 resumed testing and on 3 November J. O. Roberts flew it to Mach 2, the main objective of the thirty flights comprising Phase I of the programme. Phase II (3 December 1956-15 February 1957) used the second aircraft on thirty-two flights to test basic performance and handling. Rates of climb of up to 30,000ft (9,000m) per minute at sea level were recorded. The aircraft handled very well and was easier to trim and more stable than the F-100. Joining for the Phase III tests was the final aircraft (55-5120), incorporating an automatic variable air inlet duct (VAID), which increased the volume of 'free stream' air to the engine by 30 per cent and gave much improved performance at high altitude. Meanwhile, '118 was used for a series of

zoom climb tests that showed it could climb at Mach 1 in both normal and zoom climbs. Al White flew weapons tests in the second aircraft, including LABS drops at speeds up to Mach 1.2 and centreline 'special stores' drops at Mach 1.87. Later tests with the TX-28 store took the speed beyond Mach 2 at 35,000ft (10,700m) with clean weapons separation.

NAA's hopes were raised on 8 March 1957 by Air Defense Command's (ADC) expressed interest in a rocket-armed F-107B variant. However, this became academic when TAC made clear that it wanted the F-105 as its next aircraft, a decision that was made well before Phase II tests of the F-107A were finished. The six additional F-107As that NAA had anticipated building were cancelled.

Technically, there seemed little to choose between the two designs. The F-107A had shown early promise of being an unusually capable and reliable aircraft that fulfilled all TAC's requirements rather than simply a 'banker' for TAC against the failure of the F-105. During flight testing, the F-107A had shown far fewer developmental problems than the F-105 and in mid-1956 there seemed a real possibility that the Republic fighter would be cancelled in favour of the F-107A. Possibly Republic was favoured politically since it

had no other work in prospect, or because its design included a specialized internal nuclear weapons bay that might enable TAC to preserve its nuclear capability in the face of increasing domination by Strategic Air Command (SAC) influence.

After cancellation of further work on the F-107A in March 1957, 55-5119 continued its series of weapons tests. The other two aircraft were passed to NACA's High-Speed Flight Installation at Edwards AFB for continuation testing of their innovative design features including the VAID system, all-moving tail and ALCS. Valuable data resulted which helped in the later development of types such as the XB-70A bomber, SR-71 and a new generation of fighters including the F-15 and F-16. The third aircraft was equipped with a side-stick controller in place of the conventional 'joy stick' to prove the concept for the X-15A research vehicle. 55-5118 became 'NACA 207' but it flew very little and was soon cannibalized to keep '120 flying.

On 1 September, Scott Crossfield experienced trim-setting problems that prevented him from getting '120 airborne. The aborted take-off blew the nose-wheel tyres and on the run-out the left brake and tyre overheated, causing a fire that damaged the aircraft before a fire-truck could be brought up. The aircraft was beyond economical repair and it ended its days on Shepard AFB's fire dump. The other two F-107As were returned to USAF charge on 3 June 1960. 55-5118 ended up at Pima County Museum after spending many years deteriorating in outdoor storage and '119 was placed in the Air Force Museum at Wright-Patterson AFB.

Although TAC gained a valiant workhorse in the F-105 it also lost an exceptional aircraft in the F-107A. In common with most NAA designs it was significantly ahead of its time. In the early 1950s, the company was the foremost US defence contractor. Its determination to remain at the forefront of development led it into some technically brilliant but enormously costly projects including the Mach 3, missile-armed F-108 interceptor and the extraordinarily advanced XB-70 Valkyrie bomber. Although the company in its restructured North American Rockwell form went on to produce the B-1B bomber, the cancellation of the F-107A took it out of the fighter business.

F-100 Statistics and Performance

	YF-100	F-100A	F-100C	F-100D	F-100F
Wingspan (ft/in)	36' 7"	38' 9"	38' 9"	38' 9"	38' 9"
Length (ft/in)	46' 3"	47' 1"	47' 1"	47' 1"	50' 4"
(fuselage, excluding pitot boom)					
Height (ft/in)	14' 5"	15' 4"*	15' 4"	16' 2"	16' 2"
Wing area (sq. ft)	376	385	385	400	400
Weight (lb/kg)					
empty	18,135 (8,226)	18,135 (8,226)	19,270 (8,740)	20,638 (9,361)	21,712 (9,848)
combat	24,789 (11,244)	24,996 (11,338)	28,700 (13,018)	30,061 (13,635)	31,413 (14,248)
gross	28,561 (12,955)	28,899 (13,108)	36,549 (16,578)	38,048 (17,258)	39,122 (17,745)
Engine	XJ57-P-7	J57-P-7/P-39	J-57-P-21	J57-P-21/-21A	J57-P-21/-21A
Thrust (lb/kg)					
mil	8,700 (3,946)	9,700 (4,400)	10,200 (4,630)	10,200 (4,630)	10,200 (4,630)
afterburner	13,200 (5,990)	14,800 (6,700)	16,000 (7,250)	16,000 (7,250)	16,000 (7,250)
Max. speed (kt)					
at 35,000ft (10,700m)	634	740	803	765	760
Stalling speed (kt)	139	138	146	147	157
Service ceiling (ft/m)	52,600 (16,000)	44,900 (13,700)	38,700 (11,800)	39,600 (12,000)	38,500 (11,750)
Rate of climb (ft/m min)	–	23,800 (7,250)	21,600 (6,600)	19,000 (5,800)	18,500 (5,600)
Combat radius (miles/km)	–	358 (575)	572 (920)	520 (835)	508 (817)
Ferry range (miles/km)	–	1,294 (2,080)	1,954 (3,145)	1,995 (3,210)	1,661 (2,670)

*(F-100A with 'short' vertical stabilizer was 13' 4")

F-100 Production

Listed in order of serial allocation.

Type/Block	Quantity	AF Serials	Construction Numbers
YF-100A	2	52-5754/-5755	(Model) NAA-180-1/2
F-100A-1-NA	10	52-5756/-5765	NA-192-1/10
F-100A-5-NA	13	52-5766/-5778	NA-192-11/23
F-100A-10-NA	40	53-1529/-1568	NA-192-24/63
F-100A-15-NA	40	53-1569/-1608	NA-192-64/103
F-100A-20-NA	100	53-1609/-1708	NA-192-104/203
F-100C-1-NA	70	53-1709/-1778	NA-214-1/70
F-100C-1-NA	30	54-1740/-1769	NA-217-1/30
F-100C-5-NA	45	54-1770/-1814	NA-217-31/75
F-100C-15-NA	45	54-1815/-1859	NA-217-76/120
F-100C-20-NA	111	54-1860/-1970	NA-217-121/231
F-100C-25-NA	150	54-1971/-2120	NA-217-232/381
F-100C-10-NH	25	55-2709/-2733	NA-2221/25

F-100D-1-NA	12	54-2121/-2132	NA-223-1/12
F-100D-5-NA	19	54-2133/-2151	NA-223-13/31
F-100D-10-NA	70	54-2152/-2221	NA-223-32/101
F-100D-15-NA	82	54-2222/-2303	NA-223-102/183
F-100C-10-NH	25	55-2709/-2733	NA-222-1/25
F-100D-35-NH	10	55-2734/-2743	NA-224-1/10
F-100D-40-NH	40	55-2744/-2783	NA-224-11/50
F-100D-45-NH	80	55-2784/-2863	NA-224-51/130
F-100D-50-NH	45	55-2864/-2908	NA-224-131/175
F-100D-55-NH	46	55-2909/-2954	NA-244-176/221
F-100D-20-NA	100	55-3502/-3601	NA-223-184/283
F-100D-25-NA	100	55-3602/-3701	NA-223-284/383
F-100D-30-NA	113	55-3702/-3814	NA-223-384/496
F-100D-60-NA	60	56-2903/-2962	NA-235-1/60
F-100D-65-NA	60	56-2963/-3022	NA-235-61/120
F-100D-70-NA	120	56-3023/-3142	NA-235-121/240
F-100D-75-NA	56	56-3143/-3198	NA-235-241/296
F-100D-90-NA	148	56-3199/-3346	NA-235-297/444
F-100D-80-NH	28	56-3351/-3378	NA-245-1/28
F-100D-85-NH	85	56-3379/-3463	NA-245-29/113
F-100F-1-NA	15	56-3725/-3739	NA-243-1/15
F-100F-5-NA	30	56-3740/-3769	NA-243-16/45
F-100F-10-NA	150	56-3770/-3919	NA-243-46/195
F-100F-15-NA	100	56-3920/-4019	NA-243-196/295
F-100F-20-NA	29	58-1205/-1233	NA-255-1/29 (MDAP)
F-100F-15-NA	9	58-6975/-6983	NA-261-1/9 (MDAP)
F-100F-15-NA	6	59-2558/-2563	NA-262-1/6 (MDAP)

(F-100A-10-NA 53-1545/-1548, -1551 and -1554 were modified to RF-100As.)

Sub-totals

YF-100A/F-100	205
F-100C	476
F-100D	1,274
F-100F	339
Total production:	*2,294*

F-100Ds equipped with NAVS (Doppler Navigation System)

All FY58 F-100Fs equipped with NAVS.

F-100D-55/90

-2795, -2837, -2845, -2849, -2853, -2855/6, -2861, -2863, -2865, -2870, -2878/9, -2881, -2883, -2889, -2892, -2901, -2903/4/5, -2917, -3502, -3508, -3512, -3516, -3518, -3521/2, -3525, -3528, -3530, -3532, -3534/5, -3541, -3543, -3545, -3549, -3550, -3553, -3555, -3558/9, -3560, -3562, -3564, -3566, -3568/9, -3570, -3572/3/4, -3576, -3580/1/2, -3581, -3585, -3586, -3587, -3589, -3590/1/2/3, -3595, -3598, -3600/1/2/3/4/5/6, -3608, -3611, -3613, -3615, -3618/9, -3620, -3622/3, -3625, -3628, -3630/1/2, -3634, -3639, -3640/1/2, -3647, -3650, -3653, -3740, -3745, -3762 -3765/6, -3780, -3782, -3784/5, -3793, -3803/4, -3806, -3809, -3811/2/3/4.

F-100D-56

-2903, -3259, -3263/4/5/6/7, -3269, -3270, -3270, -3272/3, -3275/6/7/8/9, -3280, -3282/3, -3285/6/7, -3320, -3324, -3326/7/8/9, -3330, -3331/2/3/4/5/6, -3338/9, -3340/1, -3343, -3345/6.

MAIN DIFFERENCES TABLE
F-100 SERIES

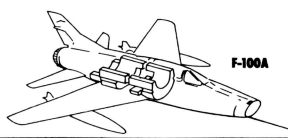

F-100A

ENGINE	J57-21A WITH AFTERBURNER
AC ELECTRICAL POWER SOURCE	THREE INVERTERS
ARMAMENT	FOUR GUNS AND MISSILES
STARTER	PNEUMATIC
DROP TANKS	TWO 275-GALLON
INTERNAL FUEL	FUSELAGE
REFUELING PROVISIONS	GRAVITY TANK FILLING
FLAPS	NO
OXYGEN SYSTEM	GASEOUS, WITH D-2 REGULATOR
AUTOPILOT	NO

ENGINE	J57-21A WITH AFTERBURNER
AC ELECTRICAL POWER SOURCE	THREE INVERTERS
ARMAMENT	FOUR GUNS AND VARIOUS COMBINATIONS OF EXTERNAL LOADS INCLUDING BOMBS, ROCKETS AND MISSILES MOUNTED ON REMOVABLE PYLONS.
STARTER	PNEUMATIC
DROP TANKS	TWO 275-GALLON AND/OR COMBINATION OF 200-GALLON (TWO 335-GALLON ON SOME AIRPLANES)
INTERNAL FUEL	FUSELAGE AND WING
REFUELING PROVISIONS	PRESSURE TYPE (SINGLE-POINT AND AIR REFUELING)
FLAPS	NO
OXYGEN SYSTEM	LIQUID, WITH D-2A REGULATOR
AUTOPILOT	NO

F-100C

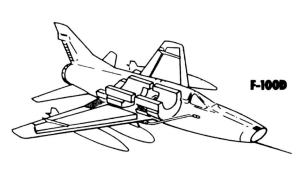

F-100D

ENGINE	J57-21A WITH AFTERBURNER
AC ELECTRICAL POWER SOURCE	ONE ENGINE-DRIVEN AC GENERATOR WITH ONE STAND-BY INVERTER
ARMAMENT	FOUR GUNS AND VARIOUS COMBINATIONS OF EXTERNAL LOADS INCLUDING BOMBS, ROCKETS, AND MISSILES MOUNTED ON FORCE EJECTION PYLONS.
STARTER	CARTRIDGE AND PNEUMATIC
DROP TANKS	TWO 275-GALLON, TWO 450-GALLON OR TWO 335-GALLON AND/OR COMBINATION OF 200-GALLON.
INTERNAL FUEL	FUSELAGE AND WING
REFUELING PROVISIONS	PRESSURE-TYPE (SINGLE-POINT AND AIR REFUELING)
FLAPS	YES
OXYGEN SYSTEM	LIQUID WITH MD-1 REGULATOR
AUTOPILOT	YES

ENGINE	J57-21A WITH AFTERBURNER
AC ELECTRICAL POWER SOURCE	ONE ENGINE-DRIVEN AC GENERATOR WITH ONE STAND-BY INVERTER
ARMAMENT	TWO GUNS AND VARIOUS COMBINATIONS OF EXTERNAL LOADS INCLUDING BOMBS, ROCKETS, AND MISSILES MOUNTED ON FORCE EJECTION PYLONS
STARTER	CARTRIDGE AND PNEUMATIC
DROP TANKS	TWO 275-GALLON TWO 450-GALLON OR TWO 335-GALLON AND/OR COMBINATION OF 200-GALLON.
INTERNAL FUEL	FUSELAGE AND WING
REFUELING PROVISIONS	PRESSURE-TYPE (SINGLE-POINT AND AIR REFUELING)
FLAPS	YES
OXYGEN SYSTEM	LIQUID WITH MD-1 REGULATOR
AUTOPILOT	YES

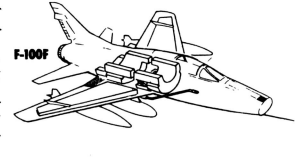

F-100F

F-100-1-00-1

F-100 Units

USAF F-100 Units

3rd TFD   F-100D/F from June 1964
Based: England AFB, Louisiana
90th TFS (light blue) *Pair o' Dice*
Deployed to Bien Hoa AB, RVN, 8 Feb 1966–31 Oct 1970. Transitioned to A-37B.
416th TFS (blue) *Silver Knights*
From 21st TFW, June 1964. Deployed to: Da Nang AB, RVN, March 1965; Tan Son Nhut AB, RVN, Nov 1965–June 1966; 37th TFW, Phu Cat AB, RVN, 15 April 1967; 31st TFW, Tuy Hoa AB, RVN, 28 May 1969 (coded SE). Non-operational from 5 Sept 1970. To 4403rd TFW, England AFB, 23 Sept 1970.
510th TFS (purple)
F-100D from March 1964. Deployed to Bien Hoa AB, RVN, 10 Nov 1965. Inactivated 15 Nov 1969.
531st TFS (red)
From 21st TFW, June 1964. Deployed to Bien Hoa AB, RVN, 8 Nov 1965. Inactivated 31 July 1970.
307th TFS
TDY from 31st TFW to Bien Hoa AB, RVN, July–Nov 1965.
308th TFS
Assigned to 3rd TFW, Bien Hoa AB, RVN, 2 Dec 1965–15 Nov 1966. Reassigned to Tuy Hoa AB, RVN, 15 Nov 1966.

Codes used at Bien Hoa: CB (90th TFS), CE (510th TFS), CP (531st TFS).

4th FDW   From F-86H to F-100C, early 1958
Based: Seymour Johnson AFB, North Carolina
333rd FDS (red) *Lancers*
334th FDS (blue) *Eagles*
335th FDS (green) *Chiefs*
336th FDS (yellow) *Rocketeers*

Transitioned to F-105B from 16 June 1959.

8th TFW *Attaquez et Conquerez*   From F-84G and F-86F to F-100D/F, late 1956
Based: Itazuke AB, Japan
35th TFS (blue)
36th TFS (red) *Flying Fiends*
80th TFS (yellow) *Headhunters*

To F-105D, May 1963, then F-4C via re-designation of 32nd TFW as 8th TFW, 1965.

18th TFW   From F-86F to F-100D/F, 1957
Based: Kadena AB, Japan
12th TFS (yellow/black/yellow) *Bald Eagles*
44th TFS (blue) *Vampires*
67th TFS (red) *Fighting Cocks*

To F-105D/F from Oct 1962.

20th TFW *Victory by Valor*   From F-84F to F-100D/F, 16 June 1957
Based: RAF Wethersfield and RAF Woodbridge, UK
55th TFS (blue) *Fighting Fifty Fifth*
Moved to RAF Upper Heyford, UK, 1 June 1970.
77th TFS (red) *Gamblers*
Moved to RAF Upper Heyford, UK, 1 June 1970.
79th TFS (yellow) *Tigers*
Based: RAF Woodbridge, UK
Moved to RAF Upper Heyford, UK, 15 Jan 1970.

To F-111E from Sept 1970.

21st TFW   From F-84G to F-100D/F, late 1958
Based: Misawa AB, Japan
416th TFS (blue) *Silver Knights*
531st TFS (red)

Transitioned to F-100D from July 1958. Deactivated June 1960, both squadrons reassigned to 3rd TFW.

27th TFW   F-100D/F from Feb 1959
Based: Cannon AFB, New Mexico
481st TFS (green)
TDYs to Takhli RTAFB, Thailand, 1963; Misawa AB, Japan and Kunsan AB, Korea, 1964; Tan Son Nhut AB, RVN, 27 June 1965–1 Jan 1966. To F-111E late 1969. Inactivated 31 Aug 1973.
522nd TFS (red) *Fireballs*
Saw Buck III TDYs to Takhli RTAB, Thailand, 13 Dec 1962–1 June 1963, TDY to Da Nang AB, RVN (6 aircraft) and Takhli (6 aircraft), 14 Aug 1964, then Da Nang (whole squadron) until 6 May 1964. TDYs to Misawa AB, Japan, May 1965, Clark AB, Philippines, late 1965. To F-111A, 1972.
523rd TFS (blue)
Reassigned to 405th TFW, Nov 1965.
524th TFS (yellow) *Hounds of Heaven*
Flew F-100D until March 1969. To F-111D, 1972.

312th TFW renumbered 27th TFW, Feb 1959. 18 aircraft Det maintained at Takhli, RTAB, May 1962–May 1964, reduced to 6 aircraft, Feb 1963. 27th TFW became F-100 RTU, 1 Jan 1966. Flew last regular USAF F-100 mission, 19 July 1972 (56-3333).
Coded from July 1968: CA (481st TFS), CC (522nd TFS), CD (524th TFS).
Common base code CC used from 1972.

31st TFW   From F-84F to F-100D/F, mid-1957
Based: Turner AFB, Georgia
306th TFS (green)
307th TFS (red)
308th TFS (yellow)
309th TFS (blue)

All air assets transferred to 354th TFW, Myrtle Beach from 15 March 1959.

31st TFW   F-100D/F from 15 March 1959
Based: George AFB, California
306th TFS (red)
Inactivated 28 Sept 1970.
307th TFS (blue)
TDY to Bien Hoa AB, RVN, June 1965. Aircraft left for use by 531st TFS. Reassigned to Torrejon AB, Spain, April 1966.
308th TFS (green) *Emerald Knights*
TDY to Bien Hoa AB, RVN, Dec 1965–Nov 1966. Reassigned to 4403rd TFW*, 15 Oct 1970.
309th TFS (yellow)
Reassigned to 4403rd TFW*, England AFB, 5 Oct 1970.

Wing formed by a 'paper' transfer on 15 March 1959 of assets of TFW, retaining markings and colours of 413th TFW. Moved to Homestead AFB, mid-1960, deployed to Tuy Hoa AB Dec 1966–15 Oct 1970, taking 306th, 308th, 309th TFS. Following units assigned at Tuy Hoa:
355th TFS
15 May 1969–30 Sept 1970, then to 354th TFW with A-7D Corsair II.
416th TFS *Silver Knights*
28 May 1969–5 Sept 1970, then to 4403rd TFW*, England AFB, 23 Sept 1970.
136th TFS New York ANG *Rocky's Raiders*
14 June 1968–25 May 1969.
188th TFS New Mexico ANG *Enchilada Air Force 7*
May 1968–June 1969.

Wing transferred to USA 'on paper', 30 Oct 1970. Aircraft passed to various ANG units.
Codes used at Tuy Hoa: SD (306th TFS), SM (308th TFS), SS (309th TFS), SP (355th TFS), SE (416th TFS), SG (136th TFS), SK (188th TFS).
* 4403rd TFW was a Provisional Wing at Homestead AFB that handled F-100 units returning from South East Asia and passed their aircraft on to ANG units. Returning squadrons were assigned for about a year, the 416th TFS being the last under its control.

35th TFW   F-100D/F from Oct 1966
Based: Phan Rang AB, RVN
352nd TFS
Active 10 Oct 1966–31 July 1971.
612th TFS, Det 1
HQ squadron using F-100F in *Misty* FAC role 10 Oct 1966–8 June 1967 and 14 April 1969–31 July 1971. (At Phu Cat AB between these dates.)
614th TFS *Lucky Devils*
Active 10 Oct 1966–31 July 1971. Reassigned to 401st TFW, Torrejon AB, Spain.
615th TFS
Active 10 Oct 1966–31 July 1971.
120th TFS
Colorado ANG (F-100C). Assigned 30 April 1968–18 April 1969.

Wing became F-100 unit through exchange of designation numbers with 366th TFW, Phan Rang AB while 35th TFW was at Da Nang AB in Oct 1966, having initially formed there in April 1966. 366th then became an F-4 Wing at Da Nang.
Codes used at Phan Rang: VM (352nd TFS), VS (612th TFS), VP (614th TFS), VZ (615th TFS), VS (120th TFS while Det 1, 612th TFS was at Phu Cat).

36th FDW   From F-86F to F-100C, 1956
Based: Bitburg AB, West Germany

22nd FDS (red)
To F-105D/F from May 1961.
23rd FDS (blue)
To F-105D/F from May 1961.
53rd FDS (yellow)
Based: Landstuhl/Ramstein AB, West Germany
To F-105D from May 1961.
461st FDS (black)
Based: Hahn AB, West Germany
Deactivated Nov 1959.
32nd FDS (green)
Based: Soesterberg AB, Netherlands
To F/TF-102A with 86th FIW, 1960.

Wing also responsible for Skyblazers Flight Demonstration Team 1956–1961. Aircraft then passed to 50th TFW. Like other FDWs and FBWs, Wing became a TFW after 1 July 1958.

37th TFW   Activated as F-100D/F unit, 1 March 1967
Based: Phu Cat AB, RVN
416th TFS *Silver Knights*
Assigned 15 April 1967–27 May 1969, then to 31st TFW, Tuy Hoa AB, RVN.
355th TFS
Assigned from 354th TFW, 3 Feb 1968–15 May 1969, then to 31st TFW, Tuy Hoa AB, RVN.
612th TFS, Det 1
(Misty FAC). From Phan Rang AB, RVN, 8 June 1967–13 April 1969, then returned to Phan Rang.
174th TFS Iowa ANG
Assigned from 14 May 1968–11 May 1969.

Codes used at Phu Cat: HE (416th TFS), HP (355th TFS), HS (612th TFS), HA (174th TFS).

45th FDS (black/yellow/black)   F-100C/D training and transition for USAFE units from March 1956
Based: Sidi Slimane AB, French Morocco

F-100Cs passed to 36th FDW, Bitburg AB, and 7272nd FTW, Wheelus AB. Replaced by F-100Ds. Deactivated 8 Jan 1958.

48th FBW *Statue de la Liberté*   From F-86F to F-100D/F, late 1956
Based: Chaumont AB, France
492nd FBS (blue) *Bolars*
493rd FBS (yellow) *Roosters*
494th FBS (red) *Panthers*

Wing transferred to RAF Lakenheath, UK by 15 Jan 1960 as 48th TFW. Transitioned to F-4D from Feb 1972.
Codes used at Lakenheath from March 1970: LR (492nd TFS), LS (493rd TFS), LT (494th TFS).

49th FBW *Tutor et Ultor*   F-100D/F from 10 Dec 1957
Based: Etain-Rouvres AB, France
7th FBS (blue)
8th TFS (yellow) *Black Sheep*
9th TFS (red) *Iron Knights*

Wing activated by re-numbering 388th FBW. Moved to Spangdahlem AB as 49th TFW, 1960. Converted to F-105D/F from Oct 1961.

50th FBW *Masters of the Sky*   From F-86H to F-100D/F, 1957
Based: Toul Rosières AB, France
10th FBS (blue)
81st FBS (yellow)
417th FBS (red)

Wing transferred to Hahn AB from 10 Dec 1959 as 50th TFW. Converted to F-4D from Oct 1966 with 81st TFS receiving F-4Cww.

57th FWW (formerly 4525th FWW)   F-100D/F 1960, Oct 1969
Based: Nellis AFB, Nevada
4536th CCTS

65th FWS from late 1969 when Wing became 57th FWW. Inactivated 31 Dec 1969.
Coded WB from Oct 1969.

72nd TFS (red)   F-100D/F 1 July 1958–9 April 1959
Based: Clark AB, Philippines

Formerly 418th FBS May–July 1958, squadron controlled by 6200th ABW. Re-designated 510th FBS with 405th FBW, 9 April 1959.
113rd TFG   F-100C/F, 26 Jan 1958–9 April 1959
Based: Myrtle Beach AFB, South Carolina
119th TFS New Jersey ANG
To F-101B, June 1970.
121 TFS District of Columbia ANG
To F-105D/F, July 1971.
HQ Flight, DC ANG

Called to active service during the Pueblo Crisis at Andrews AFB. Transferred to Myrtle Beach.
Codes used at Myrtle Beach: XA (119th TFS), XB (121st TFS), XD (HQ Flight).

312nd FBW   From F-86H to F-100D/F, late 1956
Based: Cannon AFB, New Mexico
386th FBS (red)
387th FBS (blue)
388th FBS (yellow)
477th FBS (green)

Wing became 312nd TFW, 1 July 1958. Re-designated 27th TFW, Feb 1959.

322nd FDW   From F-86F to F-100C, mid-1955
Based: Foster AFB, Texas
450th FDS (red)
451st FDS (yellow)
452nd FDS (green)

First TAC Wing with F-100C. De-activated late 1957, aircraft passed to 4th FDW and 36th FDW.

323rd FBW (323rd FBG and 386th FBG)   From F-86F to F-100D/F, Aug 1956
Based: Bunker Hill AFB, Indiana
With **323rd FBG** were:
453rd FBS (red)
454th FBS (blue)
455th FBS (yellow)
Some F-100As used initially. Deactivated summer 1957.

With **386th FBG** were:
552nd FBS
553rd FBS
554th FBS
At Bunker Hill from late 1956 until Aug 1957.

354th FBW/ TFW   F-100D/F from early 1957
Based: Myrtle Beach AFB, South Carolina
352nd TFS (yellow)
TDYs to Phan Rang Bay AB, RVN, 15 Aug–10 Oct 1966 with 366th TFW; and 10 Oct 1966–31 July 1971 with 31st TFW.
353rd TFS (red) *Black Panther*
Transitioned to F-4E 1970 and designation passed to an A-7D unit.
355th TFS (blue)
Attached to 37th TFW, Phu Cat AB, RVN, 3 Feb–15 May 1969 and 31st TFW, Tuy Hoa AB, RVN, 15 May–30 Sept 1970.
356th TFS (green) *Green Demons*
Transitioned to F-4C by Nov 1967.

Wing took over F-100D/Fs from deactivated 31st FBW, 1957. Deployed squadrons to Spain, Italy and Japan. Became 354th TFW, July 1958. Squadrons reassigned to other units by June 1968 and it moved 'on paper' to Kunsan AB replacing 4th TFW as controlling unit for two ANG F-100C/F squadrons:
127th TFS Kansas ANG (red)
5 July 1968–10 June 1969. Returned to Kansas State control 18 June 1969 and transitioned to F-105D/F 1971.
166th TFS Ohio ANG (blue)
5 July 1968–10 June 1969. Returned to Ohio State control, 19 June 1969. To F-100D/F Nov 1971.

Codes used at Kunsan: BO (127th TFS), BP (166th TFS).

366th FBW   From F-84F to F-100D/F, late 1957
Based: England AFB, Louisiana
389th FBS (red)
390th FBS (blue)
391st FBS (yellow)
480th FBS (green)
Deactivated early 1959 as 366th TFW. Reactivated at Da Nang AB, RVN, April 1966, moving to Phan Rang AB, RVN, 20 March–10 Oct 1966 controlling:
352nd TFS
15 Aug–10 Oct 1966.
614th TFS *Lucky Devils*
18 Sept–10 Oct 1966.
615th TFS
15 May–10 Oct 1966.
Wing to Da Nang AB to fly F-4 and F-100 squadrons passed to 35th TFW control, Phan Rang AB.

388th FBW   From F-86F to F-100C/F, late 1956
Based: Etain-Rouvres, France
561st FBS (yellow)
562nd FBS (blue)
563rd FBS (red)
Wing re-numbered 49th FBW, Dec 1957. 388th TFW reactivated at McConnell AFB, 1 Oct 1962 with one squadron:
560th TFS
Tasked as a training and proficiency squadron. To F-105D mid-1963 when Wing (including 561st, 562nd, 563rd TFS) reactivated on F-105D/F. 388th TFW inactivated once again, Feb 1964. Replaced by 23rd TFW before reactivating at Korat AB, 8 April 1966 with F-105D/F to replace 6234th TFW.

401st TFW *Caelum Arena Nostrum*   From F-84F to F-100D/F, late 1957
Based: England AFB, Louisiana
612th TFS (blue) *Screaming Eagles*
TDY to Da Nang AB, RVN, Sept–Nov 1964. Activated as Det 1, 612th TFS with 366th TFW, Phan Rang AB, RVN, 15 May 1966 then with 35th TFW, Phan Rang from 10 Oct 1966; 37th TFW, Phu Cat AB, RVN 8 June 1967, returning to 35th TFW, Phan Rang, 14 April 1969–31 July 1971. To F-4E in 1971 with 307th TFS assets and reassigned to Torrejon AB, Spain.
613th TFS (yellow) *Squids*
TDY to Da Nang AB, RVN, Nov 1964–July 1965. Reassigned to Torrejon AB, Spain, April 1966. To F-4E 1970.
614th TFS (red) *Lucky Devils*
TDY to Clark AB, Philippines and Da Nang AB, RVN, Nov 1964. To 35th TFW, 18 Sept 1966. Transitioned to F-4E 1971.
615th TFS (green)
TDY to Clark AB, Philippines and Da Nang AB, RVN, June 1964. To Phan Rang AB, RVN with 35th TFW, 10 Oct 1966.

When Wing transferred to Torrejon AB it had only the 613rd TFS but added:
307th TFS
From 31st TFW, Bien Hoa AB, RVN, April 1966. To F-4E 1970.
353rd TFS *Black Panthers*
From 354th TFW. To F-4E 1970.

405th FBW   From F-84F to F-100D, late 1956
Based: Langley AFB, Virginia
508th FBS (yellow)
Deactivated 1 July 1958.
509th FBS (red)
Reactivated 9 April 1959 as FIS with F-86D.
510th FBS (purple) *Buzzards*
Reactivated at Clark AB, Philippines, 9 April 1959.
511th FBS (blue)
Deactivated 1 July 1958.

First TAC F-100D unit, 405th deactivated 1 July 1958. Reactivated as 405th FW at Clark AB, Philippines, 9 April 1959 with only one F-100D unit:
510th TFS
TDY to Don Muang RTAFB, Thailand, April–Nov 1961. To 3rd TFW, England AFB, 1964.

413th FDW   From F-86H to F-100C/F, late 1957. F-100D/F, 1958
Based: George AFB, California
1st FDS (red)
21st FDS (blue)
34th FDS (green)
474th TFS (yellow)

Assigned when Wing transitioned to F-100D/F as 413rd TFW, 1958. Wing deactivated, 15 March 1959, re-designated 31st TFW.

450th FDW   From F-86F to F-100C, 1955
Based: Foster AFB, Texas
720th FDS
721st FDS (red)
722nd FDS
723rd FDS

Deactivated Dec 1958.

474th FBW   From F-86H to F-100D/F, late 1957
Based: Cannon AFB, New Mexico
428th FBS (blue) *Buccaneers*
TDY to Takhli RTAFB, Thailand 18 May–3 Sept 1962. TDY to Da Nang AB, RVN from Nov 1964 (using 522nd TFS assets) and Takhli, Aug 1964–March 1965.
429th FBS (yellow) *Black Falcons*
TDY to 6251st TFW, Bien Hoa AB, RVN, 13 July–Nov 1965. Attached to 3rd TFW, 21 Nov–16 Dec 1965.
430th FBS (red) *Tigers*
TDY to Takhli RTAFB, Thailand, 3 Sept–13 Dec 1962.
478th FBS (green)
Deactivated late 1965, reactivated on F-111A Jan 1968 with 428th, 429th, 430th TFS.

479th FDW   From F-86F to F-100A, late 1954
Based: George AFB, California
434th FDS (red)
435th FDS (green)
436th FDS (yellow)
476th FDS (blue)
Added from 8 Oct 1957.

First TAC F-100 unit. To F-100C/F by 1956, then F-104A, 1958.

506th FBW   From F-84F to F-100D/F, Sept 1957
Based: Tinker AFB, Oklahoma
457th FBS (red)
Deployed to Landstuhl AB, West Germany, 22 March–Sept 1958. (Aircraft left in place for 458th FBS.)
458th FBS (yellow)
Deployed to Landstuhl, West Germany, Sept 1958–March 1959 using 457th FBS aircraft.
462nd FBS (blue)
470th FBS (green)
Deactivated 1 April 1959.

Air National Guard (ANG) Units

Arizona ANG, 162nd TFG
152nd TFTS (yellow)
Based: Tucson IAP
From F-86F to F-100A, May 1958. From F-100A to F-102A from Feb 1966 as ADC-gained unit. To F-100C/F from mid-1969 as 152nd TFTS training ANG F-100 crews. To F-100D/F, June 1972. Began A-7D training late 1975 in parallel with F-100 training. F-100 flying ended March 1978.
Arkansas ANG, 188th TFG
184th TFS (red) *Flying Razorbacks*   From RF-101C to F-100D/F, summer 1972
Based: Fort Smith municipal airport
To F-4C, summer 1979.

Colorado ANG, 140th TFG
120th TFS (blue)   From F-86L to F-100C/F, 1 Jan 1961
Based: Buckley Field, Aurora
Called to active duty 1 Oct 1961 during Berlin Crisis but remained at Buckley ANGB. Called to active duty 26 Jan 1968 during Pueblo Crisis and deployed to Phan Rang AB, RVN, 3 May 1968. Returned to State control, 30 April 1969. To F-100D/F Oct 1971, A-7D April 1974.

Coded VS at Phan Rang AB.

Connecticut ANG, 103rd TFG
118th TFS *Flying Yankeess*   From F-86H to F-100A, summer 1960
Based: Bradley Field IAP
F/TF-102A, June 1966, F-100D/F, spring 1971, A-10A, summer 1979.
Camouflaged aircraft coded CT after 1971.

District of Columbia ANG, 113th TFG
121st TFS (red or yellow)   From F-86H to F-100C/F, mid-1960
Based: Andrews AFB
Called to active duty during Berlin Crisis, 1 Oct 1961 but remained at
Andrews AFB. Deployed to Puerto Rico, Nov 1963 and to Europe,
Aug 1964. Called to active duty 26 Jan 1968 during Pueblo Crisis and
deployed to Myrtle Beach AFB as F-100 CCTS until 18 June 1969. To
F-105D/F, July 1971.
Coded XB at Myrtle Beach AFB.

Georgia ANG, 116th TFG
128th TFS   From C-124C to F-100D/F, spring 1973
Based: Dobbins AFB
To F-105G/F, summer 1979.

Indiana ANG, 181st TFG and 122nd TFG
113rd TFS, 181st TFG From F-84F to F-100D/F, Sept 1971
Based: Hulman Field, Terre Haute
To F-4C, summer 1979.
Coded HF after 1970.
163rd TFS (yellow), *Marksmen*, **122nd TFG**   From F-84F to
F-100D/F, June 1971
Based: Baer Field, Fort Wayne
To F-4C, spring 1979.

Iowa ANG, 132nd TFG and 185th TFG
124th TFS   From F-84F to F-100C/F, April 1971
Based: Des Moines municipal airport
Phased out last F-100Cs in ANG for F-100D, 1975. To A-7D, Jan 1977.
174th TFS, 185th TFG From RF-84F to F-100C/F, summer 1961
Based: Sioux City municipal airport
To F-100D/F June 1974, then A-7D Dec 1976.

Kansas ANG, 184th TFG
127th TFS (red) *Jayhawks*   From F-86L to F-100C/F, spring 1961
Based: McConnell AFB
Called to active duty 26 Jan during Pueblo Crisis. Deployed to Kunsan
AB, Korea with 354th TFW, 5 July 1968–10 June 1969. Returned to
State control, June 1969. Converted to F-105D/F, spring 1971.
Coded BP at Kunsan AB.

Louisiana ANG, 159th TFG
122nd TFS (red, blue or green) From F/TF-102A to F-100D/F, winter
1970
Based: NAS New Orleans
To F-4C April 1979.

Massachusetts ANG, 102nd and 104th TFG
101st TFS   From F-84F to F-100D/F, May 1971
Based: Logan airport, Boston
Some F-100Cs assigned for conversion training in 1960 but unit
continued to fly F-86H instead at that time. To F-106A/B as ADC-
gained unit, 10 June 1972.
131st TFS (red), **104th TFG**   From F-84F to F-100D/F, June 1971
Based: Barnes Field, Westfield
To A-10A, July 1979.
Coded MA.

Michigan ANG, 127th TFG
107th TFS (red)   From RF-101A/C to F-100D/F, mid-1972
Based: Selfridge ANGB

To A-7D, Sept 1978.
Coded MI.

Missouri ANG, 131st TFG
110th TFS (red) *Lindbergh's Own*   From F-84F to F-100C/F, Sept 1962
Based: Lambert Field
To F-100D/F Dec 1971, then F-4C, early 1979.

New Jersey ANG, 177th TFG
119th TFS   From F-86H to F-100C/F, Sept 1965
Based: Atlantic City
Called to active duty 26 Jan 1968 during Pueblo Crisis and transferred
to Myrtle Beach AFB as F-100 RTU until 18 June 1969. To F-101B,
June 1970.
Coded XA at Myrtle Beach AFB 1968–69.

New Mexico ANG, 150th TFG
188th TFS (yellow) *Enchilada Air Force*   From F-80C to F-100A, April
1958
Based: Kirtland AFB
First ANG F-100 unit (as 188th FIS). To F-100C/F spring 1964 as
188th TFS. Called to active duty 26 Jan 1968 during Pueblo Crisis and
deployed to Tuy Hoa AB, RVN, May 1968–5 June 1969. To A-7D,
autumn 1973.
Coded SK at Tuy Hoa from 7 June 1968.

New York ANG, 107th TFG
136th TFS (yellow) *Rocky's Raiders/New York's Finest.*   From F-86H
to F-100C/F, Aug 1960
Based: Niagara Falls IAP
Called to active duty during Berlin Crisis, Oct 1961 but remained at
Niagara Falls. Called to active duty 26 Jan 1968 during Pueblo Crisis
and deployed to Tuy Hoa AB, RVN, 14 June 1968–25 May 1969. Transitioned to F-101B/F, April 1971.
Coded SG at Tuy Hoa 1968–69.

Ohio ANG 180th, 178th, 179th and 121st TFG
112th TFS (green), **180th TFG**   From F-84F to F-100D/F, Oct 1970
Based: Toledo Airport, Swanton
To A-7D, summer 1979.
162nd TFS (red), **178th TFG**   From F-84F to F-100D/F, April 1970
Based: Springfield, Ohio
To A-7D, April 1978.
164th TFS (yellow), **179th TFG**   From F-84F to F-100D/F, Feb 1972
Based: Mansfield-Lahm airport
To C-130B, winter 1975.
166th TFS (blue), **121st TFG**   From F-84F to F-100C/F, Oct 1962
Based: Lockbourne AFB
Called to active duty during Pueblo Crisis 26 June 1968 and deployed
to Kunsan AB, Korea, assigned to 354th TFW until 19 June 1969. To
F-100D/F Nov 1971, then A-7D Dec 1974.
Coded BO at Kunsan AB.

Oklahoma ANG, 138th TFG
125th TFS (blue, green or red)   From C-124C to F-100D/F, Jan 1973
Based: Tulsa
To A-7D, July 1978.

South Dakota ANG, 114th TFG
175th TFS   From F/TF-102A to F-100D/F, spring 1971
Based: Sioux Falls Municipal Airport
To A-7D, 1977.

Texas ANG, 149th TFG
182nd TFS (red)   From F-84F to F-100D/F, spring 1971
Based: Kelly AFB
To F-4C, spring 1979.

Other USAF Units

3595th CCTW   From F-84 and F-86 to F-100A from 1954
Based: Nellis AFB, Nevada
Re-designated 4520th CCTW, July 1958.

3600th CCTW, Air Training Command   F-100C/F from Dec 1957
Based: Luke AFB, Arizona
Re-designated 4510th CCTW, July 1958 then 58th TFTW, Oct 1969.

3600th Air Demonstration Flight (Thunderbirds). F-100C/F mid-1956–Dec 1963, F-100D/F June 1964–Nov 1968
Later, 3595th Air Demonstration Flight, then 4520th Air Demonstration Flight.

4510th CCTW   F-100D/F from July 1958
Based: Luke AFB, Arizona
4511th CCTS
Inactivated 18 Jan 1970 and replaced by 31st TFTS.
4514th CCTS (green)
To 58th TFTW, 15 Oct 1969. Inactivated 15 Dec 1969. Replaced by 310th TFTS with A-7D.
4515th CCTS
Activated 1 Sept 1966, inactivated 18 June 1970 and reactivated as 426th TFTS.
4517th CCTS
Assigned to 4510th CCTW, 1 Sept 1966. Reassigned to 58th TFTW, 15 Oct 1969.
All squadrons coded LA from July 1968.

58th TFTW   F-100D/F from Oct 1969
Based: Luke AFB, Arizona
311th TFTS
F-100D/F 18 Jan 1970–21 Aug 1971 with assets of 4515th CCTS.
426th TFTS
F-100D/F 18 Jan 1970–13 Sept 1971. Activated with assets of 4515th CCTS.

4520th CCTW (black/yellow chequers)   F-100A/C/D/F from July 1958
Based: Nellis AFB, Nevada
Took over F-100 training when it was transferred from Air Training Command to Tactical Air Command, July 1958. Two squadrons moved to Luke AFB, Arizona, Oct 1962. By 1969 all remaining F-100D/Fs were assigned to 4536th Fighter Weapons Squadron (coded WB) within 4525th Fighter Weapons Wing. This became 57th FWW. 4536th FWS then became 65th FWS (also coded WB) that continued to operate F-100DS until inactivated 31 Dec 1969.

4530th CCTW (yellow)   F-100C/F from July 1958
Williams AFB, Arizona
Re-designation of 3525th CCTW. Ceased F-100 operations Oct 1960.

7272nd FTW   B-57E and F-100C from Jan 1958
Based: Wheelus AB, Libya
7235th Support Squadron (red, then blue) supplied target-towing F-100Cs for USAFE units visiting Wheelus AB until 1965.

4758th DSES (Defense Systems Evaluation Squadron)   F-100C/F from July 1962
Based: Biggs AFB, Texas
Provided high-speed target towing aircraft. To Holloman AFB, New Mexico, April 1966–Oct 1970.

475th WEG (Weapons Evaluation Group)   QF-100D/F
Based: Tyndall AFB, Florida
Supported 82nd Tactical Aerial Targets Squadron, Holloman AFB, New Mexico using QF-100, April 1981–92.

ARDC (Air Research and Development Command, later Air Force Systems Command)
WADC (Wright Air Development Center)   EF-100A, JF-100A/C/F from 1954
Based: Wright Field, Ohio (later Wright-Patterson AFB)
'EF' (in EF-100A) indicated 'Exempt'. Changed in 1955 to 'JF' to avoid confusion with 'E' for 'electronic' (as in 'EB-66').
AFFTC (Air Force Flight Test Center)
Based: Edwards AFB, California
Flight test work under ARDC using various F-100s.
Aerospace Medical Division   F-100F
Based: Brooks AFB/Kelly AFB, Texas
Used for aircrew medical research under ARDC.
Air Force Special Weapons Center   F-100F
Based: Kirtland AFB, New Mexico
Atomic weapons delivery research.
4925th Test Squadron (Atomic)   F-100A
Based: Kirtland AFB, New Mexico
Air Proving Ground Command (later, Armament Development and Test Center; ADTC)

AFLC (Air Force Logistics Command)   F-100A/C/D
Based: McClellan AFB, California
Used several 'pattern' F-100s to assist with depot level maintenance work.

MATS (Military Air Transport Service)
1708th Ferrying Wing   F-100A
Trained ferry and delivery pilots on F-100.

Non-USAF Units

NACA/NASA
Several F-100A/Cs used for supersonic test programmes and to develop boundary layer control including: F-100C 53-1585 (NACA 200) and 53-1709 (NASA 703).

US Army
Several F-100D/Fs used in connection with Hawk SAM and other trials including: F-100D 56-3186, -3187, -3426 and F-100F 56-3889, -3897, -3899, -3904, -3905, -3911.

Tracor/Flight Systems
Several F-100D/Fs used for air-to-air training under civilian contracts and other experimental work in addition to QF-100 provision. Approximately ten F-100s were flying in various civilian ownership, 2000–2001.

MDAP F-100 Users

Republic of China

4th FBW   F-100A/F from Aug 1958
Chiayi AB
21st FBS (red)
22nd FBS (yellow)
23rd FBS (blue)
Later reassigned to 11th Group. F-100A phased out early 1980s, replaced by Northrop F-5E/F.

11th Group, 2nd FBW   F-100A/F from 1959
Hsinchu AB

41st FBS (red)
Transitioned at Chiayi as 17th FBS.
42nd FBS (blue)
48th FBS (red/white/blue)
Last F-100A flight, 5 Sept 1984.

4th Squadron
Taoyuan AB   RF-100A from Dec 1958 to Dec 1960

Serials of Aircraft Used

Serial followed by RoCAF Code.
(P) = preserved example, w/o = write-off through accident.

F-100-A

53-1529/0101 (P), 53-1530/0102, 53-1537/0103, 53-1539/0104, 53-1540/0105 (P), 53-1549/0106, 53-1584/0107 (w/o 7.4.72), 53-1593/0108 (w/o 21.2.72), 53-1595/0109 (w/o 11.6.69), 53-1605/0110 (w/o 26.4.60), 53-1608/0111 (w/o 30.11.71), 53-1609/0112, 53-1610/0113 (P), 53-1611/0114, 53-1613/0115 (w/o 9.3.65), 53-1614/0116, 53-1616/0117 (w/o 12.1.79), 53-1618/0118 (w/o 16.4.79), 53-1619/0119 (w/o 4.9.63), 53-1621/0120 (w/o 27.4.76), 53-1622/0121, 53-1623/0122 (w/o 16.3.82), 53-1624/0123 (w/o 26.3.65), 53-1627/0124, 53-1628/0125 (w/o 27.12.68), 53-1630/0126 (w/o 2.2.78), 53-1631/0127 (w/o 24.11.65), 53-1632/0128, 53-1633/0129, 53-1634/0130, 53-1635/0131, 53-1638/0132, 53-1640/0133, 53-1643/0134, 53-1645/0135 (w/o 23.5.69), 53-1646/0136, 53-1648/0137, 53-1649/0138, 53-1650/0139 (w/o 23.12.61), 53-1653/0140, 53-1655/0141 (P), 53-1656/0142 (w/o 19.8.69), 53-1657/0143 (w/o 3.3.77), 53-1658/0144, 53-1664/0145, 53-1665/0146 (w/o 17.8.65), 53-1666/0147, 53-1667/0148 (w/o 10.3.76), 53-1668/0149, 53-1669/0150 (w/o 23.7.77), 53-1670/0151 (w/o 5.9.61), 53-1671/0152 (w/o 7.9.75), 53-1672/0153 (w/o 10.8.63), 53-1673/0154 (w/o 5.2.63), 53-1675/0155, 53-1676/0156 (w/o 4.11.65), 53-1680/0157 (w/o 8.9.65), 53-1681/0158 (w/o 3.7.70), 53-1682/0159, 53-1683/0160, 53-1685/0161 (w/o 25.3.80), 53-1686/0162 (w/o 13.3.63), 53-1687/0163, 53-1689/0164 (w/o 18.10.70), 53-1690/0165, 53-1691/0166 (w/o 18.3.65), 53-1692/0167, 53-1693/0168 (w/o 16.3.71), 53-1695/0169 (w/o 3.3.77), 53-1696/0170, 53-1697/0171, 53-1698/0172, 53-1699/0173, 53-1700/0174 (w/o 22.1.64), 53-1702/0175, 53-1703/0176 (w/o 17.8.61), 53-1704/0177 (w/o 18.9.76), 53-1705/0178, 53-1706/0179 (w/o 15.2.74), 53-1708/0180, 53-1535/0201 (w/o 11.11.77), 53-1536/0202 (w/o 13.11.77), 53-1538/0203, 53-1541/0204, 53-1542/0205, 53-1543/0206, 53-1550/0207 (P), 53-1552/0208, 53-1555/0209, 53-1560/0210, 53-1561/0211 (P), 53-1563/0212, 53-1565/0213, 53-1571/0214 (P), 53-1577/0215 (P), 53-1582/0216, 53-1583/0217 (P), 53-1589/0218 (P), 53-1594/0219 (w/o 20.6.73), 53-1596/0220, 53-1598/0221, 53-1601/0222, 53-1602/0223 (P), 53-1603/0224, 53-1604/0225, 53-1606/0226 (w/o 30.3.76), 53-1612/0227 (w/o 4.1.73), 53-1615/0228 (w/o 19.1.78), 53-1620/0229, 53-1625/0230, 53-1626/0231, 53-1637/0232, 53-1638/0233 (P), 53-1642/0234 (P), 53-1570/0235, 53-1569/0301, 53-1581/0302 (P), 53-1651/0303, 53-1662/0304.

RF-100A

53-1545/5645, 53-1546/5646, 53-1547/5647, 53-1554/5648.

F-100F

56-3968/0001 (P), 56-3977/0002 (w/o 27.5.76), 56-3978/0003 (w/o 28.8.76), 56-3979/0004 (w/o 4.8.60), 56-3987/0005 (P), 56-3988/0006, 58-6975/0007 (w/o 17.7.64), 58-6977/0008, 58-6980/0009 (P), 59-2561/0010, 56-3753/0011, 56-3862/0012, 56-3733/0013, 56-3808/0014.

France

F-100D/Fs were assigned to Wings (Escadre de Chasse), each with two or three squadrons (Escadron de Chasse) divided into Flights (Escadrilles) with 'pooled' aircraft that carried the badges of both flights: the 1st Escadrille on the left side of the tail and the 2nd on the right. Two Escadres flew F-100s: the 3rd (1/3, 2/3) and 11th (1/11, 2/11, 3/11, 4/11).

3e Escadre
EC 1/3 *Navarre* (yellow)   F-84F to F-100D/F, Jan 1959
Escadrilles: SPA 95 ('swallow' badge), SPA 153 ('Egyptian falcon' badge).
Based: Reims-Betheny. Coded 3-IA-IZ.
Deployed to Lahr, West Germany, June 1961–Jan 1966.

EC 2/3 *Champagne* (red)   F-100D/F from Jan 1959
Escadrilles: SPA 67 ('stork' badge), SPA 75 ('falcon' badge).
Based: Reims-Betheny. Coded 3-JA-JZ.
Deployed to Lahr, West Germany, 10 June 1961–Jan 1966.

11e Escadre
EC 1/11 *Rousillon*   F-84G–F-84F, F-100D/F, May 1958
Escadrilles: GC III6-5e ('comedy mask' badge), GCIII/6-6e ('tragedy mask' badge).
Based: Luxeil-St Sauveur. Coded 11-EA-EZ.
Deployed to Bremgarten, West Germany, June 1961–Sept 1967.
Moved to Toul-Rosieres, Sept 1967–10 Oct 1975. Transitioned to Jaguar thereafter.

EC 2/11 *Vosges*   F-84G–F-84F, F-100D/F, 1 May 1958
Escadrilles: SPA 91 ('eagle and skull' badge), SPA 97 ('pennant with ermine' badge).
Based: Luxeil-St Sauveur. Coded 11-MA-MZ.
Deployed to Bremgarten, West Germany, June 1961–Sept 1967.
Moved to Toul-Rosieres, Sept 1967–1976. Transitioned to Jaguar by end of 1976.

EC 3/11 *Corse*   F-100D/F from 1 April 1966
Escadrilles: SPA 88 ('serpent' badge), SPA 69 ('cat's head' badge).
Based: Luxeil-St Sauveur. Coded 11-RA-RZ. Became F-100 OCU.
Deployed to Bremgarten, Colmar and Toul-Rosieres. Transitioned to Jaguar, 1976.

EC 4/11 *Jura*   F-100D/F, 1 Jan 1973
Escadrilles: SPA 158 ('serpentaria bird holding snake' badge), SPA 161 ('sphinx' badge).
Based: Toul-Rosieres and Djibouti. Coded 11-YA-YZ.
Activated at Djibouti, Jan 1973–12 Dec 1978. Transitioned to Jaguar 1978–79.

Esc de Convoyage EC-070
Coded MA–MZ. Tasked with ferrying F-100s to RAF Sculthorpe and USAF charge, 1977–78.

Serials of Aircraft Used

'P' = preserved example, 'ret' = an aircraft returned to USAF charge at RAF Sculthorpe 1975–77, 'wfu' = aircraft withdrawn from use for other reasons, 'w/o' = aircraft destroyed in accident.

F-100D-54-NH

-2121 (w/o 18.10.66), -2122 (w/o 26.5.75), -2123, -2124 (w/o), -2125, -2128 (ret), -2129 (w/o 24.7.73), -2130 (P), -2131(P), -2133 (w/o 17.7.75), -2135 (w/o 14.11.67), -2136, -2137 (w/o 1.10.64), -2138 (w/o 2.8.77), -2140 (w/o 17.10.58), -2141 (w/o 8.9.59), -2144 (w/o 1.6.67),

-2146 (ret), -2148, -2149 (ret), -2150 (w/o 5.9.67), -2152 (ret), -2154, -2156 (w/o 20.11.78), -2157 (ret), -2158 (w/o 10.2.77), -2160 (ret), -2162 (w/o 10.10.73), -2163 (ret), -2164, -2165 (ret), -2166 (ret), -2167 (w/o 23.6.67), -2169 (ret 2.3.76), -2171 (wfu 17.2.70), -2174 (ret), -2184 (w/o 17.8.64), -2185, -2186, -2187 (w/o), -2189 (w/o), -2194 (ret), -2195 (w/o 12.5.60), -2196 (ret), -2198 (w/o 26.1.60), -2203 (ret), -2204 (w/o 29.5.77), -2205, -2210 (w/o 13.9.66), -2211 (ret), -2212 (ret), -2213 (w/o 3.6.60), -2215 (w/o 31.12.64), -2217 (w/o 11.9.63), -2220 (w/o 15.6.60), -2223 (ret), -2226 (w/o 14.8.63), -2231 (w/o 7.10.64), -2235, -2236 (w/o 13.9.66), -2237 (w/o 22.6.61), -2239 (ret), -2243 (w/o 21.8.63), -2246 (ret), -2247 (w/o 29.1.71), -2248 (ret), -2249, -2252 (w/o 16.01.62), -2254 (ret), -2255 (w/o 31.01.64), -2257 (w/o 31.12.64), -2260 (w/o 5.3.59), -2264 (w/o 17.12.73), -2265 (ret), -2267 (wfu), -2269 (ret), -2271 (w/o 10.69), -2272 (ret), -2273 (w/o), -2293, -2295 (P).

F-100D-55-NH

-2734, -2736 (P), -2737, -2738, -2739(P), -2741 (w/o 6.72), -2745 (?29.3.61).

F-100F-56-NH

-3928, -3935 (ret), -3936 (ret), -3937 (P), -3938 (ret), -3939 (w/o 24.6.69), -3940 (wfu 18.6.71), -3941 (w/o 19.10.73), -4008 (w/o 10.7.64), -4009 (ret), -4012, -4013 (w/o 5.8.59), -4014, -4017.

Denmark

Esk 725   F-100D/F, April 1961
Based: Karup AB
To F 35/TF 35 Draken, Sept 1970.

Esk 727   F-100D/F, May 1959
Based: Karup AB
To Skrydstrup AB, April 1974–April 1981 then converted to F-16A.

Esk 730   F-100D/F, 3 July 1961
Based: Skrydstrup AB
Esk 730-100 flew last eight F-100Fs until 11 Aug 1982 while rest of squadron converted to F-16A.

Serials of Aircraft Used

F-100Ds were given codes using 'G' and the last three digits of the serial; F-100Fs had the last three digits prefixed by 'GT'.
'FS' = transfer to Flight Systems, 'P' = preserved example, 'ret' = aircraft returned to USAF charge at RAF Sculthorpe 1975–77, 'T' = aircraft transferred to Turkey, 'wfu' = aircraft withdrawn from use for other reasons, 'w/o' = aircraft destroyed in accident.

F-100D

54-2132 (w/o 14.11.62 – mid-air), 54-2134 (w/o 19.3.63 – mid-air), 54-2177 (T), 54-2179 (w/o 17.1.66 – hit sea), 54-2183 (w/o 13...77 – fuel problem), 54-2190 (w/o 4.12.64 – fuel fire), 54-2192 (w/o 10.11.62 – fuel tank explosion), 54-2199 (w/o 23.8.67 – engine blockage), 54-2206 (T), 54-2221 (w/o 9.3.61 – engine explosion), 54-2222 (T), 54-2227 (w/o 30.1.63 – hit ground), 54-2240 (w/o 3.7.63 – fuel leakage), 54-2244 (w/o 29.11.76 – hit ground), 54-2253 (w/o 12.12.63 – hit ground), 54-2256 (w/o 26.6.62 – oil pressure failed), 54-2261 (T), 54-2262 (T, w/o 29.7.83), 54-2266 (T), 54-2270 (T, w/o 11.2.82), 54-2274 (T, w/o 11.10.84), 54-2279 (wfu 9.11.76 – nose-gear collapse), 54-2283 (T, w/o 14.8.85), 54-2284 (w/o 14.11.62 – mid-air), 54-2288 (w/o 19.7.68 – drop tank hit tail), 54-2289 (w/o 5.10.67 – vertigo, night take-off), 54-2290 (T, gateguard, Aviano), 54-2300 (w/o 19.3.63 – mid-air), 54-2301 (w/o 27.7.65 – compressor failure), 54-2302 (w/o 13.4.72 – hit ground), 54-2303 (T, wfu 14.7.87), 55-2744 (T, w/o 12.8.83 – mid-air), 55-2747 (w/o 6.5.80 – fuel starvation), 55-2748 (T, wfu 14.7.87), 55-2751 (T, w/o 12.3.85), 55-2756 (w/o 8.3.68 – hit ground, night), 55-2765 (T, w/o 12.10.81), 55-2768 (T, wfu 13.6.88), 55-2769 (T, wfu 13.6.88), 55-2771 (T, wfu 13.6.88), 55-2773 (wfu 5.10.76 – nose-gear failed), 55-2775 (T, wfu 5.11.86), 55-2776 (w/o 10.3.73 – engine failure), 55-2777 (w/o 29.7.64 – adverse yaw), 55-2778 (w/o 11.8.70 – engine failure), 55-2779 (T, w/o 26.4.83), 55-2781 (w/o 4.5.77 – runaway trim), 55-2782 (T, wfu 14.5.86).

TF-100F

56-3826 FS (N414FS, w/o 11.7.94), 56-3842 FS (N417FS), 56-2844 FS (N415FS, Greco Air N26AZ), 56-3856 (w/o 16.3.76 – engine failure), 56-3870 (P, Skrydstrup AB), 56-3874 (P, Danish Aviation Museum), 56-3892 (w/o 9.6.76 – engine failure), 56-3908 (P, Skrystrup AB), 56-3916 FS (N416FS), 56-3927 (P, Danish Aviation Museum), 56-3961 (wfu 8.9.81 – nose-gear collapse), 56-3971 FS (N419FS), 56-3996 FS (N418FS).

F-100F

56-4015 (w/o 20.3.70 – adverse yaw), 56-4018 (w/o 21.2.73 – mid-air), 56-4019 (T, w/o – mid-air), 58-6976 (T, wfu 29.12.87), 58-6978 (w/o 12.5.61 – flat spin), 58-6979 (w/o 2.8.66 – ricochet, strafing), 58-6981 (w/o 7.7.64 – hit ground), 58-6982 (w/o 3.2.76 – engine failure), 58-6983 (w/o 1.6.77 – fuel pump failed), 59-2558 (w/o 25.2.76 – engine failure/oil leak).

Turkey

F-100C/D/F units. (Full squadron titles in brackets.)

1nci Ana Jet Ussu (1st Main Jet Air Base), **Eskisehir**
111 Filo *Panter* (Panther). (111nci Av-Bombardiman Filosu) Nov 1958–79.
112 Filo *Seytan* (Devil) (112nci Av-Onleme Filosu) 1962–65 and 1969–74.
113 Filo *Isik* (Light) (113ncu Av Filosu) 1959–72.

3ncu Ana Jet Ussu (3rd Main Jet Air Base), **Konya**
131 Filo *Ejder* (Dragon) (131nci Jet Egitim Filosu) 1974–78.
132 Filo *Hancer* (Dagger) (132nci Av-Bombardiman Filosu) 1974–87.

7nci Ana Jet Ussu (7th Main Jet Air Base), **Malatya**
171 Filo (re-named from 113 Filo) 1972–77.
172 Filo (renamed from 182 Filo) 1972–79.

8nci Ana Jet Ussu (8th Main Jet Air Base), **Diyarbakir**
181 Filo *Pars* (Leopard) (181nci Av-Bombardiman Filosu) 1972–86.
182 Filo *Atmaca* (Sparrowhawk) (182nci Av-Bombardiman Filosu) 1969–86.

(*Av-Bombardiman Filosu* = Fighter-Bomber Squadron; *Filo* = Squadron; *Av-Onleme Filosu* = Fighter-Interceptor Squadron; *Jet Egitim Filosu* = Jet Training Squadron.)

Serials of Aircraft Used

1958 Deliveries
F-100D-10-NA 54-2161, -2164, -2173, -2201, -2202;
F-100F-15-NA 54-2224, -2238, -2251, -2275;
F-100D-40-NH 55-2749, -2755, -2757, -2763;
F-100F-16-NA 56-3967, -3976, -3989, -3977, -3998, -4007.

1959 Deliveries

F-100D-5-NA 54-2143, -2147;
F-100D-10-NA 54-2159, -2170, -2172, -2175, -2182, -2193, -2200, -2207, -2208, -2216, -2218, -2219;
F-100D-15-NA 54-2228, -2230, -2242, -2245, -2277, -2282;
F-100D-35-NH 55-2742, -2743;
F-100D-40-NH 55-2746, -2750, -2752, -2753, -2754, -2758, -2759, -2760, -2766, -2767;
F-100F-16-NA 56-3999.

1960–62 Deliveries

F-100D-10-NA 54-2214;
F-100D-15-NA 54-2776;
F-100D-35-NH 55-2740;
F-100D-40-NH 55-2764;
F-100F-15-NA 59-2559, -2560, -2562, -2563.

1969 Deliveries

F-100D-46-NA 55-2825;
F-100D-51-NA 55-2874, 55-2888;
F-100D-56-NA 55-2910, -2916, -2940;
F-100D-20-NA 55-3596;
F-100D-26-NA 55-3700;
F-100D-31-NA 55-3718, -3721;
F-100D-61-NA 56-2951, -2960;
F-100D-71-NA 56-3083;
F-100D-81-NA 56-3355;
F-100D-86-NA 56-3399, -3457;
F-100F-15-NA 56-3946, -3952.

1970 Deliveries

F-100D-50-NH 55-2899;
F-100D-20-NA 55-3509;
F-100D-25-NA 55-3617, -3651;
F-100D-30-NA 55-3750, -3756;
F-100D-31-NA 55-3761, -3798;
F-100D-60-NA 56-2919, -2929, -2941;
F-100D-65-NA 56-2966;
F-100D-70-NA 56-3039, -3096;
F-100D-90-NA 56-3235;
F-100D-80-NH 56-3376;
F-100D-85-NH 56-3390, -3391, -3433, -3454;
F-100F-16-NA 56-3930, -3970.

1972 Deliveries

F-100C-2-NA 53-1715, -1727, -1729, -1746, -1747, -1761, -1767, -1774, 54-1759;
F-100C-6-NA 54-1793;
F-100C-16-NA 54-1826, -1844;
F-100C-21-NA 54-1870, -1872, -1875, -1888, -1925, -1929, -1944, -1950;
F-100C-26-NA 54-1978, -2022, -2056, -2074, -2077, -2084, -2087,

-2108, -2117, -2118;
F-100C-11-NH 55-2712, -2715, -2720, -2722.

Forty-three more F-100Cs delivered in 1973 from the following and the rest in 1974:
F-100C-2-NA 53-1725, -1732, -1738, -1757, 54-1741, -1749, -1755, -1756, -1766;
F-100C-6-NA 54-1777, -1780, -1782, -1787, -1794, -1798, -1800, -1804, -1805, -1807;
F-100C-16-NA 54-1818, -1835, -1838, -1850, -1858;
F-100C-21-NA 54-1868, -1877, -1883, -1891, -1903, -1908, -1915, -1919, -1920, -1921, -1926, -1932, -1934, -1937, -1939, -1942, -1945, -1948, -1949, -1959;
F-100C-26-NA 54-1989, -1999, -2013, -2031, -2032, -2034, -2042, -2046, -2047, -2052, -2053, -2057, -2058, -2059, -2060, -2066, -2068, -2070, -2076, -2083, -2089, -2091, -2092, -2097, -2100, -2103, -2104, -2113, -2115, -2120;
F-100C-11-NH 55-2716, -2721, -2724.

Also in 1972–74

F-100F-5-NA 56-3759;
F-100F-10-NA 56-3774, -3803, -3831, -3843, -3850, -3867, -3876, -3884, -3890, -3896, -3902, -3903, -3909, -3919;
F-100F-15-NA 56-3921, -3947, -3948, -3957, -3963.

1977–78 Deliveries

F-100F-6-NA 56-3766;
F-100F-11-NA 56-3895;
F-100F-16-NA 56-3950, -3958, -3966, -3992 (all in 1977);
F-100F-2-NA 56-3732, -3739;
F-100F-6-NA 56-3752;
F-100F-11-NA 56-3783, -3788, -3800, -3846, -3854, -3914 (all in 1978).

1981 Deliveries (ex-RDAF)

F-100D-10-NA 54-2177, -2206;
F-100D-15-NA 54-2261, -2266, -2270, -2274, -2283;
F-100D-15-NH 54-2303;
F-100D-40-NH 55-2744, -2748, -2751, -2765, -2768, -2769, -2771, -2775, -2779, -2782;
F-100F-16-NA 56-4019;
F-100F-15-NA 58-6976.

1982 Deliveries (ex-RDAF)

F-100D-15-NA 54-2222, -2262;
F-100D-40-NH 55-2771.
An additional F-100D (54-2290) became unserviceable on its delivery flight to Turkey and was consigned to a dump at Sigonella, Italy. It was later rescued and restored by the museum at Vigna di Valle, donated to the 31st TFW, USAF at Aviano AB and displayed on the gate as *Thor's Hammer* (309th TFS, 31st TFW, coded SS) in Vietnam camouflage. The original *Thor's Hammer* was 56-2927.

F-100C/D Nuclear Weapons Control Procedures

The Mk 7 fission weapon was the only nuclear device to be carried by F-100Cs and early F-100Ds (*see* Chapter 3). It was deployed for more than fifteen years, longer than any other US free-fall nuclear weapon and produced in nine variants between 1952 and 1967.

In the aircraft it was controlled by the T-145, T-270 (T-145) or in later F-100Ds by the T-270 control panel. The T-270, using the Fusing Selector (F-SEL) rotary switch together with two other rotary switches and five timer dials inside the weapon, pre-set before the mission, set the fusing options prior to release. The cockpit panel was installed centrally, below the front, main instrument display.

On the T-270, a top row of three indicator lights were labelled (left to right): EXT (to indicate that the Mk 7's large, lower stabilizing fin was extended or released); IN (to indicate that the separate capsule containing the nuclear fission elements was in place inside the bomb casing); and A/S (to indicate that the weapon safety switch was closed, necessary for detonation). Below this on the control panel (left to right) was the FIN EXT/RET switch (to extend or retract the bomb's fin, using battery power), OUT (showing the fission capsule was in the 'out' position)

and A/S (a switch to arm or safe the bomb). Between the IN and OUT lights was an in-flight insertion (IFI) switch to control the IFI mechanism.

In the third row was a row of five circuit-breaker switches to provide for aircraft power with circuit-breaker protection for:
1. Bomb fin operation;
2. Weapon batteries heaters;
3. IFI operation;
4. Warm-up power for the bomb's radars (two switches).

Located on the bottom of the T-270 was an F-SEL switch to control the weapon fusing options. This switch (using also the ground pre-set selections on a panel inside the Mk 7) was used to set the proper fusing option.

Using a setting between 1 and 4, the timer would start at weapon release, turn on the radar, electrically arm the bomb and allow the radar to detonate the weapon at a pre-determined altitude. On settings 5 and 6, the timer would arm the weapon and allow the contact fuse to detonate. Setting 7 would start the timer when the pilot pressed the bomb release button at the identification point (IP) in the mission route, indicated by a T/O light. It would continue to run at release and detonate at completion of the timer

period. Releasing the bomb release button, to abort the run, would cause the weapon timer to return to zero.

The last items on the bottom of the panel provided AC and DC power to the F-SEL switch so that it could set the fusing options detailed below. The NULL light, when extinguished, indicated the proper fusing option as selected by the F-SEL switch. Any special store was released by use of the bomb release button on top of the control stick.

The armament panel switches controlled the release. The MODE SELECTOR switch selected the type of release: LABS, LABS ALT, low-altitude drogue delivery (LADD) or MANUAL. The ARMAMENT SELECTOR switch selected the special store, left intermediate or centreline station. Pilots were required to memorize all these settings and procedures.

For later weapons such as the Mk 28 EX (externally carried), Mk 28 RE (retarded, externally carried) or B-43, the T-270 panel was replaced by the 'idiot proof' T-249, DCU-9A or DCU-117A version. On these, a large rotary selector switch could be set to AIR (giving a pre-set detonation at an altitude determined by the radar fuse), GND (laydown or ground contact) detonation or SAFE. 'Laydown' on weapons capable of this option had to be set on pre-flight. There were OS and SGA settings in which the panel could be locked with safety wire to allow detection of any unauthorized operation of the weapons controls. A similar locking option was used in the DCU-9A, while the DCU-117A had permissive action link (PAL) – four knobs with digits to provide a code combination for unlocking the bomb release controls. A warning light illuminated while the weapon fusing options were changed by the pilot during the mission.

F-SEL	Timer	Radar Number	Detonation Altitude	Option	Delivery Option
1		1	1	Radar	LABS OTS*
2		2	1	Radar	LABS OTS
3		1	2	Radar	LABS OTS
4		2	2	Radar	LABS OTS
5		3	–	Contact	LABS OTS
6		4	–	Contact	Dive
7		5	–	Timer	LABS IP

*LABS – low-altitude bombing system; OTS – 'over the shoulder' nuclear delivery.

F-100 Losses in South East Asia

Includes serials followed by date of both combat and operational losses.

Slashed digits indicate a loss at night.

F-100C

53-1713 (8.8.68)
53-1740 (14.3.69)
53-1741 (4.5.69)
53-1765 (27.9.68)
54-1775 (2.8.68)
54-1897 (27.3.69)
54-1912 (25.7.68)
54-1922 (23.8.68)
54-1931 (18.12.68)
54-1956 (25/26.1.69)
54-1973 (29.12.68)
54-2004 (14.7.68)
54-2030 (4.1.69)
54-2041 (31.1.69)
54-2051 (4.1.69)

F-100D

55-2795 (13.11.65)
55-2837 (31.7.65)
55-2849 (12.7.69)
55-2857 (2.3.65)
55-2875 (2.4.68)
55-2890 (9.3.70)
55-2895 (23.8.69)
55-2900 (4.7.68)
55-2901 (11.2.71)
55-2903[?] 18.9.69
55-2904 (15.9.67)
55-2911[?] (26.1.67 or 6.4.68)
55-2912 (19.3.67)
55-2914 (18.6.68)
55-2918 (22.2.69)
55-2920 (16.12.68)
55-2921 (23.10.68)
55-2923 (23.4.68)
55-2929 (17.10.68)
55-2935 (4.10.69)
55-2943 (8.7.70)
55-3071 (13.9.66)
55-3100 (3.10.66)

55-3502 (30.9.66)
55-3510 (13.6.67)
55-3511 (28.12.69)
55-3513 (21.1.69)
55-3516 (26.6.69)
55-3522 (9.5.69)
55-3534 (30.3.66)
55-3535 (25.6.68)
55-3541 (26.1.67)
55-3543 (1.10.65)
55-3548 (18.5.68)
55-3549 (12.7.67)
55-3550 (28.4.71)
55-3555 (24.5.69)
55-3559 (14.10.66)
55-3562 (8.2.69)
55-3568 (30/31.1.68)
55-3569 (9.1.70)
55-3572 (9.7.70)
55-3574 (26.1.70)
55-3581 (8.8.69)
55-3585 (10.2.70)
55-3587 (6.3.68)
55-3589 (5.7.69)
55-3600 (13.6.65)
55-3603 (6.11.66)
55-3606 (20.3.68)
55-3608 (28.7.68)
55-3611 (12.3.67)
55-3613 (29.9.65)
55-3618 (10.5.67)
55-3619 (7.1.68)
55-3625 (3.4.65)
55-3631 (31.9.65)
55-3632 (22.4.69)
55-3635 (18.3.69)
55-3639 (6.8.67)
55-3640 (14.9.66)
55-3642 (10.10.69)
55-3643 (20.4.68)
55-3647 (20.12.68)
55-3653 (16.11.68)
55-3661 (2.10.68)
55-3702 (12.6.65)
55-3704 (20.1 69)
55-3714 (15.2.67)

55-3717 (1.4.68)
55-3719 (29.12.65)
55-3722 (14.7.68)
55-3737 (24.9.69)
55-3738 (23.9.65)
55-3739 (25.7.66)
55-3749 (13.4.71)
55-3762 (26.2.68)
55-3765 (4.1.68)
55-3766 (6.6.67)
55-3773 (10.5.66)
55-3777 (13.1.70)
55-3780 (5.3.66)
55-3782 (8.5.70)
55-3783 (19.2.65)
55-3787 (11.12.66)
55-3790 (3.6.69)
55-3793 (14.3.66)
55-3803 (29.5.70)
55-3806 (16.9.70)
55-3809 (12.10.66)
56-2905 (21.7.68)
56-2907 (16.2.67)
56-2908 (2.1.65)
56-2922 (22.12.67)
56-2923 (24.9.65)
56-2924 (22.6.66)
56-2925[?] (12.2.67)
56-2927 (19.2.67)
56-2935 (16.11.68)
56-2936 (3.7.68)
56-2937 (11.4.71)
56-2949 (17.5.68)
56-2954 (12.5.67)
56-2955 (15.4.71)
56-2956 (29.7.66)
56-2960 (25.3.69)
56-2965 (21.10.67)
56-2968 (26.12.68)
56-3027 (30.3.67)
56-3040 (19.11.67)
56-3041 (2.8.67)
56-3049 (10.7.69)
56-3063 (8.12.66)
56-3066 (22.7.68)
56-3069 (14.10.69)

56-3074 (5.10.65)
56-3075 (30.4.69)
56-3085 (18.8.64)
56-3090 (6.8.69)
56-3094 (14.5.67)
56-3097 (14.1.70)
56-3113 (21.1.69)
56-3114 (18.8.67)
56-3119 (25.5.69)
56-3120 (4.4.71)
56-3121 (4.3.70)
56-3122 (2.7.68)
56-3124 (9.7.68)
56-3125 (19.11.65)
56-3132 (12.12.70)
56-3136 (26.5.70)
56-3147 (17.2.70)
56-3150 (2.3.65)
56-3151 (10.4.65)
56-3152 (23.3.68)
56-3158 (21.1.69)
56-3166 (9.1.66)
56-3167 (26.10.66)
56-3170 (20.7.65)
56-3174 (5.3.69)
56-3177 (20.9.65)
56-3180 (22.3.71)
56-3181 (11.3.71)
56-3185 (9.8.65)
56-3197 (27.1.71)
56-3237 (29.11.68)
56-3242 (30.5.70)
56-3245 (12.9.68)
56-3252 (24.7.69)
56-3261 (25.2.68)
56-3264 (22.8.67)

56-3269 (6.3.68)
56-3270 (6.3.69)
56-3275 (15.7.67)
56-3277 (15.3.67)
56-3278 (6.4.70)
56-3283 (15.8.69)
56-3285 (21.5.67)
56-3287 (30.6.70)
56-3301 (25/26.1.69)
56-3304 (14.2.68)
56-3305 (22.4.69)
56-3330 (19.9.67)
56-3332 (10.12.69)
56-3334 (21.7.65)
56-3335 (23.4.69)
56-3339 (24.6.68)
56-3340 (22.6.65)
56-3343 (24.7.66)
56-3372 (30.6.68)
56-3375 (3.8.66)
56-3380 (10.3.69)
56-3383 (25.10.70)
56-3384 (9.3.70)
56-3403 (16.4.69)
56-3415 (12.3.71)
56-3420 (16.7.69)
56-3429 (14.1.68)
56-3431 (16.11.66)
56-3435 (21.8.70)
56-3437 (1.8.67)
56-3438 (12.11.68)
56-3446 (9.11.68)
56-3448 (13.1.67)
56-3451 (12.2.67)
56-3452 (17.11.68)

F-100F

56-3731 (24.1.69)
56-3734 (9.8.69)
56-3750 (27.7.68)
56-3764 (8.11.67)
56-3772 (10.9.68)
56-3775 (20.11.68)
56-3784 (18.3.68)
56-3796 (1.11.69)
56-3827 (8.5.70)
56-3834 (17.8.68)
56-3839 (7.4.68)
56-3847 (19.1.70)
56-3863 (1.4.69)
56-3865 (16.8.68)
56-3869 (12.10.66)
56-3878 (30.12.67)
56-3886 (22.1.69)
56-3887 (24.10.69)
56-3923 (17/18.2.68)
56-3954 (26.8.67)
56-3959 (17.2.68)
56-3975 (18.1.70)
56-3980 (2.5.67)
56-3995 (12.1.69)
56-4002 (1.7.67)
56-4005 (20.12.67)
58-1212 (23.3.66)
58-1215 (11.12.69)
58-1217 (19.7.66)
58-1221 (13.3.66)
58-1226 (5.7.68)
58-1231 (20.12.65)

F-100D losses also occurred on 18/11/64 and 13/1/65 but serials of these aircraft were not recorded at the time.

Preserved, Ground Instructional and Displayed F-100 Airframes

Includes serials followed by location.

YF-100A

52-5755	Edwards AFB, California

F-100A

52-5756	18th Wing, Kadena AB, Okinawa
52-5759	37 TFW/MU Lackland AFB, Texas
52-5760	95 ABW/MU Edwards AFB, California
52-5762	Grand Haven, Michigan
52-5773	American Airpower Heritage Museum, Midland, Texas
52-5777	75 ABW/MU Hill AFB, Utah
53-1529	Chiayi RoCAF AB, Taiwan
53-1532	150 FW, NM ANG Kirtland AFB, New Mexico
53-1533	Melrose, New Mexico
53-1540	Chung-Yeng Technical School, Taipei, Taiwan
53-1550	Chung-Cheng Aviation Museum, Taiwan
53-1559	178 FW OH ANG, Springfield, Ohio
53-1561	RoCAF Museum, Taiwan
53-1571	Tam Kang, Taiwan
53-1573	17 LS, Goodfellow AFB, Texas
53-1577	GIA at Tainan High School, Taiwan
53-1578	140 SUG, CO ANG Aurora, Colorado
53-1581	Chung Chen Institute, Taiwan
53-1583	Taitung City Stadium, Taiwan
53-1589	National University of Taiwan
53-1610	Cheng Kuang, Taiwan
53-1639	Hualien City, Taiwan
53-1642	Chung Hsin, Taiwan
53-1655	Hsinchu AB, Taiwan

F-100C

53-1712	Grissom AFB Museum, Indiana
53-1716	56 EMS Luke AFB, Arizona
53-1784	366 LG, Mountain Home AFB, Idaho
54-1752	Dyess AFB, Texas
54-1573	Air Force Museum, Wright-Patterson AFB
54-1784	Octave-Chanute Museum, Rantoul, Illinois
54-1785	Octave-Chanute Museum, Rantoul, Illinois
54-1786	March Field Museum, March ARB, California
54-1823	Pima Air Museum, Tucson, Arizona
54-1851	78 ABW, Robins AFB, Georgia
54-1986	96 ABW, Eglin AFB, Florida
54-1993	184 BW, KS ANG, McConnell AFB, Kansas
54-2005	185 FG, IA ANG, Sioux City, Iowa
54-2089	Turk Hava Muzesi, Ataturk Airport, Istanbul, Turkey
54-2106	WI ANG CRTC, Camp Douglas, Wisconsin
54-2145	Hampton, Virginia

F-100D

54-2130	Savigny-les-Beaune, France
54-2131	Toul-Rosieres, France
54-2136	Schawbisches bavern und Technik Museum, Stuttgart, West Germany
54-2151	82 TRW, Sheppard AFB, Texas
54-2157	North East Aircraft Museum, Tyne-and-Wear, UK
54-2163	Dumfries and Galloway Aviation Museum, UK
54-2165	American Air Museum, Duxford, UK
54-2174	Midland Air Museum, Baginton, UK
54-2187	Savigny-les-Beaune, France
54-2196	Norfolk and Suffolk Aviation Museum, Bungay, UK
54-2212	422 ABS, RAF Croughton, UK
54-2223	Newark Air Museum, UK
54-2239	Musée de l'Air et de l'Espace, Paris, France
54-2265	Militaire Luchtvaart Museum, Soesterberg, Netherlands
54-2269	48 FW, RAF Lakenheath, UK
54-2281	Glendale, Arizona
54-2290	Aviano AB, Italy
54-2294	Homestead ARS, Florida
54-2299	Palmdale, California
55-2734	Chatillon-en-Dois Campsite, France
55-2736	Musée de l'Air et de l'Espace, Paris, France
55-2739	Savigny-les-Beaume, France
55-2855	180 FW OH ANG, Swanton, Ohio
55-2884	121 ARW, OH ANG, Columbus, Ohio
55-3503	Fred E. Weisbrod Aircraft Museum, Pueblo, Colorado
55-3595	57 LG, Nellis AFB, Nevada
55-3650	138 FW, OK ANG, Tulsa, Oklahoma
55-3667	131 FW, MO ANG, Bridgeton, Missouri
55-3678	42 LG, Maxwell AFB, Alabama
55-3754	Air Force Museum, Wright-Patterson AFB
55-3805	103 FW CT ANG, East Granby, Connecticut
56-2928	116 CG, GA ANG, Robins AFB, Georgia
56-2940	27 LG Cannon AFB, New Mexico
56-2967	Myrtle Beach, California
56-2993	107 ARW, NY ANG, Niagara Falls, New York
56-2995	102 FW, MA ANG, Otis ANGB, Massachusetts
56-3000	149 FW, TX ANG, Kelly AFB, Texas
56-3008	104 FW, MA ANG, Westfield, Connecticut
56-3020	LA ANG, New Orleans, Louisiana
56-3022	179 AW, OH ANG, Mansfield, Ohio
56-3025	127 WG, MI ANG, Selfridge ANGB, Michigan
56-3055	162 FW, AZ ANG, Tucson, Arizona
56-3154	Lone Star Flight Museum, Galveston, Texas
56-3187	114 FW, SD ANG, Sioux Falls, South Dakota
56-3210	122 LG IN ANG, Fort Wayne, Indiana
56-3220	49 LG, Holloman AFB, New Mexico
56-3288	77 ABW, McClellan AFB, California
56-3299	140 SUG, CO ANG, Aurora, Colorado
56-3320	181 FW, IN ANG Terre Haute, Indiana
56-3426	132 FW, IA ANG Des Moines, Indiana
56-3434	AR ANG, North Little Rock, Arkansas

F-100F

56-3727	355 LG, Davis-Monthan AFB, Arizona
56-3730	USAF Academy, Colorado
56-3812	Duncan, Arizona
56-3813	Independence, Kansas
56-3814	Texas City, Texas
56-3819	Saint Maries, Idaho
56-3822	Lineville, Alabama
56-3825	Aurora, Nebraska
56-3855	Las Cruces, New Mexico
56-3862	Air Force Museum, Wright-Patterson AFB
56-3870	Skrydstrup AB, Denmark
56-3874	Danish Aviation Museum, Billund, Denmark
56-3894	127 WG, MI ANG, Selfridge ANGB, Michigan
56-3897	177 FW, NJ ANG, Egg Harbor Township, New Jersey
56-3898	Lashenden Air Warfare Museum, Ashford, Kent, UK
56-3908	Skrydstrup AB, Denmark
56-3927	Danish Aviation Museum, Billund, Denmark
56-3929	La Grange, Texas
56-3949	Karup AB, Denmark
56-3963	Lago Vista, Texas
56-3990	Burnet, Texas
58-1232	70 ABG, Brooks AFB, Texas
58-3837	Air Force Museum, Wright-Patterson AFB

QF-100 Conversions

Conversion number followed by serial.
All were F-100Ds apart from examples with an asterisk, indicating an F-100F.

Sperry Conversions

092/56-3414, 093/55-3610, 094/56-3048, 095/55-3669, 096/56-2979, 097/56-3984*, 098/56-2912, 099/56-2978, 100/56-3324, 101/55-2809, 102/56-3006, 103/55-2816, 104/55-2789, 105/55-2828, 106/55-2821, 107/55-2823, 108/55-2845, 109/55-3657, 110/55-3663, 111/55-3662, 112/55-3712, 113/55-3668, 114/55-3726, 115/55-3692, 116/56-2947, 117/56-2977, 118/56-2982, 119/55-3746, 120/56-2987, 121/56-3037, 122/56-3056, 123/56-3143, 124/56-3251, 125/56-3044, 126/56-3239, 127/56-3253, 128/56-3291, 129/56-3313, 130/56-3310, 131/56-3328, 132/56-3389, 133/55-3673, 134/56-3402, 135/56-3410, 136/56-3176, 137/55-2841, 138/55-2877, 139/55-2860, 140/55-2867, 141/55-3620, 142/55-3593, 143/55-2898, 144/55-3623, 145/55-2889, 146/55-2949, 147/55-2856, 148/55-3564, 149/55-3724, 150/55-3710, 151/55-3674, 152/55-3797, 153/56-2942, 154/56-2950, 155/56-3068, 156/56-2975, 157/56-2961, 158/56-3107, 159/56-3118, 160/56-3133, 161/56-3218, 162/56-3153, 163/56-3233, 164/56-3123, 165/56-3129, 166/56-3183, 167/56-3109, 168/56-3309, 169/56-3276, 170/56-3369, 171/56-3439, 172/55-2801, 173/56-3400, 174/55-2834, 175/55-3752, 176/55-3788, 177/55-2830, 178/55-3812, 179/55-2833, 180/55-3545, 181/55-2827, 182/56-3298, 183/56-3010, 184/56-2980, 185/56-3205, 186/56-3017, 187/56-3256, 188/56-2992, 189/56-3162, 501/56-3801*, 502/56-3740*.
All the above were ex-ANG lost during flights from Tyndall or Holloman AFBs.

Flight Systems Conversions

F-100D

201/55-2863, 202/55-2925, 203/55-2939, 204/55-3666, 205/55-2951, 206/55-3528, 207/55-3578, 208/55-3601, 209/55-3566, 210/55-3709, 211/55-3744, 212/56-2915, 213/55-3775, 214/56-2918, 215/56-2920, 216/56-2944, 217/56-2959, 218/56-3231, 219/56-2981, 220/56-2989, 221/56-3117, 222/56-3034, 223/56-3184, 224/56-3248, 225/56-3130, 226/56-3191, 227/56-3210, 228/56-3241, 229/56-3232, 230/55-3689, 231/55-3679, 232/55-3727, 233/55-3683, 234/56-2999, 235/55-3685, 236/56-3011, 237/56-3213, 238/56-3260, 239/56-3295, 240/56-3422, 241/55-3558, 242/55-3688, 243/56-3234, 244/56-3201, 245/56-3255, 246/55-3690, 247/55-2846, 248/56-2910, 249/55-2870, 250/55-3604, 251/55-3508, 252/56-3003, 253/55-3505, 254/55-3570, 255/56-3140, 256/56-3259, 257/56-3265, 258/56-3303, 259/56-3306, 260/56-3296, 261/56-3311, 262/56-3356, 263/56-3371, 264/56-3381, 265/56-3393, 266/56-3413, 267/56-3426, 268/56-3443, 269/56-3019, 270/56-3031, 271/55-3672, 272/56-3072, 273/55-3703, 274/56-3315, 275/55-3811, 276/56-3405, 277/56-3331, 278/55-3630, 279/55-3740, 280/55-3705, 281/55-2865, 282/55-2873, 283/55-2927, 284/55-3733, 285/55-3770, 286/55-3580, 287/56-3397, 288/56-3412, 289/55-3552, 290/56-3135, 291/56-3141, 292/56-3307, 293/56-3462, 294/56-3345, 295/55-3758, 296/56-3155, 297/56-3365, 298/55-3759, 299/55-2942, 300/55-3616, 301/56-2974, 302/56-3163, 303/55-2793, 304/55-3664, 305/55-2807, 306/55-2813, 307/55-2818, 308/55-2826, 309/56-3171, 310/55-2853, 311/55-2859, 312/55-2879, 313/55-2881, 314/55-3665, 315/56-2917, 316/56-2932, 317/56-3007, 318/56-2952, 319/56-3024, 320/56-2953, 321/56-3028, 322/56-3033, 323/56-3035, 324/56-3053, 325/56-3054, 326/56-3195, 327/55-2905, 328/55-2917, 329/55-2933, 330/55-2945, 331/55-2952, 332/55-3521, 333/55-3567, 334/55-3557, 335/55-3576, 336/55-3622, 337/55-3634, 338/55-3644, 339/56-3081, 340/56-3101, 341/56-3082, 342/56-3112, 343/56-3168, 344/56-3169, 345/56-3173, 346/56-3187, 347/56-3190, 348/56-3194, 349/56-3198, 350/56-3221, 351/55-3757, 352/55-3771, 353/55-3784, 354/55-3741, 355/56-2970, 356/56-3427, 357/56-3179, 358/56-3463, 359/56-3222, 360/56-3404, 361/56-3093, 362/56-3425, 363/56-3279, 364/56-3361, 365/56-3046, 366/56-3406, 367/56-3385, 368/56-3333, 369/55-3804.

F-100F

370/56-3868, 371/56-3737, 372/56-3748, 373/56-3751, 374/56-3754, 375/56-3760, 376/56-3763, 377/56-3762, 378/56-3765, 379/56-3787, 380/56-3795, 381/56-3746, 382/56-3805, 383/56-3818, 384/56-3830, 385/56-3840, 386/56-3836, 387/56-3859, 388/56-3860, 389/56-3882, 390/56-3891, 391/56-3893, 392/56-3883, 393/56-3906, 394/56-3898, 395/56-3907, 396/56-3910, 397/56-3915, 398/56-3917, 399/56-3922, 400/56-3928, 401/56-3951, 402/56-3956, 403/56-3962, 404/56-3791, 405/56-3994, 406/56-3738, 407/56-4001, 408/56-3768, 409/56-3773, 410/56-3794, 411/56-3812, 412/56-3813, 413/56-3814, 414/56-3819, 415/56-3855, 416/56-3822, 417/56-3861, 418/56-3825, 419/56-3832, 420/56-3880, 421/56-3837, 422/56-3889, 423/56-3897, 424/56-3904.
Conversions 411–421 returned to AMARC in 1991, 422/423/424 transferred to US Army. The others were destroyed during flights from Tyndall or Holloman AFBs.

Glossary

AAA	anti-aircraft artillery		HEI	high explosive/incendiary
AB	air base		HVA(R)	high velocity aircraft (rocket)
a.b.	afterburner			
ACM	air combat manoeuvring		ICBM	intercontinental ballistic missile
ACT	air combat tactics		IFF	identification, friend or foe
ADC	Air Defense Command		IFR	instrument flight rules
ADF	automatic direction finding		IOC	initial operational capability
AFB	Air Force Base		IP	identification point/initial point/Instructor Pilot
AGL	above ground level			
AIM	air intercept missile		IR	infra-red
AMARC	Aerospace Maintenance and Regeneration Center		IRAN	inspect and repair as necessary
ANG	Air National Guard		KIAS	knots, indicated airspeed
APU	auxiliary power unit		kt	knots
ARS	Air Refuelling Squadron			
ATC	Air Training Command		LABS	low-altitude bombing system
			LADD	low-altitude drogue delivery
BUFF	B-52 bomber		LOX	liquid oxygen
BW	Bomb Wing			
			MASDC	Military Aircraft Storage and Disposition Center
CAS	close air support		MiGCAP	combat air patrol to counter enemy air defences
CBU	cluster bomb unit			
CCTS/CCTW	Combat Crew Training Squadron/Wing		MMS	Munitions Maintenance Squadron
CO	commanding officer			
CONUS	continental USA		NAA	North American Aviation
CRT	cathode ray tube		NAVS	Doppler navigation system
CSD	constant speed drive		NOLO	no live operator onboard
			NOTAM	notice for airmen
DEFCON	defense condition		NVA	North Vietnamese Army
ECM	electronic countermeasures		OCU	Operational Conversion Unit
ELINT	electronic intelligence		OIC	Officer in Charge
EPR	engine pressure ratio		ORI	Operational Readiness Inspection
EWO	electronic warfare officer		OTS	'over the shoulder' nuclear delivery
FAC	forward air controller		PACAF	Pacific Air Force
FBS/FBW	Fighter-bomber Squadron/Wing		PAL	permissive action link
FDS/FDW	Fighter (Day) Squadron/Wing		PCS	permanent change of station
FFAR	folding fin aircraft rocket		POW	prisoner of war
FS/FG	Fighter Squadron/Group		PSP	pierced steel planking
FSAT	full-scale aerial target			
			RADAN	radar navigation system
GAR	guided air rocket		RAT	ram-air turbine
GCA	ground controlled approach		ResCAP	combat air patrol over recovery of downed aircrew
GCI	ground controlled interception			
GE	General Electric		RHAW	radar homing and warning
GP	general purpose (bomb)		RoCAF	Republic of China Air Force
			RTAFB	Royal Thai Air Force Base
HEAP	high explosive/armour piercing		RTU	Replacement Training Unit

SAC	Strategic Air Command	TO	Technical Order
SADS	surface-to-air defence system	TOT	time-over-target
SAM	surface-to-air missile		
SAR	search and rescue	USAFE	United States Air Forces Europe
SEAD	suppression of enemy air defences		
SEATO	South East Asia Treaty Organization	VC	Viet Cong
SOP	standard operational procedure	VFR	visual flight rules
SOS	Special Operations Squadron	VNAF	Vietnamese Air Force (South Vietnam)
		VPAF	Vietnamese Peoples' Air Force (North Vietnam)
TAC	Tactical Air Command		
TACAN	tactical air navigation		
TBO	time between overhauls	WADC	Wright Air Development Center
TDY	temporary duty	WP	white phosphorus
TFS/TFG/TFW	Tactical Fighter Squadron/Group/Wing	WW	Wild Weasel
TFTS/TFTW	Tactical Fighter Training Squadron/Wing		
THK	Turk Hava Kuvvetleri (Turkish AF)	ZEL	zero-length launch
TIC	troops in contact		

Index